European Yearbook of International Economic Law

EYIEL Monographs - Studies in European and International Economic Law

Volume 13

EYIEL Monographs is a subseries of the European Yearbook of International Economic Law (EYIEL). It contains scholarly works in the fields of European and international economic law, in particular WTO law, international investment law, international monetary law, law of regional economic integration, external trade law of the EU and EU internal market law. The series does not include edited volumes. EYIEL Monographs are peer-reviewed by the series editors and external reviewers.

More information about this subseries at http://www.springer.com/series/15744

Kriton Dionysiou

CETA's Investment Chapter

A Rule of Law Perspective

Springer

Kriton Dionysiou
Nicosia, Cyprus

ISSN 2364-8392 ISSN 2364-8406 (electronic)
European Yearbook of International Economic Law
ISSN 2524-6658 ISSN 2524-6666 (electronic)
EYIEL Monographs - Studies in European and International Economic Law
ISBN 978-3-030-66991-1 ISBN 978-3-030-66992-8 (eBook)
https://doi.org/10.1007/978-3-030-66992-8

This Springer imprint is published by the registered company Springer Nature Switzerland AG.
The registered company address is: Gewerbestrasse 11, 6330 Cham, Switzerland

A son never forgets

Preface

Despite a backlash against investment treaty arbitration from several states and the civil society, the European Union (EU) and Canada have recently concluded the "Comprehensive Economic and Trade Agreement (CETA)" whose investment chapter contains such a dispute settlement mechanism. According to EU and Canadian officials, CETA's Investment Chapter represents a decisive response to the legitimacy crisis facing investment treaty arbitration. Such a declaration, nevertheless, should not be treated as self-evidential. In light of the above, the monograph attempts to assess whether CETA's Investment Chapter constitutes a positive response to the legitimacy crisis facing investment treaty arbitration.

For this purpose, the study begins by tracing the historical roots of the legitimacy crisis facing investment arbitration and the tension between its private foundations and the public law nature of these investment disputes. This historical analysis leads to the realization that the legitimacy crisis reflects fundamentally a Rule of Law crisis within investment treaty arbitration. Subsequently, the monograph proceeds with a theoretical exploration of the Rule of Law in the third chapter. In that chapter, it will be argued that the Rule of Law incorporates the idea that public authority should be accountable to an independent, transparent, and accessible judicial body that fundamentally aims to guard a number of goals, paramount of these goals are human rights principles and legal certainty. The third chapter concludes that the Rule of Law is not only the principal normative and causal assumption on which legitimacy concerns are based, but it could and should be utilized as a platform for future reforms.

Chapters 4 to 7 then use the Rule of Law as a normative framework to analyze CETA's Investment Chapter to assess its impact on the legitimacy crisis. Eventually concluding that CETA's Investment Chapter is unlikely to completely solve the legitimacy crisis simply because it is just a patchwork of reforms rather than a comprehensive reinvention of the substantive and procedural aspects of investment treaty arbitration. Finally, the monograph draws meaningful insights about the way the challenges presented by investment treaty arbitration should be addressed by scrutinizing CETA's Investment Chapter from a Rule of Law perspective.

Nicosia, Cyprus Kriton Dionysiou

List of Treaties, Conventions, Guidelines, and Resolutions

Arbitration Rules of the Arbitration Institute of the Stockholm Chamber of Commerce (2017).

Basel Convention on the Control of Transboundary Movements of Hazardous Wastes and their Disposal (1992).

Chinese Model BIT (2003).

Council Negotiating Directives (Canada, India, and Singapore) (2011).

Council of the European Union, Negotiating Directives for a Convention Establishing a Multilateral Court for the Settlement of Investment Disputes (2018).

Drago-Porter Convention (1907).

Energy Charter Treaty (1991).

EU-Canada Comprehensive Economic and Trade Agreement (2016).

European Convention on Human Rights (1953).

General Agreement on Tariffs and Trade (1947).

General Treaty for the Renunciation of War (1928).

Germany-Pakistan BIT (1959).

German Model Treaty (2008).

Guiding Principles for Global Investment Policymaking—G20 (2016).

Havana Charter of 1948.

IBA Guidelines on Conflicts of Interest (2014).

ICTY Statute—International Criminal Tribunal for the former Yugoslavia (1993).

International Labor Organization Convention (1998).

International Centre for Settlement of Investment Disputes Convention (2006).

Interpretation of NAFTA Chapter 11—Provisions adopted by the NAFTA Free Trade Commission (2001).

Joint Interpretative Instrument on the Comprehensive Economic and Trade Agreement (CETA) between Canada and the European Union and its Member States (2016).

Kyiv Recommendations on Judicial Independence in Eastern Europe, South Caucasus, and Central Asia (2010).

Kyoto Protocol (1992).

Magna Carta (1215).

Nagoya Protocol on Access to Genetic Resources and the Fair and Equitable Sharing the Benefits arising from their Utilization to the Convention on Biological Diversity, October (2010).

North American Free Trade Agreement (1994).

Rome Statute of the International Criminal Court (2002).

Strategic Partnership Agreement (2017).

UK Act of Settlement (1701).

UK Model BIT (2005).

UNESCO Convention on the Means of Prohibiting and Preventing the Illicit Import, Export, and Transport of Ownership of Cultural Property (1970).

UNCITRAL Rules on Transparency in Treaty-based Investor-State Arbitration (2014).

Universal Declaration of Human Rights (1948).

United States Bill of Rights (1791).

UNGA Resolution 1803.

UNCITRAL Arbitration Rules (2010).

USA-Czech Republic BIT (2004).

US-OMAN FTA (2009).

Treaty on European Union (2012).

Treaty on Sustainable Investment for Climate Change Mitigation and Adaptation.

Vienna Convention on the Law of Treaties (1980).

Contents

Abbreviations

AAA	American Arbitration Association
BIT	Bilateral Investment Treaty
CETA	Comprehensive Economic and Trade Agreement
CJEU	Court of Justice of the European Union
DSU	Dispute Settlement Understanding
ECHR	European Convention on Human Rights
EFILA	European Federation for Investment Law and Arbitration
EU	European Union
FDI	Foreign direct investment
FET	Fair and equitable treatment
FTA	Free trade agreement
FTC	Free trade commission
GATT	General Agreement on Tariffs and Trade
IBA	International Bar Association
ICC	International Chamber of Commerce
ICC	International Criminal Court
ICCA	International Council for Commercial Arbitration
ICJ	International Court of Justice
ICS	Investment Court System
ICSID	International Centre for Settlement of Investment Disputes
ICTY	International Criminal Tribunal for the former Yugoslavia
IIA	International Investment Agreement
ILA	International Law Association
ILC	International Law Commission
ILO	International Labour Organization
ISDS	Investor-state dispute settlement
LCIA	London Court of International Arbitration
MFN	Most-favored-nation
MIGA	Multilateral Investment Guarantee Agency
UN	United Nations

UNGA	United Nations General Assembly
PCA	Permanent Court of Arbitration
SCC	Stockholm Chamber of Commerce
USD	United States Dollar
TPF	Third-party funding
NAFTA	North American Free Trade Agreement
NGO	Non-governmental organization
OECD	Organisation for Economic Co-operation and Development
OIC	Organization of Islamic Conference
SPA	Strategic partnership agreement
TTIP	Transatlantic Trade and Investment Partnership
TPP	Trans-Pacific Partnership
UK	United Kingdom
UNESCO	United Nations Educational, Scientific and Cultural Organization
UNCITRAL	United Nations Commission on International Trade Law
USA	United States of America
VCLT	Vienna Convention on the Law of Treaties
WTO	World Trade Organization

Table of Cases

Adel A Hamadi Al Tamimi v. Sultanate of Oman, ICSID Case No. ARB/11/33
ADF Group Inc. v. United States of America, ICSID Case No. ARB (AF)/00/1
Alpha Projektholding GmbH v. Ukraine, ICSID Case No. ARB/07/16
Armed Activities on the Territory of the Congo (New Application: 2002) (Democratic Republic of the Congo v. Rwanda), ICJ Reports 2005
Asian Agricultural Products Ltd. v. Republic of Sri Lanka, ICSID Case No. ARB/87/3
Bernhard von Pezold and Others v. Republic of Zimbabwe, ICSID Case No. ARB/10/15
Biloune and Marine Drive Complex Ltd v Ghana Investments Centre and the Government of Ghana, UNCITRAL Award 6/1990
Biwater Gauff (Tanzania) Ltd. v. United Republic of Tanzania, ICSID Case No. ARB/05/22
Cargill, Incorporated v. United Mexican States, ICSID Case No. ARB(AF)/05/2
Case Concerning Barcelona Traction, Light, and Power Company, Ltd (1970), ICJ Reports 1970
Camuzzi International S.A. v. The Argentine Republic, ICSID Case No. ARB/03/2
CME Czech Republic BVv The Czech Republic, UNCITRAL Award 9/2001
CMS Gas Transmission Company v. The Republic of Argentina, ICSID Case No. ARB/01/8
Charanne and Construction Investments v. Spain, SCC Case No. V 062/2012
Chemtura Corporation v. Government of Canada, UNCITRAL (formerly Crompton Corporation v. Government of Canada)
Chevron Corporation and Texaco Petroleum Corporation v. The Republic of Ecuador, PCA Case No. 2009-23
Compañia del Desarrollo de Santa Elena S.A. v. Republic of Costa Rica, ICSID Case No. ARB/96/1
Consortium RFCC v. Royaume du Maroc, ICSID Case No. ARB/00/6
Eastern Sugar B.V. (Netherlands) v. The Czech Republic, SCC Case No. 088/2004
EDF (Services) Limited v. Romania, ICSID Case No. ARB/05/13

Emilio Agustin Maffezini v The Kingdom of Spain, ICSID Case No. ARB/97/7
Enron Corporation and Ponderosa Assets, L.P. v. Argentine Republic, ICSID Case No. ARB/01/3
European Communities and Certain Member States — Measures Affecting Trade in Large Civil Aircraft, WT/DS316/40/Rev.1
Muhammet Çap & Sehil Inaat Endustri ve Ticaret Ltd. Sti. v. Turkmenistan, ICSID Case No. ARB/12/6
EuroGas Inc. and Belmont Resources Inc. v. Slovak Republic, ICSID Case No. ARB/14/14
Fraport AG Frankfurt Airport Services Worldwide v. The Republic of the Philippines, ICSID Case No. ARB/03/25
Gami Investments, Inc. v. The Government of the United Mexican States, UNCITRAL
Glamis Gold, Ltd. v. The United States of America, UNCITRAL Award 6/2009
Grand River Enterprises Six Nations, Ltd., et al. v. United States of America, UNCITRAL
Gustav F W Hamester GmbH & Co KG v. Republic of Ghana, ICSID Case No. ARB/07/24
Hesham T. M. Al Warraq v. Republic of Indonesia, UNCITRAL Award 11/2014
Holiday Inns SA/Occidental Petroleum v Morocco, ICSID Case No. ARB/72/1
İçkale İnşaat Limited Şirketi v. Turkmenistan, ICSID Case No. ARB/10/24
Inceysa Vallisoletana S.L. v. Republic of El Salvador, ICSID Case No. ARB/03/26
Gustav F W Hamester GmbH & Co KG v. Republic of Ghana, ICSID Case No. ARB/07/24
International Thunderbird Gaming Corporation v. The United Mexican States, UNCITRAL
Ioan Micula, Viorel Micula, S.C. European Food S.A, S.C. Starmill S.R.L. and S.C. Multipack S.R.L. v.Romania, ICSID Case No. ARB/05/20
Kasikili/Sedudu Island, Botswana v Namibia, Judgment, Merits, ICJ Reports 1999
Loewen Group, Inc. and Raymond L. Loewen v. United States of America, ICSID Case No. ARB(AF)/98/3
L. F. H. Neer and Pauline Neer (U.S.A.) v. United Mexican States, Reports of International Arbitral Awards (15th October 1926)
LG&E Energy Corp., LG&E Capital Corp., and LG&E International, Inc. v Argentine Republic, ICSID Case No. ARB/02/1
Maestri v Italy, Appl. No. 39748/98 Strasbourg, Judgment 17th February 2004
Metalclad Corporation v. The United Mexican States, ICSID Case No. ARB (AF)/97/1
Merrill and Ring Forestry L.P. v. Canada, ICSID Case No. UNCT/07/1
Methanex Corporation v United States of America, UNCITRAL Award 8/2005
Mondev International Ltd. v. United States of America, ICSID Case No. ARB (AF)/99/2
MTD Equity Sdn. Bhd. and MTD Chile S.A. v. Republic of Chile, ICSID Case No. ARB/01/7
Noble Ventures, Inc. v. Romania, ICSID Case No. ARB/01/11

OPIC Karimum Corporation v. The Bolivarian Republic of Venezuela, ICSID Case No. ARB/10/14
Pac Rim Cayman LLC v. Republic of El Salvador, ICSID Case No. ARB/09/12
Petur Thor v. Iceland, App. No. 39731/98 Strasbourg, Judgment 10th April 2003
Perenco Ecuador Ltd. v. The Republic of Ecuador and Empresa Estatal Petróleos del Ecuador (Petroecuador), ICSID Case No. ARB/08/6
Phoenix Action, Ltd. v. The Czech Republic, ICSID Case No. ARB/06/5
Piero Foresti, Laura de Carli & Others v. The Republic of South Africa, ICSID Case No. ARB(AF)/07/01
Pope & Talbot v. Canada, UNCITRAL Award 5/2002
PSEG Global Inc et al v Turkey, ICSID Case No. ARB/02/05
R v Sussex Justices, Ex parte McCarthy [1924] 1 KB 256
Railroad Development Corporation v. Republic of Guatemala, ICSID Case No. ARB/07/23
Renta 4 S.V.S.A, Ahorro Corporación Emergentes F.I., Ahorro Corporación Eurofondo F.I., Rovime Inversiones SICAV S.A., Quasar de Valors SICAV S.A., Orgor de Valores SICAV S.A., GBI 9000 SICAV S.A. v. The Russian Federation, SCC No. 24/2007
Republic of Ecuador v. United States of America, PCA Case No. 2012-5
Right of Passage over Indian Territory, Portugal v India, (1960) ICJ Reports 1960
Romak S.A (Switzerland) v The Republic of Uzbekistan, PCA Case No. AA280
Ronald S. Lauder v The Czech Republic, UNCITRAL Award 9/2001
Saipem S.p.A. v. The People's Republic of Bangladesh, ICSID Case No. ARB/05/07
Salini Costruttori S.p.a and Italstrade S.p.A v Hashemite Kingdom of Jordan, ICSID Case No. ARB/02/13)
Saluka Investments B.V. v. The Czech Republic, UNCITRAL Award 3/2006
Saint-Gobain Performance Plastics Europe v. Bolivarian Republic of Venezuela, ICSID Case No. ARB/12/13
Sempra Energy International v. The Argentine Republic, ICSID Case No. ARB/02/16
SGS Société Générale de Surveillance S.A. v. Republic of the Philippines, ICSID Case No. ARB/02/6
Southern Pacific Properties (Middle East) Limited v. Arab Republic of Egypt, Decision on Jurisdiction, ICSID Case No. ARB/84/3
Slowakische Republik v Achmea BV (Case C-284/16), 6 March 2018
Siemens A.G. v. The Argentine Republic, ICSID Case No. ARB/02/8
S.D. Myers, Inc. v. Government of Canada, UNCITRAL Award 12/2002
Spyridon Roussalis v. Romania, ICSID Case No. ARB/06/1
Suez, Sociedad General de Aguas de Barcelona, S.A.and Vivendi Universal, S.A. v. Argentine Republic, ICSID Case No. ARB/03/19
Sürmeli v. Germany, App. no. 75529/01 Strasbourg, Judgment 8th June 2006
Técnicas Medioambientales Tecmed, S.A. v. The United Mexican States, ICSID Case No. ARB (AF)/00/2
Telefónica S.A. v. United Mexican States, ICSID Case No. ARB(AF)/12/4

Tidewater Inc., Tidewater Investment SRL, Tidewater Caribe, C.A., et al. v. The Bolivarian Republic of Venezuela, ICSID Case No. ARB/10/5
Tokios Tokelés v. Ukraine, ICSID Case No. ARB/02/18
Urbaser S.A. and Consorcio de Aguas Bilbao Bizkaia, Bilbao Biskaia Ur Partzuergoa v. The Argentine Republic, ICSID Case No. ARB/07/26
United States-Import Prohibition of Certain Shrimps and Shrimp Products, Appellate Body Report WT/DS58/R, 12 October 1998
United Parcel Service of America Inc. v. Government of Canada, ICSID Case No. UNCT/02/1
Urbaser S.A. and Consorcio de Aguas Bilbao Bizkaia, Bilbao Biskaia Ur Partzuergoa v. The Argentine Republic, ICSID Case No. ARB/07/26
Veteran Petroleum Limited (Cyprus) v. The Russian Federation, PCA Case No. AA 228
Vito G. Gallo v. The Government of Canada, PCA Case No. 55798
Waste Management, Inc. v. United Mexican States, ICSID Case No. ARB (AF)/00/3

Chapter 1
Introduction

In recent decades, international investment law has seen immense development. As a result, the international investment law landscape currently consists of thousands of investment treaties and distinct legal rules of foreign investment protection. At the same time, investment treaty arbitration has become the preferred method for investment dispute resolution resulting in hundreds of cases over the past few decades.[1] It is not surprising, that it has been characterised by prominent scholars as one of the most active and fastest-growing areas of public international law.[2] In the fitting words of Jackson, an attempt to follow the developments in international investment law is as if one is attempting to describe the image out of the window of a train in motion—the events tend to move speedier that one can narrate them.[3]

According to a leading study, there are three interdependent principles that underpin the reasons behind the development of international investment law and the rapid increase of international investment agreements (IIAs).[4] The first principle is that international investment flows increase prosperity. This belief is a central component of the states' strategies to promote economic growth and development.[5] However, without strong legal assurances, foreign investors would be unwilling to commit capital in a host state. Accordingly, the second principle underpinning the development of international investment law is that legal protection of property promotes investment flows, which then promote growth and development.[6] International investment law rests on a third principle rooted in legal internationalism. Following the fall of the Soviet Union and as awareness of the common fate of states grew, it was suggested that every state should genuinely be interested in confining

[1] *See generally* UNCTAD (2018), ch 3.

[2] Salacuse (1990); Juilliard (2009), p. 273.

[3] Jackson in Tietje et al. (2008), p. 5.

[4] Bonnitcha et al. (2017), p. 8.

[5] *ibid.*

[6] *ibid*, p. 9.

K. Dionysiou, *CETA's Investment Chapter*, European Yearbook of International Economic Law 13, https://doi.org/10.1007/978-3-030-66992-8_1

itself within the limits of international law.[7] This realisation has brought to the forefront the principle of *pacta sunt servanda* ('agreements must be honored'), without which the international legal system of investment protection would not be able to function.[8]

The principal method through which IIAs protect foreign investments and uphold the above principles is investment treaty arbitration, also known as investor-state dispute settlement mechanism (ISDS). Generally, an IIA stipulates that any dispute between a host state and a foreign investor is to be resolved through arbitration. Based on these agreements, foreign investors can commence arbitration proceedings against host states claiming that sovereign acts are in violation of substantive protection standards included in an IIA. According to Susan Franck, there is ample evidence to suggest that arbitration is an efficient and fair method of settling investment disputes.[9] Yet, over recent years the use of investment arbitration as a dispute settlement mechanism has drawn controversy and criticism.[10] In particular, investment treaty arbitration faces strong opposition from states, local populations and the civil society regarding a number of its procedural and substantive aspects.

As a result of this backlash, the exponential increase of IIAs has since slowed down in recent years. The United Nations (UN) data indicate that the effective termination of IIAs exceeded the number of new IIAs conclusions for the first time in 2018.[11] Alongside the recent decline in the signing of new IIAs, nowadays there seems to be a wave of radical voices calling for the abandonment of this system and for a return to the more orthodox state-to-state dispute resolution framework.[12] Some states already even begun denouncing the convention on the International Centre for Settlement of Investment Disputes (ICSID) and withdrawing from IIAs. For example, Bolivia, Ecuador, India and Indonesia have decided to discontinue existing IIAs,[13] while South Africa, Brazil and Australia have undertaken serious steps towards alternatives of IIAs for investment protection.[14] In the same vein, in response to a consultation process initiated by the European Union (EU) on the draft Transatlantic Trade and Investment Partnership (TTIP), the vast majority of respondents expressed their concerns about the ISDS mechanism included in TTIP.[15] The

---

[7] *ibid*, p. 10.

[8] *ibid*, p. 11.

[9] Franck (2009).

[10] Waibel et al. (2010), Corporate Europe Observatory (2012) and UN Commission on International Trade Law (2018).

[11] UNCTAD, p. 88.

[12] Public Statement on the International Investment Regime (Osgoode Law School, 2010). The statement declares that there is a strong moral as well as policy case for States to withdraw from international investment treaties and to oppose investment treaty arbitration, including by refusal to pay arbitration awards against them where an award for compensation has followed from a good faith measure that was introduced for a legitimate public policy objective.

[13] Rivera and Viscarra (2017) and Jailami (2015).

[14] Kurtz (2011) and Muniz et al. (2017).

[15] European Commission (2015).

next question that should be answered is why the legitimacy crisis facing investment arbitration emerged in the first place.

One of the main criticisms made against investment arbitration is that it fails to defend the Rule of Law. As Santiago Montt once observed, the legitimacy of investment arbitration is severely compromised as several aspects of this system are at odds with the Rule of Law.[16] For example, many cases are reaching inconsistent and conflicting decisions on even the most basic principles of investment protection, which in turn makes international investment law unpredictable.[17] On top of that, the proceedings in investment arbitration are kept behind closed doors which fuels the suspicion harbored by many commentators that arbitrators are biased in favor of foreign investors and capital-exporting states.[18] A further criticism leveled at this system was recently highlighted in a letter signed by a hundred law professors stating that this kind of investor protection provisions undermine the Rule of Law due to the lack of sufficient safeguards ensuring independence and impartiality.[19]

Other criticisms concerns the high litigation costs of investment disputes[20] and the fact that investment tribunals excessively interfere with the exclusive regulatory power of States.[21] In the words of Sornarajah, 'investment arbitration has become an instrument of protection for foreign investment to the exclusion of other interests such as the environmental, health, access to essentials like medicines, electricity, and water, positive discrimination to advantage underprivileged groups and human rights.'[22]

Despite these misgivings, the continuing conclusion of IIAs indicates that several states still maintain a belief that both IIAs and investment arbitration are beneficial to their interests. As a result, and instead of completely abandoning investment arbitration, States have been attempting to recalibrate the substantive and procedural aspects of this dispute settlement mechanism.[23] In particular, both the EU and Canada have tried to circumvent this legitimacy crisis with the inclusion of certain safeguards in the recently signed CETA. These safeguards include, among others, provisions on greater transparency and procedural fairness, an appelate mechanism and an Investment Court System (ICS). Accordingly, in its new investment policy, the EU attempts to provide significant impetus for correcting mistakes of the past, by

[16]As will be explained later on, Montt failed to completely unfold the concept of the Rule of Law in the domain of investment arbitration. *See generally* Mont (2009), ch. 3.

[17]Franck (2005).

[18]Malintoppi (2008).

[19]Legal Statement on investment protection and investor-state dispute settlement mechanisms in TTIP and CETA (October 2016).

[20]Gaukrodger and Gordon (2012), pp. 17–23.

[21]Cotula (2014) and Wagner (2014).

[22]Sornarajah (2015), p. 392. Along the same line, a group of UN experts highlighted the risks that investment arbitration poses on the States' obligations to comply with their international human rights obligations. *See generally* UNCITRAL (2019).

[23]Reinisch (2009), pp. 908–915; UNCTAD (2017); Morosini (2017).

utilising CETA as a blueprint for the future of the investment policy of the EU.[24] There are, in other words, reasons to assume that CETA might be considered an appropriate response to the doubts and reservations that have engulfed investment arbitration. Regardless of the contracting parties' bold statements regarding the improvements made on both the substantive and procedural provisions of the investment chapter therein, the present study critically evaluates CETA's Investment Chapter to assess the real reach and impact of these supposed improvements.

According to the contracting parties, CETA adopts a new approach to investment protection as it attempts to improve the investment arbitration system and make it more acceptable to the wider public by adopting a number of measures.[25] One of the most important measures adopted is the declared aim that investment disputes under CETA will be adjudicated in full accordance with the Rule of Law.[26] However, the basic question the literature has failed to examine is whether CETA's Investment Chapter actually lives up to its stated goals. To address this gap in knowledge, the monograph will use CETA as case-study to investigate both the relevance of the Rule of Law in the context of investment arbitration and the compatibility of CETA's Investment Chapter with this important concept. The monograph's main objective is, therefore, to answer whether CETA's Investment Chapter is consistent with the Rule of Law.

Answering this crucial question requires a number of distinct, albeit interconnected, sub-inquiries. On this front, the study will first identify the roots of the legitimacy crisis facing investment arbitration, and analyse the deeper causes behind it. More specifically, the second chapter provides a brief historical overview of investment arbitration and then turns to the normative foundations of investment arbitration. The objective of the second chapter is to analyse the reasons behind the legitimacy crisis in investment arbitration and to conclude with an important realisation: The backlash against investment arbitration reflects fundamentally a Rule of Law crisis within investment law's dispute settlement mechanism. It is, subsequently, illustrated that the sub-elements driving the legitimacy crisis can be grasped and unified under the concept of the Rule of Law. For example, certain practices of investment tribunals that have attracted criticism do not align with the Rule of Law principles of legal certainty, transparency, procedural fairness and access to justice. There are also concerns that investment tribunals are reluctant to protect human rights as a result of the drafting of the substantive provisions of IIAs.

In essence, the second chapter articulates the principal normative and causal assumption on which existing arguments against investment arbitration are based. This explanation is useful for the ongoing debates since greater clarity about the reasons behind the legitimacy crisis can shed new light on the ways it can be addressed in the future. In other words, a problem may have within it the seeds of its own solution. It is no coincidence that a principal method in public law

---

[24]Marceddu (2016), Titi (2015) and Kleinheisterkamp (2012).

[25]European Commission (2016).

[26]*ibid.*

scholarship to enhance the legitimacy of public authority is through the notion of the Rule of Law. Due to the public law character of investment arbitration, the arbitral process should satisfy public law standards. Conceptualising the Rule of Law in the domain of investment arbitration is a way through which the legitimacy of investment arbitration can be enhanced. Despite the somewhat descriptive nature of this part, this is an essential element of the research undertaken by the study because it permits to explore and assess the causes of the legitimacy crisis rather than its symptoms.

Second, the study will clearly delimitate the scope, content and constituent elements of the Rule of Law, which itself is a vital concept in the arena of international investment law. The study will then present arguments to explain the necessity and appropriateness of the use of the Rule of Law as an assessment tool for the purpose of the study. On this front, the third chapter highlights the substantive and procedural components of the Rule of Law and argues that the Rule of Law can serve as a normative framework for investment arbitration. Furthermore, the chapter finds that the Rule of Law incorporates the idea that public authority should be accountable to an independent, transparent and accessible judicial body that fundamentally aims to guard human rights and provide legal certainty. In that sense, the third chapter provides a detailed theoretical framework that will be used to evaluate CETA's Investment Chapter in the chapters that follow. Hence, Chaps. 2 and 3 are necessary to justify why the research question of the monograph is worth answering in the first place.

Finally, the study will evaluate CETA's Investment Chapter via the framework of the Rule of Law while pointing out the significance of its findings in the current debates about the legitimacy of investment treaty arbitration. In light of this, the following four chapters analyse to what extent specific aspects of CETA's Investment Chapter are consistent with the Rule of Law. Namely, the study focuses on legal certainty, human rights, procedural fairness, and access to justice and transparency. Accordingly, Chap. 4 analyses whether the drafting of the investment provisions in CETA, the binding interpretive rules, the appellate mechanism, and the mechanisms to deal with conflicting awards and multiple proceedings further legal certainty. Chapter 5 examines whether CETA's Investment Chapter better integrates human rights law and investment obligations. Both the traditional methods of integration and the novel mechanisms introduced in CETA are scrutinised to assess whether the relevant provisions could ease the tension between human rights law and investment protection.

Chapter 6 seeks to evaluate whether the institutional safeguards in CETA's Investment chapter have the potential to ensure procedural fairness during the arbitration proceedings. In particular, the chapter evaluates the code of conduct and ethics introduced in CETA to examine whether the risk of biased adjudicators determining investment disputes has been effectively alleviated. It is further examined whether the enforcement mechanism of this set of behavioral standards is adequate for the purpose of challenging adjudicator's impartiality. Lastly, the chapter delves into whether the so-called Investment Court System in CETA has addressed the institutional bias for which investment arbitration has been accused.

Chapter 7 examines the extent to which the contracting parties have achieved greater transparency and access to justice. In particular, the seventh chapter looks into whether CETA provisions provide access to documents and open hearings as well as the opportunity to third parties to access the arbitral proceedings. Last, but not least, the chapter analyses whether the parties have confronted the challenges pertaining to access to justice resulting from the high litigation costs of investment disputes. Apart from highlighting the theoretical implications of the monograph, the last chapter will provide an answer to the research question of the study and, subsequently, share some thoughts on the way forward.

References

Bonnitcha J et al (2017) The political economy of the investment treaty regime. Oxford University Press, Oxford

Corporate Europe Observatory (2012) Profiting from injustice: how law firms, arbitrators and financers are fuelling an investment arbitration boom

Cotula C (2014) Do investment treaties unduly constrain regulatory space?. Questions of international law

European Commission (2015) Report on the online public consultation on investment protection and investor-to-state dispute settlement (ISDS) in the Transatlantic Trade and Investment Partnership Agreement (TTIP). trade.ec.europa.eu/doclib/docs/2015/january/tradoc_153044.pdf

European Commission (2016) CETA: EU and Canada agree on new approach on investment and trade agreement. europa.eu/rapid/press-release_IP-16-399_en.htm. Accessed 17 May 2020

Franck S (2005) The legitimacy crisis in investment treaty arbitration: privatizing public international law through inconsistent decisions. Fordham Law Rev 73:1521

Franck S (2009) Developments and outcomes in investment treaty arbitration. Harv Int Law J 50:2

Gaukrodger D, Gordon K (2012) Investor-state dispute settlement: a scoping paper for the investment policy community. OECD Working Papers on International Investment No. 2012/13

Jailami A (2015) Indonesia's perspective on review of international investment agreements. Investment Policy Brief 1

Juilliard P (2009) The law on international investment law. Can the imbalance be redressed? In: Sauvant Karl P (ed) Yearbook of international investment law and policy 2008-2009. Oxford University Press, Oxford

Kleinheisterkamp J (2012) European policy space in international investment law. ICSID Rev Foreign Invest Law J 27:2

Kurtz J (2011) The Australian trade policy statement on investor - state dispute settlement. Am Soc Int Law 15:22

Legal Statement on investment protection and investor-state dispute settlement mechanisms in TTIP and CETA (October 2016) stop-ttip.org/wp-content/uploads/2016/10/13.10.16-Legal-Statement-1.pdf. Accessed 5 May 2020

Malintoppi L (2008) Independence, impartiality and duty of disclosure of arbitrators. In: Muchlinski P et al (eds) The Oxford handbook of international investment law. Oxford University Press, Oxford

Marceddu ML (2016) The emerging profile of the European IIAs. Transnational Dispute Settlement 13:1

Montt S (2009) State liability and investment treaty arbitration: global constitutional and administrative law in the BIT generation. Hart Publishing, Oxford

Morosini F (ed) (2017) Reconceptualizing international investment law from the global south. Cambridge University Press, Cambridge

Muniz J et al (2017) The new Brazilian BIT on cooperation and facilitation of investments: a new approach in times of change. ICSID Rev 32:2

Public Statement on the International Investment Regime (Osgoode Law School, 2010). www.osgoode.yorku.ca/public-statement-international-investment-regime-31-august-2010/. Accessed 10 Apr 2020

Reinisch A (2009) The future of investment arbitration. In: Christina B et al (eds) International investment law for the 21st century: essays in honour of christoph schreuer, Oxford University Press, Oxford, pp 908–915

Rivera J, Viscarra M (2017) Life After ICSID: 10th anniversary of Bolivia's withdrawal from ICSID. Wolters Kluwer Arbitration. arbitrationblog.kluwerarbitration.com/2017/08/12/life-icsid-10th-anniversary-bolivias-withdrawal-icsid/. Accessed 22 May 2020

Salacuse J (1990) BIT by BIT: the growth of bilateral investment treaties and their impact on foreign investment in developing countries. Int Lawyer 24:3

Sornarajah M (2015) Resistance and change in the international law of foreign investment. Cambridge University Press, Cambridge

Tietje C et al (2008) Once and forever?' The legal effects of a denunciation of ICSID telc.jura.uni-halle.de/sites/default/files/altbestand/Heft74.pdf. Accessed 10 May 2020

Titi C (2015) International investment law and the European Union: towards a new generation of international investment agreements. Eur J Int Law 26:3

UN Commission on International Trade Law, Report of Working Group III (Investor-State Dispute Settlement Reform) on the Work of its thirty-fifth session (New York, 14 May 2018)

UNCITRAL WGIII, 37th Session (New York, 1–5th April 2019). www.ohchr.org/Documents/Issues/Development/IEDebt/OL_ARM_07.03.19_1.2019.pdf

UNCTAD's (2017) Reform package: for the international investment regime. https://investmentpolicy.unctad.org/publications/1183/unctad-s-reformpackage-for-the-international-investment-regime-2017-edition

United Nations Conference on Trade and Development (2018) World Investment Report

Wagner M (2014) Regulatory space in international trade law and international investment law. Univ Pa J Int Law 36:1

Waibel M et al (eds) (2010) The backlash against investment arbitration: perception and reality. Kluwer Law International, Alphen aan den Rijn

Chapter 2
The Backlash Against Investment Treaty Arbitration: Treat the Cause and Not the Symptom

2.1 Introduction

This chapter explores the cause behind the backlash against investment arbitration, and subsequently, identifies the method through which the contracting parties to CETA have responded. For this purpose, the chapter provides a brief historical account of investment arbitration and then turns to its normative foundations. The inquiry in the first two parts lays the groundwork for better explaining the root cause behind the backlash against this dispute settlement mechanism. The chapter then outlines the concerns driving the legitimacy crisis and, subsequently, looks at the public law framework that was used by the contracting parties to CETA in an effort to respond to the criticism against investment arbitration. It is subsequently argued that the legitimacy crisis in investment arbitration can be explained only if it is acknowledged that investment disputes go beyond the mere interest of States. Because of this function, the main issue with investment arbitration is its nonconformity with public law rules and principles that aim to protect a number of interests that go beyond States' interests. On this basis, it is finally argued that the backlash against investment arbitration reflects fundamentally a Rule of Law crisis within investment law's dispute settlement mechanism. Since the legitimacy crisis is rooted in a deeper Rule of Law crisis, it appears that the latter constitutes the principal normative assumption on which existing arguments against investment arbitration are based. In other words, this chapter argues that the legitimacy crisis in investment arbitration is *a priori* a Rule of Law crisis.

K. Dionysiou, *CETA's Investment Chapter*, European Yearbook of International Economic Law 13, https://doi.org/10.1007/978-3-030-66992-8_2

2.2 Brief Historical Account of Investment Treaty Arbitration

2.2.1 Colonial Era

In order to fully understand the reasons behind the backlash against investment arbitration, one should understand how and why this system emerged in the first place. The part that follows illustrates how certain historical events have played a role in shaping international investment law into a decentralised regime consisting of thousands of similarly drafted IIAs that contain vaguely construed standards of treatment. As will be argued in the parts the follow, such features have played a catalytic role in enhancing the backlash against investment arbitration.

The current framework of investment arbitration is a product of historical development first surfaced in the Middle Ages.[1] During the early days of international investment law and until the nineteenth century, an international framework of investment protection remained underdeveloped. This is mostly because the international community assumed that each state would protect foreign investments in its jurisdiction. Accordingly, a domestic scheme of protection would be sufficient for that purpose.[2] The alien property was to be treated the same way as the nationals of a host state with reference to its domestic laws.

In order to understand this stance towards foreign direct investments (FDIs), special reference should be made to Gunboat diplomacy. During the colonial era, an injury to another state's national was considered an injury to the state itself. This communal view of property dates back to Vattel in *The Law of Nations* where a citizen was considered the property of their state of nationality.[3] On this basis, the injured state was resorting to state-to-state dispute resolution to settle a claim. That period was further characterised by interdependence between States and investors.[4] Not only was there a merging of interests between States and investors, but also European companies played an active role in developing legal doctrines and state policies favorable to their needs.[5] Colonial and commercial objectives were merged with the clearest examples of such merger being the Dutch and English East India Companies. For this reason, it comes as no surprise that in the most extreme situations, capital-exporting States were resorting to the violent imposition of their investors' interests, known as gunboat diplomacy.[6]

---

[1]Newcombe and Paradell (2008), p. 2.

[2]Dolzer and Schreuer (2012), p. 3.

[3]Vattel (2008), p. 315.

[4]Miles (2013), p. 33.

[5]*ibid.*

[6]Newcombe and Paradell (2008), pp. 1–10. A famous example of 'gunboat diplomacy' is the dispatch of a European armada to Venezuela as a response to the unwillingness of Venezuela's government to repay its debt. *See* Hood (1977).

Therefore, the assumption by States that domestic protection for FDIs would suffice should be viewed against a period of colonialism where investment protection was primarily exercised through diplomatic espousal and the use of force.[7] In the words of Sornarajah, 'power was the final arbiter of foreign investment disputes.'[8] An international legal system of investment protection, therefore, seemed unnecessary during the colonial era since adequate protection to FDIs was provided through political coercion.

2.2.2 *Late Nineteenth and Early Twentieth-Century*

The colonial practices of coercion led to the incorporation of a convention in 1907, known as Drago—Porter Treaty, and to the General Treaty for the Renunciation of War that prohibited the use of force as a way to resolve investment disputes.[9] The prohibition of the use of force led to the establishment of arbitration courts and venues for state-to-state arbitration, such as claims commissions.[10] The determination of an investment dispute by a neutral third party contributed to the 'juridification' of investment disputes. In the absence of institutionalised dispute settlement mechanisms during that period, such a development was considered a novelty.[11]

Despite these positive developments, there were more fundamental challenges than just pacifying the dispute settlement mechanism.[12] Such challenges were manifested in the ideological clash during the late nineteenth century between the United States (US) and several Latin American countries. On one hand, certain Latin American countries, in response to the constant political tensions arising from investment disputes, championed the idea that an alien should receive the same treatment as nationals of the host state.[13] On the other hand, the US promoted the idea that foreign investors should be treated in accordance with international legal standards against unacceptable policies of a host state. In this way, US citizens investing abroad were expected to enjoy international legal protection regardless of the legal and political regime of the home state.

The Latin American position is mostly associated with the Argentine jurist Carlos Calvo who proclaimed that foreign investors should be treated the same way as the nationals of the host state, no matter what the level of protection afforded to these

---

[7]A usual method of redress was diplomatic espousal, where an investor's home government was espousing the investor's cause of action. *See generally* Dugan et al. (2008), pp. 26–33.

[8]Sornarajah (2011), p. 20.

[9]Newcombe and Paradell (2008), p. 10.

[10]Bray (2018), pp. 111–118.

[11]Lauterpacht (1991), p. 15.

[12]Schefer (2016), p. 7.

[13]Preziosi (1989), p. 656.

nationals.[14] In other words, the appropriate treatment to foreign investors should be one of national treatment. Furthermore, according to Calvo, States should not be able to interfere with another state's FDIs protection policies and foreign investors should only be able to seek justice at a domestic level.[15] Calvo's doctrine, though, left aliens without any assurance as to whether host States will uphold strong protection guarantees for investments.

Despite the rejection of Calvo's doctrine by capital-exporting countries, the Russian revolution in 1917 and the subsequent establishment of communist regimes across the world revitalised Calvo's doctrine.[16] In specific, it was advanced that foreign investment protection was primarily a domestic issue that should not have any international law dimension.[17] The reason behind this was the communist encouragement of numerous expropriations of foreign investments and several other interferences on private properties. According to Montt, Calvo's ideas were converted into a novel and opportunistic one: expropriation without compensation.[18] The communist views on property protection sparked debates about the legitimacy of those interferences and the appropriate standards of FDI protection in terms of international law.[19]

In the following decades, a dispute between the US and Mexico, following nationalization of a US interests company by Mexico, gave birth to what it would later be known as the 'Hull Rule'. The US Secretary of State Cordell Hull in 1938 in a letter addressing his Mexican counterpart spelled out that expropriation of a foreign investment requires prompt, adequate and effective compensation.[20] According to Hull, this standard of compensation required Mexico to comply with international law. Mexico argued that in the case of expropriation it was only required to pay compensation in accordance with its domestic law. The Mexican position not only reaffirmed its proximity with Calvo's doctrine but also foreshadowed future disagreements among States about the legal status of FDIs.[21]

---

[14]Garcia-Mora (1950), pp. 205–208.

[15]*ibid.*

[16]Dolzer and Schreuer (2012), p. 45.

[17]*ibid,* p. 45.

[18]Montt (2009), p. 57.

[19]Thomas and Gimblett (2011), pp. 661–662.

[20]'Mexico – United States: Expropriation by Mexico of Agrarian properties owned by American citizens' (1938), p. 181.

[21]Lipson (1985), pp. 16–19.

2.2.3 Post-World War II Developments

In the aftermath of World War II, FDI flows increased around the world.[22] Subsequently, the growing importance of investments worldwide forced the major capital-exporting States to insist that FDIs were entitled to international legal protection.[23] The unlimited prerogatives of States in regard to the treatment of aliens in their jurisdiction were at odds with the new economic reality. This new economic reality had international consequences for which an international legal framework was necessary.[24] This dynamic opened the floor for the development of customary international law by capital-exporting States and specifically for the so-called international minimum standard of protection.[25] According to this standard, aliens should be legally protected by international law against the host state's treatment. Most importantly, this protection should be provided even if the host State treats its own nationals in a manner that falls below the international minimum standard of protection. Although the standard's content is a matter of debate, it has been frequently applied in respect to fundamental human rights, denials of justice as well as against arbitrary expropriation.[26]

Regardless of this development, States did not manage to reach a consensus as to the exact content of the international minimum standard of protection. Even though the colonial era ended, several States maintained the position that FDIs were merely a new version of colonial attempts to impose their will over them.[27] As a response to the international minimum standard of protection, the majority of these new States were challenging the extent to which the natural resources concession rights granted by colonial powers were to be honored.[28] The standard of compensation for the expropriation of those concession rights was also under dispute.[29]

In that sense, several States were attempting to ensure that FDIs in their jurisdiction would have a minimum impact on their ability to exercise public authority. The Havana Charter of 1948, one of the first attempts to codify a universal code for investment protection, stipulates that a state should be able 'to ensure that foreign investment is not used as a basis for interference in its internal affairs or national policies'.[30] This provision demonstrates that the concerns regarding the

[22]Dolzer and Schreuer (2012), p. 49.

[23]*ibid.*

[24]Braun (2010), pp. 491–492.

[25]Root (1910).

[26]*Halsbury's Laws* (2010), paras. 462–463.

[27]For a study on decolonization and international investment law *See* Pahuja (2013), Ch. 4.

[28]*See generally* Dolzer (1986).

[29]*See* UNGA Resolution 1803, promoted by developing countries and communist regimes, which sets forth that FDIs remain subject to the domestic law of the host state and the compensation for expropriation should be 'appropriate' rather than 'prompt, adequate and effective'.

[30]Havana Charter for an International Trade Organization, Art. 12.

encroachment of the regulatory powers of States by investment protection instruments are not a recent phenomenon.

This concern was put forward in the United Nations (UN) through a set of concrete proposals, known as 'New International Economic Order.'[31] According to the proposal, every State was entitled to exercise their sovereign powers, including possession, use, and disposal its natural resources.[32] Those sovereign powers were to be upheld even if that required interfering with FDIs. Most importantly, the declaration stated that no state should be subjected to any kind of coercion to prevent the exercise of these rights.[33] In view of this, the adopting States maximised the risk for foreign investment in their territory as they were not obliged to guarantee strong legal protection, thus, creating a hostile environment for FDIs.

These conditions for FDIs lasted until the collapse of the Soviet Union in the 1990s. Eventually, the 'Washington consensus' was embraced by the vast majority States and subsequently reinforced the promotion of FDIs and the enforcement of property rights.[34] The 'Washington Consensus' promoted the liberalization of capital, the abolition of trade and investment restrictions and the privatization of state-owned companies.[35] According to the 'Washington Consensus', all of the above were prerequisites for developing States to flourish economically.[36] Foreign investments were no longer conceived as a threat but were now regarded as a tool for economic development and democratization. Still, for the 'Washington Consensus' to be successful, legal and regulatory uniformity is required across the world. This realization contains an inherent 'bias' in favor of market-based policies and pro-investor approaches to international regulation. It also requires limits upon the regulatory power of States.[37] For this reason, the next section explains how in the years that followed, States made efforts to live up to the economic legacy of the 'Washington consensus'.

2.2.4 Modern Regime of Investment Treaty Arbitration

Following the Soviet collapse and the subsequent Western dominance, the trend with regard to FDIs legal protection changed. The majority of capital-importing States not only stopped opposing foreign investment protection but also sought to grant foreign

---

[31]For the efforts of developing countries to perpetuate the dominance of Western nations through International Law *See generally* Linarelly et al. (2018), Ch. 3.

[32]*ibid.*

[33]UN General Assembly, Declaration on the Establishment of a New International Economic Order (1974). www.un-documents.net/s6r3201.htm. Accessed 1/5/2020.

[34]For the history of the 'Washington Consensus' *See* Williamson (2004).

[35]*ibid.*

[36]*ibid.*

[37]Muchlinski (2011), p. 4.

investors more legal rights.[38] In this context, States began to conclude investment treaties on a massive scale.[39] Indicatively, between 1989 and 1999, more than 1200 international investment agreements (IIAs) were signed between States.[40] The rapid increase of IIAs across the world indicates that FDIs have an immensely important role to play in securing economic and social goals.

The World Bank accompanied this new state of affairs with the establishment of ICSID a few decades earlier in an effort to set up a neutral forum for investment dispute settlement.[41] The establishment of ICSID made arbitration the most popular method for resolving investment disputes between States and foreign investors.[42] One of the most fundamental features of this new regime is that arbitration proceedings are to be initiated by the private foreign investor and not the state of nationality.[43] As a result, capital-exporting States waived their right to espouse and enforce their citizens' investment claims. Alongside with the exponential increase of IIAs, ICSID shifted foreign investment protection from the realm of politics and diplomatic protection to a rule-based system of investment protection. In that sense, the ICSID convention contributed to the 'depoliticization' of investment disputes by transferring the burden of enforcement from States to an arbitration venue.[44]

From the perspective of foreign investors, the ICSID convention provides strong assurances for a claim. Under ICSID, an investor is assured that a state party cannot frustrate the proceedings once it has consented to arbitrate,[45] while ICSID awards are to be enforced 'as if it were a final judgment of the courts of a constituent state.'[46] In contrast, under customary international law, it was the state of nationality that would eventually decide whether to proceed with a claim. By the same token, the entitlement to receive compensation in the case of diplomatic espousal belongs to the home state and not the investor. As a result of this, the home state was not obliged to pass the compensation to the claiming investor. Foreign investors were also at the mercy of local courts, whose proceedings occasionally proved to be lengthy and

[38]*See generally* Salacuse (1999).

[39]The first BIT was concluded between Germany and Pakistan in 1959. For a brief history of BITs *See* Vandevelde (2009).

[40]*See generally* UNCTAD (2000), pp. 1–6; Salacuse (2007).

[41]History of the ICSID Convention: Documents Concerning the Origin and the Formulation of the Convention on the Settlement of Investment Disputes between States and Nationals of Other States (ICSID Publications, 2009), p. 484.

[42]ICSID Website, Index. icsid.worldbank.org/en/Pages/about/default.aspx. Accessed 15/3/2020.

[43]Parlett argues that foreign investment protection challenged the doctrine of diplomatic protection as individuals were given the right to initiate claims directly against sovereign States. *See generally* Parlett (2011), pp. 103–119.

[44]*See generally* Shihata (2009).

[45]ICSID Convention, Art. 35.

[46]ICSID Convention, Section 6, para. 54.

inefficient.[47] Another issue that could arise at the domestic level is that courts are frequently unable to scrutinise acts of sovereign nations due to the doctrine of state immunity. The doctrine of sovereign immunity stipulates that a sovereign state cannot be sued without its consent.[48] This meant that it would be hard, if not impossible, for foreign investors to seek redress at the domestic level.

According to Reisman, ICSID was selected to take part in a more specified and intrusive and assertive role in monitoring governance arrangements within States.'[49] ICSID should, therefore, be appreciated for its effort to address both substantive and procedural limitations of the international legal system at the time.[50] However, and as it will be discussed later on, the ICSID established that investment arbitration is to be conducted in a similar way as international commercial arbitration. This meant that public law disputes concerning the regulatory power of States were to be settled in accordance with the procedural rules of commercial law, including confidentiality and party autonomy.[51] These historical features of investment arbitration have contributed to the legitimacy crisis and subsequently forced the study to consider whether CETA offers a substantially different investment dispute settlement mechanism.

Despite these developments, most States remained divided as to the content of the international minimum standard.[52] The enthusiasm for attracting FDIs did not leave States undivided as to the legal protection of aliens. This division was highlighted by the International Court of Justice (ICJ), in its decision in the *Barcelona Traction* case where the court held that international investment law is 'characterised by intense conflict of systems and interests.'[53] The court added that 'no generally accepted rules in the matter have crystallised on the international plane.'[54]

It is not surprising to conclude that the substantive protection standards in IIAs are somewhat opaque. The adoption of vague standards of treatment in IIAs has been a political choice aimed at reducing the likelihood of renewed dissent and with respect to the scope of protections in customary international law.[55] Hence, no real effort was made to give a concrete meaning to the substantive protections in IIAs. In

[47]For a relatively recent example of these difficulties *See Sürmeli v. Germany*, no. 75529/01, §§ 62–74, ECHR 2006-VII.

[48]Yang (2016).

[49]Reisman (2017), p. 12.

[50]For example, the International Court of Justice has played a minor role in investment dispute settlement. Very limited cases involving investment disputes have been brought to the court for which several of them the court rejected jurisdiction. The *Barcelona Traction* and *ELSI* cases demonstrate the inadequacy of the ICJ to settle investment disputes. *See generally* Desierto (2012).

[51]It is interesting to note that the drafters of ICSID did not have in mind that investment arbitration would be used for treaty dispute settlement, but to resolve disputes arising from contracts between foreign investors and States. *See* Lowenfeld (2009), p. 55.

[52]For an overall view on the 'minimum standard of protection' *See* Dumberry (2016), Ch. 2.

[53]*Case Concerning Barcelona Traction, Light, and Power Company, Ltd* (1970) ICJ 1, para. 89.

[54]*ibid*, para. 89.

[55]Calamita (2015), p. 111.

particular, the risk that the negotiations about the ICSID Convention would collapse as a result of the disagreements about the substantive content of the new treaty, advanced the programmatic formula that procedure should be put ahead of substance.[56] Ironically enough, the reluctance of States at that particular moment of history to agree on the substantive content of IIAs has led to negative implications on the long run, as will explained later in this monograph.

Additionally, Poulsen argues that many developing countries failed to appreciate the potential implications of IIAs.[57] As such, many IIAs were concluded without careful negotiations and with little consideration of their legal consequences. John argues that the rise of the ISDS made States to realise that the outcome of this system do not represent its framers' intentions, instead it has unintended consequences in relation to the outcomes of disputes.[58] As discussed in the following sections, tribunals not only have been reaching inconsistent interpretations but also have been excessively interfering with the exclusive regulatory power of States. Both the legitimacy crisis facing investment arbitration and this study is centered around the implications of investment awards on the regulatory power of States.

Unsurprisingly, many attempts for the creation of a universal code of investment protection were initiated, but to no avail. For example, the negotiations over the Multilateral Agreement on Investment in the 1990s and the subsequent efforts to develop investment protection standards by the World Trade Organization (WTO) collapsed.[59] These failures were mainly due to the fact that developing countries knew that they might be able to utilise their bargaining power against weaker States in a bilateral context, yet in a multilateral setting this power would be considerably diminished.[60] Thus, developing countries were more willing to enter a bilateral treaty, rather than opening their economy to the world.[61] Ultimately, the attempts to create a multilateral framework for investment protection failed because of the imbalance of interests among interested States.[62]

This systematic failure to reach a consensus created a wave of uncertainty for the protection of foreign investments. Without a multilateral framework of investment arbitration, only a few contested customs and questionable general principles of law were in place for the protection of foreign investors at the international level. These contrasting trends, namely the lack of a multilateral framework and the increase of FDIs flows across the world, have been the driving force of the exponential increase of IIAs over the last decades. On one hand, the 'Washington consensus' contributed to the attraction of FDIs and enhanced the protection of investment rights through

---

[56]Dolzer and Schreuer (2012), p. 54.

[57]*See generally* Poulsen (2015), Ch. 2.

[58]*See generally* St John (2018), Ch. 1.

[59]*See generally* Subedi (2016), Ch. 3.

[60]*ibid.*

[61]Salacuse and Sullivan (2005), p. 78.

[62]Fatouros further added that most of the attempts to conclude a multilateral treaty failed because the draft codes of investment protection were unbalanced and one-sided. *See* Argyrios (1961), p. 99.

IIAs. At the same time, the ICSID convention provided a robust mechanism to resolve investment disputes. On the other hand, this new trend coincided with economic nationalism with most States being unwilling to reach a global consensus on a multilateral framework of international investment protection.

To sum up, unlike other legal regimes that are centered on a multilateral instrument or an international organization, international investment law is a decentralised regime of investment protection. Accordingly, this regime is dominated by thousands of similarly drafted IIAs that contain vaguely construed standards of treatment.[63] In contrast with other fields of public international law, modern international investment law is distinguished by the investor's right to initiate a claim in a diversity of arbitral institutions directly against the host state. These features make investment arbitration a unique method of international dispute settlement. As discussed in the following section, these characteristics have contributed to the backlash against investment arbitration.

2.3 Normative Foundations of Investment Treaty Arbitration

2.3.1 Preliminary Observations

In order to fully understand the reasons behind the backlash, the objective and function of investment arbitration should also be discussed. In other words, it is of paramount importance to analyse the normative foundations of investment arbitration to understand in what way the above historical events have played a role in boosting the legitimacy crisis. Starting with some general remarks, various scholars claim that IIAs primarily seek to protect foreign investors against host state actions that have an adverse effect on their investment.[64] There are also suggestions that IIAs seek to compensate the distrust for governments who are often accused to be susceptible to populist pressures.[65] Effectively, IIAs provide strong commitments to property rights protection and, thus, send a message about the existence of an investment-friendly state. Schneiderman adds that IIAs constitute a regime performing constitution-like functions preoccupied with the protection of private property.[66]

---

[63]Jagdish Bhagwati once described this complex network of international agreements as a 'spaghetti bowl.' *See* Bhagwati (1995).

[64]Despite that international investment law consists of thousand of IIAs, their substantial and procedural similarities (standards of treatment and dispute settlement mechanism) allows us to draw certain general conclusions. These similarities have led scholars to characterise this body of IIAs as an international investment regime. *See generally* Salacuse (2010) and Schill (2009).

[65]For a discussion *See* Echandi (2011).

[66]Schneiderman (2016a), p. 23.

In the well-known book of Dolzer and Schreuer *Principles of International Investment Law*, the scholars explain that investment treaties are treated as admission tickets to foreign investment markets. Their restraining impact on the sovereign powers of States, contentious as it may be, is a necessary repercussion to the objective of establishing an investment-friendly environment.[67]

Following this reasoning, numerous scholars argue that FDI protection is the primary objective of the investment treaty regime. For example, scholars such as Garcia Bolivar,[68] Vandevelde,[69] and Vaughan Lowe[70] argue that IIAs are necessary to provide international protection to foreign investments so that States are better positioned to attract FDIs. While Salacuse and Sullivan find that 'a BIT between a developed and a developing country is founded on a grand bargain: a promise of protection of capital in return for the prospect of more capital in the future.'[71] Tribunals have supported this view as well. In *SGS v. Philippines*, the tribunal held that the IIA's object and purpose is the protection of covered investments.[72]

In summary, there is a consensus that attracting investments is the fundamental goal of IIAs; certain actions by host States are the problem, with investment agreements being the solution to the problem. Comprehensive as it may sound, this positivist conceptualization of investment arbitration leaves behind important aspects of the function of investment arbitration that could shed light on the causes behind the legitimacy crisis.

In particular, this positivist approach in international law, also known as traditional approach, promotes the idea that international law is a system of objective principles and neutral rules that emanate from States.[73] Anything that goes beyond State consent and the text of treaties is conceptually overlooked by legal positivism. The traditional concepts of international law fail to provide a comprehensive and convincing narrative behind the legitimacy crisis in investment arbitration. Consequently, debates on the hidden structures in the international investment law, its functionality or the values underlying its rules are uncommon in this setting. In the same vein, the way investment arbitration interacts with non-State actors cannot be grasped by a positivist approach to international law that perceives this mechanism

[67]Dolzer and Schreuer (2012), p. 14.

[68]Bolivar (2005), p. 751.

[69]Kenneth (1998), p. 4.

[70]Vaughan (2007), p. 37.

[71]Salacuse and Sullivan (2005), p. 77.

[72]*SGS Société Générale de Surveillance S.A. v. Republic of the Philippines*, ICSID Case No. ARB/02/6, para. 116.

[73]Bianchi (2016), p. 21.

in a mono-dimensional manner.[74] A distinction must therefore be made between what *is* the objective of investment arbitration and what it actually *does*.[75]

In simple terms, understanding investment arbitration simply as a mechanism through which a State aims to protect foreign investments in its jurisdiction does not leave much room to examine in what way this mechanism affects the local communities or third parties in general. Ultimately, this positivist understanding of investment arbitration does not provide justification as to why comprehensive reforms, that do not serve the strict interest of States, would enhance the legitimacy of investment arbitration. Legal positivism provides a narrow way of examining the ontology of this legal system and is insufficient to analyse investment arbitration from an external point of view.[76]

For example, by accepting that investment arbitration simply represents a bargain between sovereign States, it would not be possible to explain why the legitimacy of investment tribunals would be enhanced with greater transparency for third parties. Along the same lines, this positivist understanding of investment arbitration fails to explain why confidentiality during the arbitral proceedings should raise any concerns in the first place. States have given their consent for individual tribunals to decide investment disputes behind closed doors, while States have access to the arbitral proceedings. By the same token, despite that the vague wording of IIAs has attracted controversy, they were drafted in that way with the consent of the state parties. Failing to include in a framework all those points of criticism concerning investment arbitration, which are overlooked by legal positivism, evaluating any reform proposals would be pointless.

In the absence of an alternative framework of analysis, the legitimacy crisis is going to be tainted by self-referentiality. In order to avoid this, it is of cardinal importance to conceptualise both the function of investment tribunals and the legitimacy crisis facing investment arbitration into a coherent theory. It is, therefore, necessary to depart from legal positivism to better comprehend the function of investment tribunals, to capture and rationalise the criticism against them and assess whether any reform proposal addresses the legitimacy crisis.

In light of the weaknesses of legal positivism, it is necessary for the study to use the normative approach in order to argue how investment arbitration should be and how it should operate.[77] Without a normative framework to reform proposals in the context of investment arbitration, any argument regarding their impact on the legitimacy crisis facing investment arbitration will be weak. Therefore, while the

[74]*See generally* Rosado de Sa Ribeiro and Jose Guterres Costa Junior (2015), pp. 421–426; Cassese (2005), p. 692.

[75]For a comprehensive outline of the conceptual and methodological approaches on International investment law *See* Schill (2011b).

[76]For example D'Aspremont explains that although is necessary to draw a bright line between law and non-law, legal formalism is unable to describe the entire phenomenon of law. *See generally* D'Aspremont (2011), Ch. 2.

[77]*See generally* Coleman (2002).

study maintains its doctrinal core,[78] it endeavors to accommodate theoretical analysis within the legal research framework in order to provide a more comprehensive analytical framework for investment arbitration.

As illustrated in the following sections, investment tribunals go far beyond standard international tribunals by functioning as public law bodies that are able to determine the legality of sovereign acts while arbitral awards may have an impact on the wider public interest of States.[79] As explained above, IIAs are the products of public international law since they are signed by States. Nonetheless, most of these IIAs enable private individuals to challenge sovereign acts based on procedural and substantive rights that are mostly associated with a private dispute settlement mechanism.[80] This feature empowers arbitrators to determine the proper boundaries between FDI protection and state intervention, boundaries that are of vital importance for the public good.[81] In that sense, investment tribunals are very powerful bodies in terms of public policy that essentially function as courts with judicial review powers, while arbitrators function like judges at the domestic level as they are able to rule upon the legality of sovereign acts. A critical issue that emerges is that investment tribunals are able to determine the outcome of disputes with a public element in the absence of transparency, consistency and without considering the public interest of States.

As discussed in the following section, the ability of investment tribunals to review sovereign acts in combination with the private dispute settlement foundations of this system, provokes pressing legitimacy questions.

2.3.2 *Investment Arbitration as a Private Dispute Settlement Mechanism*

Despite that investment arbitration functions in a similar way to a public law system, this mechanism is modeled after international commercial arbitration. This paradoxical situation has caused considerable tensions since investment tribunals deal with the regulatory powers of States while international commercial arbitration is an

[78] *See generally* Hutchinson (2017).

[79] This is discussed in detail in the following sections. For indicative reading *See* Schill (2010).

[80] For a thorough analysis *See* Douglas (2003) and Roberts (2015).

[81] For a case that involves environmental laws and investment protection *See Compañia del Desarrollo de Santa Elena S.A. v. Republic of Costa Rica*, ICSID Case No. ARB/96/1. In para. 72 the tribunal held that expropriatory environmental measures—no matter how beneficial to society as a whole—are similar to any other expropriatory measures that a government may take in order to implement its policies. Furthermore, according to the tribunal, where property is expropriated, even for environmental purposes, whether domestic or international, the state's obligation to pay compensation remains. Also *See* Martinez-Fraca and Ryan Reetz (2014) and Titi (2014).

alternative dispute settlement mechanism used to resolve private disputes.[82] This sub-section argues that the legitimacy crisis is a result of the fact that public law disputes are resolved on the basis of a private model of adjudication. This situation presents major negative implications to States and the wider public.

It must be noted that international commercial arbitration emerged in an effort to support the autonomy of the mostly private parties to resolve their private disputes in a cost-effective, speedy and confidential manner.[83] The characteristics of international commercial arbitration suggest that its foundational normative bedrock is the concept of *lex mercatoria. Lex mercatoria* is an ancient legal concept utilised by private parties to solve disputes.[84] Since *Lex mercatoria* is a legal concept developed by merchants, it emphasises on contractual freedom and the alienability of property, while promoting *ex aequo to bono* judgments and avoiding procedural formalities commonly found in domestic law.[85]

In this regard, by analysing investment arbitration through the lens of international commercial arbitration, there is no room for greater transparency or *amicus* briefs during the arbitral proceedings. Thomas Walde supports this approach, and suggests that such procedural reforms will have a negative effect on the arbitration procedures.[86] Similarly, the debates whether investment arbitration processes should be confidential are greatly influenced by the way we perceive investment arbitration. The more the private element of investment arbitration is appreciated, the less the voices for greater transparency.

Moreover, there is no precedent in international commercial arbitration, thus it does not aim to create a consistent legal framework.[87] Accordingly, investment arbitration is merely viewed as a dispute settlement procedure with no lawmaking functions, no obligation to publish awards and relatively low standards of due process. After all, in commercial arbitration, the parties are usually expected to appoint the arbitrators. The idea behind this procedure is merely a pursuit for civilised closure with no thirst for legal orthodoxy.[88] Along the same lines, the finality of an arbitral award is prioritised at the expense of correctness and the right to appeal an award.[89] Instead of aiming for systematization, harmonization, and legal

---

[82] Blackaby and Partasides (2015), Ch. 1.

[83] *ibid.*

[84] Lando (1985), p. 747.

[85] *ibid*, pp. 747–748.

[86] Walde (2010), p. 177.

[87] *Romak S.A (Switzerland) v The Republic of Uzbekistan* PCA Case No. AA280, Award (26 November 2009). The reasoning in para. 171 represents this view. According to the tribunal, the panel has not been entrusted, by the Parties with a mission to ensure the coherence or development of jurisprudence. Furthermore, in the panel's view, its mission is to resolve the present dispute between the parties in a reasoned and persuasive manner, irrespective of the unintended consequences that the tribunal's analysis might have on future disputes in general.

[88] Paulsson (2013), p. 13. For a detailed survey on the world of commercial arbitrators *See* Dezalay and Garth (1996), Ch. 1.

[89] *See generally* Christopher Thomas and Kaur Dhillon (2017), pp. 476–480.

certainty arbitrators are merely seen as dispute resolution service providers with mostly little concerns in achieving coherence and consistency.[90]

Lastly, the private dispute settlement foundations of investment arbitration force tribunals to treat IIAs as commercial contracts. As was rightly argued by Perrone, the transactional model that investment arbitration has been based on may not always be satisfactory especially when States try to achieve other social goals.[91] The *Eastern Sugar v Czech Republic* case illustrates how a style characteristic to commercial arbitration surfaces in investment arbitration. In this case, the tribunal devoted attention to procedural details and facts, but did not devote the same amount of attention to the substance of the case and, in particular, whether a trade quota violates an IIA.[92] This style reflects the culture of commercial arbitration where the main focus is on procedure and facts.[93]

This considerable shift of power from States to private individuals and investment tribunals has caused dramatic public law implications to many States that have been subjected to claims by foreign investors.[94] Notable examples are the Argentine crisis which resulted in a wave of successful claims by foreign investors, Ecuador ordered to pay billions following an investment award, and Czech ordered to pay an award of an equivalent amount to its health budget.[95] Ignoring the public function of the host state and treating its relationship with the foreign investor as a purely commercial one sidesteps vital public policy considerations. At the domestic level, administrative and constitutional courts challenge sovereign acts. Quite paradoxically, in the realm of investment arbitration, the legality of sovereign acts is decided on the basis of a private law framework.

Consequently, drawing analogies from international commercial arbitration finds many States and stakeholders in opposition.[96] The private law framework on which investment arbitration is based contemplates the disputing parties, as having a horizontal commercial relationship, regardless of the fact that one of the parties is a sovereign state exercising its public authority.[97] The resulting lack of transparency, procedural safeguards, legal certainty and the perceived lack of concern about the public policy implications of arbitral awards is problematic.[98] Put another way,

---

[90]Mills (2011), p. 469. Also *See* UN General Assembly – International Law Commission, 'Fragmentation of International Law: Difficulties arising from the Diversification and Expansion of International Law'.

[91]Perrone (2016), p. 621.

[92]*Eastern Sugar B.V. (Netherlands) v. The Czech Republic*, SCC Case No. 088/2004.

[93]Walde (2009), p. 727.

[94]*See generally* Miller and Hicks (2005), pp. 8–10.

[95]*ibid.*

[96]*See generally* Bockstiegel (2012).

[97]*Glamis Gold, Ltd. v. The United States of America*, UNCITRAL. In para. 3 the tribunal held that the investment chapter of NAFTA which contains an ISDS mechanism is 'a significant public system of private investment protection'.

[98]For the sociological dimension of the investment arbitration community and how its commercial law foundations influence decisions *See* Hirsch (2014). On page 154, the author argues that panels

businessmen courts are not suited to adjudicate public policy issues.[99] This view was supported in the case of *International Thunderbird Gaming v Mexico*, where it was rightly stated that the legal principles or methods used to analyzing the factual situation and styles from commercial arbitration are not suitable guidelines for investment treaty arbitration.'[100]

In a nutshell, the private law foundations of investment arbitration have resulted in the lack of transparency, consistency in decision-making as well as in the absence of an appellate mechanism. Along the same lines, arbitrators usually have no legal obligation to consider the public policy implications of their awards. These features appear to be in tension with the public element of investment disputes. Basically, the *modus operandi* of investment tribunals is inappropriate taking into consideration the objective and function they were tasked to perform. At this point, it is necessary to go through the reasons behind the legitimacy crisis facing investment arbitration in detail.

2.4 The Backlash Against Investment Treaty Arbitration

2.4.1 Preliminary Observations

Due to the private law foundations of investment arbitration, proceedings are conducted on an *ad hoc* and confidential manner in a similar manner to international commercial arbitration. The ambiguously construed standards of treatment in IIAs, coupled with the absence of an appellate mechanism, contribute to greater legal uncertainty. This uncertainty coupled with the decentralised network of IIAs and arbitration venues, lead to a lack of transparency and predictability. As explained above, these features appear to be in contrast with the public law nature of investment arbitration. The World Investment Report issued by the UN Conference on Trade and Development sketches the main causes of this legitimacy crisis that should be addressed. In particular, the report points out that investment treaty arbitration provides foreign investors more rights than domestic investors in a way that generate the risk of a "regulatory chill" on the policy-making powers of States.[101] Furthermore, investment treaty arbitration results in inconsistent arbitral

that give weight to their law-making role are more likely to take into account public policy objectives and seek a balance between the competing interests. On the other hand, panels that emphasize their role in settling a dispute between the disputing parties are less prone to give weight to broader policy issues involved in the dispute.

[99]Van Harten (2007), p. 152.

[100]*International Thunderbird Gaming Corporation v. The United Mexican States*, Separate Opinion, UNCITRAL, para. 12.

[101]United Nations Conference on Trade and Development (2015), p. 128. Kahale, a well-established practitioner in the field, characterised the ISDS as the 'wild west' of international law and arbitration. *See* Kahale (2018).

awards and is inadequate in terms of guaranteeing procedural fairness, ensuring transparent proceedings and independent and impartial arbitrators.[102]

In the same report, it is highlighted that the absence of a multilateral framework in a highly multilayered and decentralised network of IIAs results in conceptual gaps and inconsistencies. This decentralization ultimately opens the system to a myriad of competing analogies.[103] Similarly, the proliferation of investment tribunals, which frequently two or more of them have jurisdiction over the same investment dispute, slows down the process of convergence.[104] Finally, a report by the Organization for Cooperation and Development (OECD) indicates that another disadvantage of investment arbitration is the considerably high costs associated with the resolution of investment disputes.[105]

That said, the above criticism it not universally accepted. There are a number of scholars who claim that the critiques against investment arbitration are largely based on inaccuracies, hypothetical fears, and lacking moral grounding.[106] The study does not share this view for a number of reasons, as will be explained in the following sections. For this purpose, the backlash against investment arbitration will be categorised into four different parts: (1) multiple proceedings and conflicting awards (2) public interest concerns (3) perceived bias and (4) confidentiality and high costs.

2.4.2 *Multiple Proceedings and Conflicting Awards*

The phenomenon of multiple proceedings and conflicting awards takes many forms. Firstly, there are situations where investment tribunals issue diverging awards dealing with the same or similar legal issues. Indicatively, tribunals have been giving diverging views as to the content of the Most-Favoured-Nation (MFN) clauses. In *Emilio Agustin Maffezini v The Kingdom of Spain*, the tribunal held that MFN clauses extent to procedural matters allowing a foreign investor to invoke a clause of another IIA that Spain has concluded in order to speed up the arbitral proceedings.[107] In contrast, the tribunal in *Salini Costruttori and Italstrade v The Kingdom of Jordan* held that an MFN clause should not be extended to procedural matters with reference to other IIAs of the respondent state.[108]

Secondly, there are situations where investment tribunals reach different legal conclusions for the same factual events. For example, in a claim by *CMS*

---

[102] *ibid.*

[103] *ibid.*

[104] *See generally* Dupuy and Vinuales (2013).

[105] Gaukrodger and Gordon (2012), pp. 17–23.

[106] *See generally* Brower and Blanchard (2014), Franck (2015) and Nelson (2010).

[107] *Emilio Agustin Maffezini v The Kingdom of Spain*, ICSID Case No. ARB/97/7, para 54.

[108] *Salini Costruttori S.p.a and Italstrade S.p.A v Hashemite Kingdom of Jordan*, ICSID Case No. ARB/02/13, para 119.

Corporation v Argentine Republic, the tribunal rejected Argentina's plea of emergency and necessity. The relevant measures by Argentina were taken to avert an economic disaster following a monetary crisis.[109] However, in a dispute between Argentina and LG&E Energy Corporation, regarding the same state measure, the tribunal accepted that Argentina was in a state of necessity, thus should be absolved from responsibility.[110]

Finally, there are situations where different investment tribunals issue diverging awards for the same dispute. This phenomenon is known as parallel proceedings. Parallel proceedings are defined as 'multiple arbitrations between States and investors of the same identity, which concern the particular state measure compliance with the state's international investment obligations.'[111] The Lauder/CME arbitrations are an illustrative example of parallel proceedings, where two different investment tribunals arrived at two different decisions over what amounted to the same dispute. It should also be taken into consideration that the standards of treatment in both IIAs were essentially the same. The first investment tribunal in London, between the Czech Republic and a US investor, held that the actions of the Czech Republic did not amount to a breach of USA-Czech Republic BIT.[112] A couple of days after, the second tribunal in Stockholm, under the provisions of an IIA signed between the Netherlands and the Czech Republic, held otherwise. It was held that the Czech Republic breached its obligations towards the Dutch-registered company of the US investor.[113]

As the foregoing suggests, the phenomenon of parallel proceedings takes place as a result of the fact that States are usually bound by parallel obligations stemming from different legal instruments regulating the same conduct. Furthermore, due to the *ad hoc* nature of investment arbitration and the proliferation of tribunals, multiple dispute settlement mechanisms are available for the purposes of enforcing these obligations. In turn, foreign investors shop around for the most suitable venue and legal rules to settle their disputes with home States. This phenomenon is known as 'treaty-shopping'.[114] 'Treaty-shopping' leaves open the possibility for a state to be found in breach of more than one obligation, yet for the same measure. Having in mind that one of the objectives of an IIA is to establish a predictable and stable legal framework for investment protection, such a shortcoming poses a serious threat to the system's legitimacy.

---

[109] *CMS Gas Transmission Company v. The Republic of Argentina*, ICSID Case No. ARB/01/8.

[110] *LG&E Energy Corp., LG&E Capital Corp., and LG&E International, Inc. v Argentine Republic*, ICSID Case No. ARB/02/1.

[111] Hansen (2010), p. 524.

[112] *Ronald S. Lauder v The Czech Republic*, UNCITRAL Award 9/2001.

[113] *CME Czech Republic BVv The Czech Republic*, UNCITRAL Award 9/2001.

[114] Kreindler (2010), p. 127.

2.4.3 *Public Interest Concerns*

Achieving greater consistency would benefit States and eventually the system as a whole. But consistent awards might still be able to excessively interfere with the regulatory power of States. Jan Paulsson two decades ago made a striking estimation about the 'delicate mechanism' of investment arbitration, as he calls it. According to Paulsson, a single incident of a daring arbitrator exceeding the strict scope of his jurisdiction may generate a backlash.[115] Another critique made against investment arbitration is that investment tribunals favor foreign investors' interests over the host state's interests and policy-making powers. In other words, there are disagreements as to the right balance between the protection provided by IIAs to foreign investors and the powers of the States to regulate and maintain legitimate government policies for the public welfare.[116]

From a wider perspective, economic globalization is premised on the strong protection of property and the private capital in general. For this reason, international mechanisms are necessary to guard these interests from potential threats. These threats often include democratic processes and sovereign acts taken by States, which are often labeled as extreme. Unsurprisingly, the recent financial crisis has pushed many States to resist economic globalization and revoke associated legal constraints to their sovereignty, including IIAs.[117] This protectionist response is further attributed to the slow but steady decline of state autonomy and the subsequent weakening of their ability to regulate their domestic affairs. In simple terms, many States currently share the belief that their interests are inadequately served through the present system of investment arbitration.[118]

One of the most notable examples used by the proponents of this criticism involves the latest economic collapse of Argentina. Facing a financial crisis in 2002, Argentina promulgated legislative measures as a means to mitigate the effects of a financial collapse. These legislative measures, however, affected large corporations in which foreign investors had invested. The measures taken by Argentina led to the devaluation of their investments. For this reason, many of these foreign investors issued claims against Argentina on the basis of various IIAs.

Notwithstanding the contradicting awards issued by various tribunals over Argentina's measures, the vast majority of tribunals did not accept Argentina's necessity defense.[119] For example in *Enron Corporation v Argentina*, the tribunal held that Argentina did not produce sufficient evidentiary support that events had

[115]Paulsson (1995), p. 257.

[116]McLachlan et al. (2017), p. 23.

[117]*See* generally Schneiderman (2016b), Karl (2008), Caron and Shirlow (2018) and Fowles (2015).

[118]Miller and Hicks (2005).

[119]ILC Articles, Art. 25.

become unmanageable or out of control.[120] In the same case, the tribunal observed that Argentina's previous conduct contributed to the financial crisis, and the measures taken were not the only way to deal with the financial crisis, thus not necessary.[121] The paradigm of Argentina was seen by many as a direct attack by tribunals on a sovereign state's ability to take measures to avert social unrest and financial collapse.[122]

Another prominent example of the tension between the regulatory powers of States and foreign investors interests involves the exact demarcation between legitimate regulation and violation of investment standards.[123] Some scholars suggest that this is a result of the ambiguous and largely unqualified content and scope of the standards of treatment, which raises doubts about their interpretation and demarcation.[124] In turn, this equivocalness allows unpredictable outcomes that do not sufficiently balance all competing interests. As Appleton explains, a failure properly interpret an investment treaty, as prescribed by the Vienna Convention on the Law of Treaties and the ILC Draft Articles on State Responsibility, may result in inconsistent decisions between panels dealing with the same subject-matter and even result in an excess of jurisdiction or an error of law.[125]

For instance, in the case of *Metalclad v Mexico*,[126] the tribunal adopted an expansive meaning of the regulatory measures that could be considered as expropriation under NAFTA.[127] Another prominent example is *Pope & Talbot v Canada* where the tribunal held that foreign investors are entitled to the international law minimum, *plus* the fairness elements.'[128] In this way, the tribunal suggested that the FET standard in NAFTA provides greater protection than customary international law. As a result of these awards, the NAFTA Free Trade Commission (FTC) issued an interpretative declaration in an effort to limit the expansive approaches of investment tribunals when it comes to interpreting standards of treatment.[129]

The expansive interpretation of IIAs has raised concerns since several States have been ordered to pay compensation to foreign investors for public policies aiming to improve the well-being of their citizens. On top of these concerns, it has been demonstrated that the fear of arbitration occasionally prevents States from enacting

---

[120] *Enron Corporation and Ponderosa Assets, L.P. v. Argentine Republic*, ICSID Case No. ARB/01/3, para 307.

[121] *ibid*, para 300.

[122] For a detailed analysis of the awards dealing with Argentina's financial collapse *See* Kurtz (2010).

[123] *See generally* Korzun (2017), pp. 373–380.

[124] Salacuse (2010), p. 453.

[125] Appleton (2013), p. 25.

[126] *Metalclad Corporation v. The United Mexican States*, ICSID Case No. ARB(AF)/97/1.

[127] *See generally* Munro (2005).

[128] *Pope & Talbot v. Canada* UNCITRAL, Award in Respect of Damages of 31 May 2002, para. 110.

[129] Interpretation of NAFTA Chapter 11 – Provisions adopted by the NAFTA Free Trade Commission.

bona fide regulatory measures that might excite claims by foreign investors.[130] This phenomenon is known as 'regulatory chill'. An illustrative example is New Zealand's reluctance to introduce legislation as a result of a pending arbitration dealing with comparable policy measures taken by Australia.[131] Unsurprisingly, following Australia's successful defense, New Zealand introduced similar measures.

2.4.4 Perceived Bias

O'Sullivan once wrote in the *Diary of an Irish Countryman* that there is little utility in using the law against the devil while the hearing will take place in hell.[132] Allegorical as it may be, this vivid passage illustrates a real concern in investment arbitration. Due to the lack of judicial independence and procedural fairness, investment arbitration has been accused for being biased in favor of foreign investors. For this reason, investment arbitration procedures are faced with skepticism by States.

In regard to accusations about bias, it has been observed that arbitrators usually act both as counsel and arbitrator giving rise to concerns about conflicts of interest.[133] It has been suggested that 'double-hatting' creates incentives for arbitrators to interpret IIA in a way that favors them in other cases acting in a different role.[134] On top of that, due to the fact that only investors can bring claims, it has been argued that a business culture is cultivated by arbitrators that makes them to interpret IIAs in favor of investors to gain repeat business.[135] In contrast with other systems of adjudication, arbitrators have limited checks on their power to interpret the law and limited avenues for the disputing parties to challenge the awards. Along the same lines, arbitrators are appointed on a case-by-case basis, while many of them come from a commercial law background.

A claim about the lack of impartiality arose in the case of *Occidental Petroleum v Morocco*.[136] After the dispute's registration, it materialised that the arbitrator appointed by the claimant was also appointed in a senior managerial position of Occidental Petroleum. Furthermore, in a series of joined cases, known as *Suez v Argentina*, Argentina challenged an arbitrator based on a conflict of interest.[137] The rest of the arbitrators, however, considered that Argentina to succeed must indicate

[130] Kyla (2011), p. 609. *See generally* Cote (2014).
[131] Peterson (2013).
[132] O'Sullivan (1979), p. 112.
[133] For a seminal paper *See* Langford et al. (2017).
[134] Van Harten (2007).
[135] *ibid.*
[136] *Holiday Inns SA/Occidental Petroleum v Morocco*, ICSID Case No. ARB/72/1.
[137] *Suez, Sociedad General de Aguas de Barcelona, S.A. and Vivendi Universal, S.A. v. Argentine Republic*, ICSID Case No. ARB/03/19.

'a manifest lack of impartiality or independence.'[138] Unsurprisingly, Argentina failed to meet that standard.

In comparison with domestic law standards where the challenging party normally must prove credible suspicion of conflict or likelihood of bias, the standard in investment arbitration is much higher. In investment arbitration, the challenging party is usually placed in a difficult position to prove a conflict of interest instead of proving credible suspicion of a conflict of interest.[139] As explained above, the investment arbitration system is considered necessary because domestic courts are not considered sufficiently neutral. The fairness of the procedures is largely dependent on the arbitrators. Therefore, it becomes imperative for arbitrators to act in an objective manner. In the absence of a suitable mechanism to assess conflict of interests, the objections against investment arbitration will be further legitimised.[140]

2.4.5 Confidentiality and High Costs

Concerns about confidentiality in investment arbitration are viewed in light of the limited obligations by tribunals to supply information and the inability of third parties to advance private or public interests before a tribunal.[141] The degree of secrecy varies depending on the arbitration rules and the applicable IIAs. To a substantial extent, though, investment arbitration follows the paradigm of international commercial arbitration by keeping the procedures and awards of arbitration in full secrecy. Unlike other legal proceedings, the content and outcome of the proceedings is usually not made known to the public. In certain occasions the existence of arbitration proceedings remains secret.[142] In *Telefonica v México*, the tribunal held that in the absence of any rules of confidentiality and publicity,[143] the former should prevail over the latter. However, it is doubtful whether these features are appropriate taking into consideration the public element in investment disputes.[144]

Another issue of concern is the high costs associated with the resolution of investment disputes. As to this, it has been observed that arbitration costs have averaged over US$8 million with some investment disputes exceeding 30 million.[145]

---

[138] Decision on the Proposal for the Disqualification of a member of the Tribunal. Para. 30. Also *See* ICSID Convention, Article 57.

[139] Art. 57 of the ICSID Convention stipulates that for a disqualification application to succeed, the applicant must establish *manifest lack* of independent judgment.

[140] Nicole Cleis (2017), p. 4.

[141] Adeleke (2015), p. 7.

[142] Bonnitcha et al. (2017), p. 246.

[143] *Telefónica S.A. v. United Mexican States*, ICSID Case No. ARB(AF)/12/4, Dissent to Procedural Order No. 1 (Unofficial English Translation) para. 27.

[144] For further discussion *See* Sarkinovic (2016).

[145] Gaukrodger and Gordon (2012), p. 19.

The largest components are the fees and expenses incurred for legal counsel and arbitration fees.[146] Due to high costs, there are growing policy concerns and in particular the possibility of such costs acting as a barrier to justice.[147] For example, developing States or small and medium investors with little resources find it difficult to participate in investment disputes. Eventually, high costs play to the advantage of financially stronger parties on either side of investment disputes.[148] For this reason, recent attempts have been made by the EU and the UN to limit the costs in investment arbitration.

To sum up, the backlash against investment arbitration is primarily caused by multiple proceedings, the intrusive jurisprudence of tribunals against sovereign acts and the lack of transparency and impartiality. Taking into consideration that a legal system depends on the trust by those subject to it, the backlash against investment arbitration is particularly detrimental. Multiple proceedings and conflicting awards have been giving rise to double compensation, diverging verdicts, and uncertainty as to the locus of settlement. As it has been rightly argued, multiple proceedings are 'problematic because they pose an intrinsic risk of inconsistent legal results.'[149] As a result, this phenomenon leads to legal uncertainty, which makes it more difficult for States to comply with their obligations under IIAs.

Further, both the actual arbitration awards and the fear of a possible penalization by investment tribunals have led to a high degree of legal uncertainty for States. The resulting legal uncertainty expands to the ability of States to adopt and enforce policy measures that are necessary for the public welfare. The procedural aspects of investment arbitration have also been raising concerns. Both the lack of sufficient procedural safeguards for conflicts of interest and the lack of transparency are two of the reasons that have fueled the backlash against investment arbitration. Lastly, the high costs associated with the resolution of investment disputes have been raising concerns. Despite that many find these accusations groundless,[150] opponents of this system flag up an old maxim that it is not only important that justice should be done but that it should also be seen to be done.[151]

[146]*ibid*, p. 19.

[147]*ibid.*

[148]*ibid*, p. 23.

[149]Kreindler (2010), p. 526.

[150]*Supra* note 105.

[151]For an English case discussing this principle *See* R v Sussex Justices, Ex parte McCarthy [1924] 1 KB 256.

2.5 Responses to the Backlash Against Investment Treaty Arbitration

2.5.1 The Way Forward

These critiques have raised legitimate concerns about the sustainability of investment arbitration. Criticism against investment arbitration, however, should begin by recognising that a globalised economy that benefits both rich and poor States requires its own legal rules. Bringing again diplomatic protection, through espousal of claims, as a means to settle investment disputes could undermine FDIs protection and repoliticise investment disputes. By way of rebuttal, some scholars suggest that IIAs are obsolete since foreign investors have the option to negotiate internationalised contracts with States for their protection.[152] This might hold true for foreign investors with sufficient negotiating powers to conclude internationalised private contracts with a host state. However, the rest of the foreign investors might find themselves in a difficult position. Further, foreign investors do not share the same political rights as the citizens of the host state and they might find it even more difficult to influence public policy. On this basis, abandoning investment arbitration might also take away the certainty and the strong enforcement possibilities it provides.[153]

The present system should neither be accepted as it stands nor abandoned totally. One cannot disregard the tension that exist in investment arbitration between the private dispute settlement foundations on which it is modeled after and the public policy implications of the arbitral awards it delivers. Yet, those who argue that exiting investment arbitration is the appropriate solution ignore that this dispute settlement system emerged to address the shortcomings of investment dispute settlement mechanisms of previous decades. In addition to the voices urging States to exit investment arbitration, many States and stakeholders have suggested that reforming this system is the best way forward. As will be argued in the following chapters, the study takes the view that using the Rule of Law framework is the most appropriate method to proceed with reforming investment arbitration.

As a result of the above issues, several States have initiated public consultations in an effort to tackle the modern challenges surrounding the international framework of FDI protection. The G20 States adopted the Guiding Principles for Global Investment Policymaking with the objective to establish an open, transparent and predictable framework for investments protection that should be based on the Rule of Law.[154] In parallel, the EU has initiated a consultation process to improve the

---

[152]For this argument *See* Yackee (2008).

[153]In defence of investment arbitration *See* Brower and Schill (2009). For a critical discussion *See* Van Harten (2010).

[154]The G20 is a forum for the governments from 19 States and the EU. G20 Guiding Principles for Global Investment Policymaking (July 2016).

investment arbitration system and make it more acceptable to those concerned.[155] This could be achieved by drawing a better balance between the policy-making power of States and the need to protect foreign investors.[156] In CETA, both parties claim to have drafted this agreement in accordance with the principles of public judicial making.[157] As will be shown in the following section, the parties have approached investment arbitration as a public law system. Ultimately, the study adopts the view of the G20 and the EU and argues that adopting the methods and principles associated with public law is key in enhancing the legitimacy of investment tribunals.

2.5.2 *Investment Arbitration as a Public Law System*

In the previous sections, it was demonstrated how the private dispute settlement foundations of investment arbitration have contributed to the current legitimacy crisis. In response to this legitimacy crisis, both the EU and Canada have utilised a different approach to draft CETA. According to the EU, in order to deal with the concerns regarding investment arbitration, it is necessary to consider the framework in which the current system operates. This method permits to juxtapose the existing system of investment arbitration with other legal systems with similar characteristics and, subsequently, to identify the ways other similar systems managed to deal with similar criticism.[158]

In particular, a public law analogy has been used to shape the investment dispute settlement mechanism in CETA.[159] Turning to the substantive nature of investment arbitration, tribunals are very powerful bodies in terms of shaping public policy that essentially function as courts with judicial review powers. As States conclude IIAs to increase FDI flows they automatically set up a framework centered on investment arbitration for the control of public—decision-making at the domestic level.[160] This view is easier to accept by having in mind that investment arbitration was developed in the context of ICSID as a functional substitute for those administrative and judicial mechanisms in host States that were insufficient and inaccessible to foreign

---

[155] Hoffmeister and Alexandru (2014), pp. 380–381. For a study on EU Foreign Investment Law *See* Dimopoulos (2012).

[156] *ibid*, pp. 380–381.

[157] Council Negotiating Directives (Canada, India and Singapore) (2011). *See generally* Council of the European Union, Negotiating Directives for a Convention Establishing a Multilateral Court for the Settlement of Investment Disputes, (2018); Schreuer (2016), pp. 737–738.

[158] The EU accepts that investment arbitration resembles a public law system as it deals with the relationship between individuals and States. *See generally* European Commission (2017).

[159] *See generally* Vadi (2015), pp. 41–43; Von Bogdandy and Venzke (2014), Ch. 3. On analogies and investment arbitration *See* Paparinskis (2014) and Roberts (2006).

[160] Ortino (2012), p. 6; Schill (2011a).

investors.[161] In the same manner, the substantive obligations in IIAs are relatively indeterminate in the sense that they set down general legal provisions intended to apply in multiple fact patterns, much like constitutional provisions.[162] This means that investment tribunals are mainly tasked to further refine the meaning of these broadly construed standards of treatment.

Schill and Kingsbury argue that investment tribunals function as review mechanisms that assess the balance a State has struck between foreign investor protection and other fundamental public purposes.'[163] In a far more radical view, Van Harten and Loughlin argue that investment treaty arbitration is not just an evolving system of global administrative law but it may constitute the only model of global administrative law yet to have emerged.[164]

In particular, the public law analogy places greater emphasis on the regulatory power of States and the public interest. It is this recognition of a States' role as the representative of a particular population that provides the basis for the public law approach and distinguishes investment arbitration from private dispute settlement.[165] This approach takes as its premise that States should be entitled to change their legal framework, subject to certain restrictions, even if those actions have an adverse impact on FDIs. Therefore, arbitrators should acknowledge that investment protection should not be championed automatically at the expense of other public policy considerations. At the same time, the public law framework recognises that States should be held accountable for their actions against private individuals.

Ultimately, arbitrators should be seen as dealing with the judicial control of public authority, where they must fulfill the expectations of a wider audience and its demands for legal certainty, access to justice, procedural fairness, transparency and legitimate outcomes.[166] The fact that tribunals deal with the exercise and control of public authority, in conjunction with the criticism made against investment arbitration, calls for a public law framework in an effort to advance legal standards that satisfy contemporary expectations of legitimacy.[167]

In addition to the substantive aspect of investment arbitration, the procedural aspect of this system resembles a public law procedural mechanism. For the purpose of concluding investment treaties, States consent to the compulsory arbitration of disputes with an unknown number of foreign investors. An investor does not need to

---

[161]*See generally* Franck (2007), pp. 365–366; Ginsburg (2006).

[162]Council of the European Union, Negotiating Directives for a Convention Establishing a Multilateral Court for the Settlement of Investment Disputes, (2018).

[163]Kingsbury and Schill (2009), p. 1.

[164]Van Harten and Loughlin (2006), p. 122.

[165]*See generally* Lowe (2010), Ch. 1.

[166]Kingsbury et al. (2005), p. 17. For another seminal paper on Supranational Governance and Global Administrative Law *See* Esty (2006).

[167]Glamis Gold, Ltd. v. The United States of America, UNCITRAL. The tribunal held that a case-specific mandate is not license to ignore systemic implications. To the contrary, it arguably makes it all the more important that each panel renders its specific decision with sensitivity to the position of future panels and an awareness of other systemic implications.

have a contract with a state to initiate proceedings against the host state. The option to arbitrate under the provisions of an IIA is open to everyone that satisfies the conditions for initiating a claim. Furthermore, in investment arbitration States cannot bring a claim against foreign investors. Investment disputes, therefore, do not arise in the context of a reciprocal relationship as it happens in international commercial arbitration. On the contrary, investment arbitration resembles a governing arrangement where individuals are entitled to damages if an action by a State is found to be illegal. Accordingly, the State is the governor and the foreign investor is governed.

As was pointed by Van Harten, only the States have the power to consent to arbitration because only them have the authority to regulate individuals in their jurisdiction and to sanction the adjudication of disputes between them and foreign investors who are subject to their regulatory powers.[168] In this way, the general consent provided in investment treaties transform investment treaty arbitration from an arrangement of consensual adjudication of disputes into a governing arrangement.'[169]

Treating investment arbitration as a public law mechanism has received support among some arbitrators as well. In *Saipem v Bangladesh*, the tribunal held that it has a responsibility to adopt solutions established in a series of consistent cases.[170] The tribunal added further that it should provide to the development of investment law and thereby to meet the legitimate expectations of States and foreign investors towards certainty of the rule of law.[171]

As explained earlier in this chapter, the core tenets of legal positivism in international law, such as state consent, are incapable of explaining why reforms are necessary in the context investment arbitration, thereby casting doubts on whether this approach can be seen as a solution to the crisis. The above realization calls for a re-examination as to the ways this legal system is studied in order to comprehend the nature of investment arbitration.[172] For these reasons, investment tribunals can no longer be considered as mere agents of States.[173] A public law framework, therefore, is a necessary tool both for understanding the legitimacy crisis in investment arbitration and for dealing with it.[174]

---

[168]Van Harten (2007), p. 64.

[169]*ibid.*

[170]*Saipem S.p.A. v. The People's Republic of Bangladesh*, ICSID Case No. ARB/05/07, para. 90.

[171]*ibid*, para. 90.

[172]Indicatively, Ulfstein argues that the international judiciary, including investment tribunals, may interfere in most subjects of constitutional concern, thus making the distinction between international and domestic issues blurred. Additionally, the combination of the vague standards with the 'evolutive' interpretation of international tribunals speak to the fact that these tribunals are conferred with sovereign powers that could hardly be foreseen at the treaty's adoption and ratification. Eventually, the constitutional functions of international tribunals raise concerns regarding accountability. *See generally* Ulfstein (2009).

[173]*See generally* Stone Sweet and Grisel (2017).

[174]Chen attempts to provide a 'superior' solution to the legitimacy crisis through a traditional approach, yet his arguments are limited to the regulatory power of States. In particular, he argues

Investment tribunals should be considered as judicial bodies that exercise public functions as their decisions affect the regulatory powers of States and non-disputing parties. Resolving whether a sovereign act has met a standard of treatment is a core element of the judicial function in public law. It is this ability of investment tribunals that has shifted the focus from concerns regarding State sovereignty and consent to the legitimacy of tribunals to regulate the conduct of others. More specifically, the criticism focuses on the ability of tribunals to unilaterally determine disputes with public interest implications. The public law function of investment tribunals, in conjunction with the criticism made against investment arbitration, subsequently call for a public law framework in an effort 'to develop legal standards for ensuring that they satisfy contemporary expectations of legitimacy.'[175]

To this end, the EU in a concept paper introduced a path for reforms towards the realisation of a new era for investment arbitration. According to this concept paper, a new investment policy is required that does not affect the ability of the EU and the Member States to regulate in the public interest.[176] In order to do so, reforms are required for both the substantive and procedural aspects of the current investment arbitration mechanism.[177] Furthermore, the Joint Interpretative Instrument on CETA asserts that both parties recognise the importance of the right to regulate in the public interest. The same legal instrument reaffirms both parties' commitment to transparent procedures and judicial consistency. Further, it is stated that CETA moves decisively from the traditional approach of investment arbitration and is inspired by the principles of public judicial making in the EU and Canada.[178] After all, Article 21 of the Treaty on European Union stipulates that the EU external actions shall be guided by the principles of the Rule of Law and human rights.[179]

Last, but not least, the EU took the initiative to establish a multilateral investment court in an effort to create a consistent and uniform jurisprudence in international investment law.[180] As will be argued in the chapters that follow, the success of this initiative will depend on the number of States willing to join this court.

To sum up, in response to the backlash a variety of States and stakeholders have approached investment arbitration as a system of judicial review for the control of

---

that by focusing on states' intentions when interpreting the standards of treatment it will be possible for states to take back control and protect their regulatory powers. Nevertheless, he fails to mention other aspects of the legitimacy crisis i.e. impartiality, transparency and multiple proceedings. *See generally* Chen (2015).

[175]Von Bogdandy et al. (2009), pp. 4–5. For the purposes of the study, legitimacy is understood very broadly as the desirability or the appropriateness of legal rules and institutions. *See generally* Franck (1990), Ch. 1; Grossman et al. (2018).

[176]European Commission (2015), p. 1.

[177]*ibid,* p. 1.

[178]Council of the European Union (2016) Joint Interpretative Instrument on the Comprehensive Economic and Trade Agreement (CETA) between Canada and the European Union and its Member States.

[179]TEU, Article 21.

[180]CETA. Art. 8. 29.

public decision-making. Given the procedural and substantive aspects of investment arbitration, it is argued that this system of law resembles a public law system. Ultimately, the monograph argues that treating investment arbitration as a public law system and adopting the methods associated with it is key to enhancing the legitimacy of investment arbitration.

2.6 Conclusion

This chapter attempted to identify the reasons behind the backlash against investment arbitration and explain the method through which the parties to CETA have responded to this backlash. As indicated in this chapter, History shows that the current decentralised regime of IIAs is a result of world-changing political events and heated ideological conflicts between economic globalization and economic nationalism. All of them essentially centered on intense debates about the legal status of FDIs and private property. The lack of a multilateral framework for investment protection, the proliferation of tribunals coupled with their *ad hoc* nature has contributed to the academic and political uproar against investment arbitration. As James Crawford accurately explains, a struggle of the twentieth century that is continuing until today is a struggle for permanence against *ad hoc* arrangements for dispute settlement.[181]

Furthermore, the fact that investment arbitration has been modeled after international commercial arbitration plays a key role in enhancing the backlash. The basic features of the private law framework that investment arbitration is currently based on, namely confidentiality and flexibility, do not translate well in a legal system that resembles a public law system of adjudication. As was illustrated in this chapter, the paradox with investment arbitration is that investment tribunals vested with the power to review and control the exercise of public authority are largely unrestrained and inconsistent in their decision-making abilities. Compared with other dispute settlement methods, arbitration provides more flexibility and a correspondingly lower degree of predictability about the outcome of an investment dispute. Accordingly, the confidentiality of the arbitral proceedings results in lack of transparency, the flexibility of the private law framework results in arbitrariness and institutional bias, and the high costs associated with the resolution of investment arbitration raise concerns over access to justice.

Additionally, the opaque nature of the standards of treatment led scholars to raise concerns over the legal uncertainty. The inconsistent awards further complicate the situation since States and affected non-disputing parties are unable to clearly identify the scope of their obligations and rights under IIAs. All the above have led to an intrusive interference of investment tribunals, which often rule inconsistently, over sovereign acts. In parallel, investment tribunals have demonstrated a reluctance to

[181] Crawford (2010), p. 13.

take into consideration human rights. It is the above criticism that fueled the legitimacy crisis and, subsequently, forced States to demand the redrafting of several procedural and substantive aspects of IIAs.

The public law nature of investment arbitration, in conjunction with the legitimacy crisis, calls for a public law framework in an effort to advance legal standards to ensure that such a mechanism satisfies contemporary expectations of legitimacy. Moreover, the sub-elements driving the legitimacy crisis in investment arbitration can be articulated through the vocabularies of public law and the Rule of Law. By taking a closer look. one will notice that the normative standpoints of legitimacy crisis are norms and principles of liberal constitutionalism—transparency, legal certainty, procedural fairness, access to justice and fundamental rights. These principles form part of the Rule of Law: the uniting legal principle from which the legitimacy concerns in investment arbitration stem.

An analogous situation with domestic courts taking decisions under the same conditions as investment tribunals would make it really hard to deny the existence of a Rule of Law crisis. As the third chapter will argue, the backlash against investment arbitration reflects fundamentally a Rule of Law crisis within investment law's dispute settlement mechanism. The relevance of this explanation lies in the fact that it provides greater clarity about the reason behind the legitimacy crisis since it identifies the cause of the legitimacy crisis, rather than its symptoms. It is, therefore, possible to reconstruct widespread, but often incomplete, critiques of this dispute settlement system. In turn, this clarity lays the ground for the ways in which this crisis could be confronted. It is therefore argued that the concept of the Rule of Law is not only able to identify the source of the legitimacy crisis in investment arbitration but it can also become a source of inspiration for reforms.

That said, it must be noted that the parties to CETA claim that its investment chapter ensures that investment disputes will be adjudicated in full accordance with the Rule of Law. Against this background, the monograph will focus on CETA's Investment Chapter and ask whether it fits with the public law paradigm and, more specifically, the Rule of Law framework. However, before proceeding on a detailed evaluation of CETA, it is necessary to provide in the next chapter a robust theoretical analysis of the Rule of Law framework and, in particular, its scope and content in the context of investment arbitration.

References

Adeleke F (2015) The role of law in assessing the value of transparency and the disconnect with the lived realities under Investor-State Dispute Settlement. SECO working papers no. 06/2015

Appleton B (2013) The song is over: why it's time to stop talking about an International Investment Arbitration Appellate Body. Proc Am Soc Int Law 107:23

Argyrios F (1961) An international code to protect private investment-proposals and perspectives. Univ Toronto Law J 14:1

Bhagwati JN (1995) US trade policy: the infatuation with FTAs. Discussion paper series no. 726

Bianchi A (2016) International law theories: an inquiry into different ways of thinking. Oxford University Press
Blackaby N, Partasides C (2015) Redfern and hunter on international arbitration, 6th edn. Oxford University Press
Bockstiegel KH (2012) Commercial and investment arbitration: how different are they today? Arbitr Int LCIA 28:4
Bolivar G (2005) The teleology of international investment law: the role of purpose in the interpretation of international investment agreements. J World Invest Trade 6:5
Bonnitcha J et al (2017) The political economy of the investment treaty regime. Oxford University Press
Braun T (2010) Part V Chapter 21: Globalization: the driving force in international investment law. In: Waibel M, Kaushal A et al (eds) The backlash against investment arbitration. Kluwer Law International
Bray HL (2018) Understanding change: evolution from international claims commissions to investment treaty arbitration. In: Schill S et al (eds) International investment law and history. Elgar Publications, pp 111–118
Brower C, Blanchard S (2014) What's in a meme? The truth about investor-state arbitration: why it need not, and must not be repossessed by states. Columbia J Transl Law 52
Brower C, Schill S (2009) Is arbitration a threat or a boon to the legitimacy of international investment law. Chic J Int Law 9
Calamita NJ (2015) The rule of law, investment treaties, and economic growth: mapping normative and empirical questions. In: Jowell J et al (eds) The importance of the rule of law in promoting development. Singapore Academy of Law, p 111
Caron D, Shirlow E (2018) Dissecting backlash: the unarticulated causes of backlash and its unintended consequences. In: Follesdal A, Ulfstein G (eds) The judicialization of international law: a mixed blessing? Oxford University Press
Cassese S (2005) Administrative law without the state? The challenge of global regulation. N Y J Int Law Polit, p 692
Chen R (2015) A contractual approach to investor-state regulatory disputes. Yale J Int Law 40:2
Christopher Thomas J, Kaur Dhillon H (2017) The foundations of investment treaty arbitration: the ICSID convention, investment treaties and the review of arbitration awards. ICSID Rev 32 (3):476–480
Coleman J (2002) Methodology. In: Coleman J, Shapiro S (eds) The Oxford handbook of law of jurisprudence and philosophy of law. Oxford University Press
Cote C (2014) A chilling effect? The impact of international investment agreements on national regulatory autonomy in the areas of health, safety and environment. LSE thesis repository
Council Negotiating Directives (Canada, India and Singapore), 12 September 2011. www.bilaterals.org/?eu-negotiating-mandates-on
Council of the European Union (2016) Joint interpretative instrument on the Comprehensive Economic and Trade Agreement (CETA) between Canada and the European Union and its Member States. data.consilium.europa.eu/doc/document/ST-13541-2016-INIT/en/pdf. Accessed 20 May 2020
Council of the European Union, Negotiating Directives for a Convention Establishing a Multilateral Court for the Settlement of Investment Disputes, 1 March 2018 (Brussels). data.consilium.europa.eu/doc/document/ST-12981-2017-ADD-1-DCL-1/en/pdf
Crawford J (2010) Continuity and discontinuity in international dispute settlement: an inaugural lecture. J Int Dispute Settlement 1:13
D'Aspremont J (2011) Formalism and the sources of international law: a theory of the ascertainment of legal rules. Oxford University Press, Ch. 2
Desierto D (2012) The International Court of Justice in the settlement of international investment disputes. J Dispute Prev Resolution 1:1
Dezalay Y, Garth BG (1996) Dealing in virtue: international commercial arbitration and the construction of a transnational legal order. The University of Chicago Press, Ch. 1

Dimopoulos A (2012) EU foreign investment law. Oxford University Press
Dolzer R (1986) Permanent sovereignty over natural resources and economic decolonization. Hum Rights Law J 7:217
Dolzer R, Schreuer C (2012) Principles of international investment law, 2nd edn. Oxford University Press, p 3
Douglas Z (2003) The hybrid foundations of investment treaty arbitration. Br Yearb Int Law 74:51
Dugan C et al (2008) Investor – state arbitration. Oxford University Press, pp 26–33
Dumberry P (2016) The formation and identification of rule of customary international law in international investment law. Cambridge University Press, Ch. 2
Dupuy P, Vinuales E (2013) The challenge of proliferation: an anatomy of the debate. In: Romano C et al (eds) The Oxford handbook of international adjudication. Oxford University Press
Echandi R (2011) What do developing countries expect from the international investment regime? In: Alvarez J, Sauvant K (eds) The evolving international investment regime. Oxford University Press
Esty DC (2006) Good governance at the supranational level: globalizing administrative law. Yale Law J 115:7
European Commission. Investment in TTIP and beyond: the path for reform: concept paper (2015), p 1. trade.ec.europa.eu/doclib/docs/2015/may/tradoc_153408.PDF. Accessed 20 May 2020
European Commission. The identification and consideration of concerns as regards investors to state dispute settlement, 20 November 2017. trade.ec.europa.eu/doclib/docs/2017/november/tradoc_156402.pdf
Fowles S (2015) The subtle revolution: TTIP, CETA and the Sovereignty of Parliament. Mishcon de Reya
Franck T (1990) The power of legitimacy among nations. Oxford University Press, Ch. 1
Franck S (2007) Foreign direct investment, investment treaty arbitration, and the rule of law. Glob Bus Dev Law J 19:365–366
Franck S (2015) Conflating politics and development? Examining investment treaty arbitration outcomes. Virginia J Int Law 55
G20 Guiding Principles for Global Investment Policymaking (July 2016) trade.ec.europa.eu/doclib/docs/2016/july/tradoc_154790.pdf. Accessed 21 May 2020
Garcia-Mora M (1950) The Calvo Clause in Latin American constitutions and international law. Marquette Law Rev 33(4):205–208
Gaukrodger D, Gordon K (2012) Investor-State Dispute Settlement: a scoping paper for the investment policy community. OECD working papers on international investment no. 2012/13
Ginsburg T (2006) International substitutes for domestic institutions: bilateral investment treaties and governance. Illinois Law and Economics Working Paper Series
Grossman N et al (eds) (2018) Legitimacy and international courts. Cambridge University Press
Halsbury's Laws (5th edition, 2010) vol 61, paras 462–463
Hansen R (2010) Parallel proceedings in Investor – State Treaty Arbitration: responses for treaty – drafters, arbitrators and parties. Mod Law Rev 73(4):524
Hirsch M (2014) The sociology of international investment law. In: Douglas Z et al (eds) The foundations of international investment law: bringing theory into practice. Oxford University Press
History of the ICSID Convention: Documents Concerning the Origin and the Formulation of the Convention on the Settlement of Investment Disputes between States and Nationals of Other States (2009) ICSID Publications, p 484
Hoffmeister F, Alexandru G (2014) A first glimpse of lights of the emerging invisible EU model BIT. J World Investment Trade 15:380–381
Hood M (1977) Gunboat diplomacy, 1895–1905, great power pressure in Venezuela. South Brunswick Publications
Hutchinson T (2017) Doctrinal research. In: Watkins D et al (eds) Research methods in law, 2nd edn. Routledge
Kahale G (2018) ISDS: the wild, wild west of international practice. Brooklyn J Int Law 44:1

Karl J (2008) International investment arbitration: a threat to state sovereignty? In: Shan W et al (eds) Redefining sovereignty in international economic law. Hart
Kenneth V (1998) The political economy of bilateral investment treaty. Am J Int Law 92(621):4
Kingsbury B, Schill S (2009) Investor-state arbitration as governance: fair and equitable treatment, proportionality and the emerging global administrative law. New York University School of Law, Public Law & Legal Theory Research Paper Series, p 1
Kingsbury B et al (2005) The emergence of global administrative law. New York University Public Law and Legal Theory Working Paper 17, p 17
Korzun V (2017) The right to regulate in investor-state arbitration: slicing and dicing regulatory carve – outs. Vanderbilt J Trans Law 355:373–380
Kreindler R (2010) Part II Chapter 6: parallel proceedings: a practitioner's perspective. In: Waibel M, Kaushal A et al (eds) The backlash against investment arbitration. Kluwer Law International, p 526
Kurtz J (2010) Adjusting the exceptional at international investment law: security, public order and financial crisis. Int Comp Law Q 59:2
Kyla T (2011) Regulatory chill and the thread of arbitration: a view from political science. In: Brown C, Miles K (eds) Evolution in investment treaty law and arbitration. Cambridge University Press, p 609
Lando O (1985). The Lex Mercatoria in international commercial arbitration. Int Comp Law Q 34:747
Langford M et al (2017) The revolving door in International investment arbitration. J Int Econ Law
Lauterpacht E (1991) Aspects of the administration of international justice. Cambridge University Press, p 15
Linarelly J et al (2018) The misery of international law: confrontations with injustice in the global economy. Oxford University Press, Ch. 3
Lipson C (1985) Standing guard: protecting foreign capital in the nineteenth and twentieth centuries. University of California Press, pp 16–19
Lowe V (2010) Private disputes and the public interest in international law. In: French D et al (eds) International law and dispute settlement: new problems and techniques. Hart, Ch. 1
Lowenfeld A (2009) The ICSID Convention: origins and transformations. Georgia J Int Comp Law 38(47):55
Martinez-Fraca PJ, Ryan Reetz C (2014) Public purpose in international law: rethinking regulatory sovereignty in the global era. Cambridge University Press
McLachlan C et al (2017) International investment arbitration – substantive principles, 2nd edn. Oxford University Press, p 23
Mexico – United States: Expropriation by Mexico of Agrarian properties owned by American citizens, (1938) 33 American Journal of International Law, p 181
Miles K (2013) The origins of international investment law: empire, environment and the safeguarding of capital. Cambridge University Press, p 33
Miller S, Hicks G (2005) Investor-State Dispute Settlement: a reality check. Rowman & Littlefield, Centre for Strategic & International Studies, pp 8–10
Mills A (2011) Antinomies of public and private at the foundations of international investment law and arbitration. J Int Econ Law 14(2):469
Montt S (2009) State liability and investment treaty arbitration: global constitutional and administrative law in the BIT generation. Hart, p 57
Muchlinski P (2011) Corporation and the uses of law: international investment law arbitration as a 'Multilateral Legal Order'. Onati Socio-Legal Series 1(4):4
Munro M (2005) Expropriating expropriation law: the implications of the metalclad decision on Canadian expropriation law and environmental land-use regulation. Asper Rev Int Bus Trade Law 5:75
Nelson T (2010) History ain't changed: why investor-state arbitration will survive the 'New Revolution'. In: Waibel M, Kaushal A et al (eds) The backlash against investment arbitration. Kluwer Law International

Newcombe A, Paradell L (2008) Law and practice of investment treaties. Kluwer Law International, p 10
Nicole Cleis M (2017) The independence and impartiality of ICSID Arbitrators. Brill Publications, p 4
O'Sullivan H (1979) Diary of an Irish Countryman. Mercier Press, p 112
Ortino F (2012) The investment treaty system as judicial review. King's College London Dickson Poon School of Law Legal Studies Research Paper Series, p 6
Pahuja S (2013) Decolonizing international law: development, economic growth and the politics of universality. Cambridge University Press, Ch. 4
Paparinskis M (2014) Analogies and other regimes of international law. In: Douglas Z et al (eds) The foundations of international investment law: bringing theory into practice. Cambridge University Press
Parlett K (2011) The individual in the international legal system: continuity and change in international law. Cambridge University Press, pp 103–119
Paulsson J (1995) Arbitration without privity. ICSID Rev 10:257
Paulsson J (2013) The idea of arbitration. Oxford University Press, p 13
Perrone N (2016) International investment regime after the global crisis of neoliberalism: rupture or continuity? Indiana J Glob Legal Stud 23(2):621
Peterson L (2013) First heating in Philip Morris v Australia arbitration is pushed into 2014, as New Zealand reveals its awaiting outcome of Australian cases. IA Reporter. www.iareporter.com/articles/first-hearing-in-philip-morris-v-australia-arbitration-is-pushed-into-2014-as-new-zealand-reveals-it-is-awaiting-outcome-of-australian-cases/
Poulsen L (2015) Bounded rationality and economic diplomacy: the politics of investment treaties in developing countries. Cambridge University Press, Ch. 2
Preziosi A (1989) The Andean Pact's Foreign Investment Code Decision 2020: an agreement to disagree. Univ Miami Inter-American Law Rev 20:656
Reisman M (2017) The empire strikes back: the struggle to reshape ISDS. SSRN database, p 12. papers.ssrn.com/sol3/papers.cfm?abstract_id=2943514
Roberts A (2006) Clash of paradigms: actors and analogies shaping the investment treaty regime. Eur J Int Law 17:1
Roberts A (2015) Triangular treaties: the extent and limits of investment treaty rights. Am J Int Law 56:2
Root E (1910) The basis of protection to citizens residing abroad. Am J Int Law 4:517
Rosado de Sa Ribeiro M, Jose Guterres Costa Junior O (2015) Global governance and investment treaty arbitration: the importance of the Argentine crisis for future dispute. Law Pract Int Courts Tribunals 14:421–426
Salacuse J (1999) From developing countries to emerging markets: a changing role of law in the third world. Int Lawyer 33
Salacuse J (2007) The treatification of international investment law. Law Bus Rev Am 13:155
Salacuse J (2010) The emerging global regime for investment. Harv Int Law J 51
Salacuse J, Sullivan N (2005) Do BITs really work?: an evaluation of bilateral investment treaties and their grand bargain. Harv Int Law J 46:78
Sarkinovic TB (2016) Investor-state arbitration: between private and public interests. Manchester J Int Econ Law 13:250
Schefer K (2016) International investment law: text, cases and materials, 2nd edn. Elgar Publications, p 7
Schill S (2009) The multilateralization of international investment law. Cambridge University Press
Schill S (2010) Crafting the international economic order: the public function of investment treaty arbitration and its significance for the role of the arbitrator. Leiden J Int Law 3
Schill S (2011a) Enhancing international investment law's legitimacy: conceptual and methodological foundations of a new public law approach. Virginia J Int Law 52
Schill S (2011b) W(h)ither fragmentation? On the literature and sociology of international investment law. Eur J Int Law 22:3

Schneiderman D (2016a) Global constitutionalism and international economic law: the case of international investment law. In: Bungenberg M et al (eds) European yearbook of international economic law. Springer, p 23
Schneiderman D (2016b) Resisting economic globalization: critical theory and international investment law. Palgrave Press
Schreuer C (2016) The development of international law by ICSID tribunals. ICSID Rev 31 (3):737–738.
Shihata I (2009) Towards a greater depoliticization of investment disputes: the roles of ICSID and MIGA. In: Lu K et al (eds) Investing with confidence: understanding political risk management in the 21st century. The World Bank Group
Sornarajah M (2011) The international law on foreign investment, 3rd edn. Cambridge University Press, p 20
St John T (2018) The rise of investor-state arbitration: politics, law and unintended consequences. Oxford University Press, Ch. 1
Stone Sweet A, Grisel F (2017) The evolution of international arbitration: judicialization, governance, legitimacy. Oxford University Press
Subedi S (2016) International investment law: reconciling policy and principle, 3rd edn. Hart, Ch. 3
Thomas O, Gimblett J (2011) From gunboats to BITs: the evolution of modern international investment law. In: Sauvant K (ed) Yearbook of international investment law & policy. Oxford University Press, pp 661–662
Titi A (2014) The right to regulate in international investment law. Nomos
Ulfstein G (2009) The international judiciary. In: Klabbers J et al (eds) The constitutionalization of international law. Oxford University Press
UN General Assembly, Declaration on the Establishment of a New International Economic Order (1974). www.un-documents.net/s6r3201.htm. Accessed 1 May 2020
United Nations Conference on Trade and Development, World Investment Report (2015), p 128
Vadi V (2015) Analogies in international investment law and arbitration. Cambridge University Press, pp 41–43
Van Harten G (2007) Investment treaty arbitration and public law. Oxford University Press, p 152
Van Harten G (2010) Five justifications for investment treaties: a critical discussion. Trade Law Dev 2(1):19
Van Harten G, Loughlin M (2006) Investment treaty arbitration as a species of global administrative law. Eur J Int Law 17:122
Vandevelde K (2009) Brief history of international investment agreements. In: Sauvant K, Sachs L (eds) The effect of treaties on foreign direct investment treaties: bilateral investment treaties, double taxation treaties, and investment flows. Oxford University Press
Vattel E (2008) The law of nations or principle of natural law. First published 1758. Liberty Fund 2008, p 315
Vaughan L (2007) Changing dimensions of international investment law. University of Oxford Faculty of Law Legal Studies Research Paper Series, p 37
Von Bogdandy A, Venzke I (2014) In whose name? A public law theory of international adjudication. Oxford University Press, Ch. 3
Von Bogdandy A et al (2009) Developing the publicness of public international law: towards a legal framework for global governance activities. In: Von Bogdandy A et al (eds) The exercise of public authority by international institutions: advancing international institutional law. Springer, pp 4–5
Walde T (2009) Interpreting investment treaties: experiences and examples. In: Binder C et al (eds) International investment law for the 21st century: essays in honour of Christoph Schreuer. Oxford University Press, p 727
Walde T (2010) Equality of arms' in investment arbitration: procedural challenges. In: Small KY (ed) Arbitration under international investment agreements: a guide to key issues. Oxford University Press, p 177
Williamson J (2004) The strange history of the Washington Consensus. J Post Keynesian Econ 27:2

Yackee J (2008) Do we really need BITs? Toward a return to contract in international investment law. Asian J WTO Int Health Law Policy 121

Yang X (2016) Sovereign immunity. Oxford International Law. www.oxfordbibliographies.com/view/document/obo-9780199796953/obo-9780199796953-0018.xml. Accessed 28 Apr 2020

Chapter 3
Investment Treaty Arbitration and the Rule of Law: Tensions and Solutions

3.1 Introduction

Given that the legitimacy crisis against investment arbitration is essentially a Rule of Law crisis, the aim of this chapter is to highlight the substantive and procedural components of the Rule of Law in the context of investment arbitration. To that end, the first part of this chapter will provide a brief overview of the historical origins of the Rule of Law. In the second part, both the procedural and the substantive aspects of the Rule of Law will be examined in order to highlight its significance and relevance in investment disputes. Finally, the third part of this chapter elaborates on the way the concept of the Rule of Law interacts with certain aspects of investment arbitration, and, most importantly, how it could contribute to ending the legitimacy crisis. Eventually, the chapter argues that the Rule of Law constitutes a concrete theoretical framework to evaluate investment arbitration. This argument builds on the understanding that the Rule of Law could be and should be utilized as a framework through which legal developments in investment treaty arbitration can be analysed, compared, and evaluated. This in turn will help us address the research problem of this monograph.

3.2 Historical Origins of the Rule of Law

3.2.1 Classical Origins

In order to take full advantage of the Rule of Law and to establish on which terms it is useful in the context of investment arbitration, one should focus on locating the historical origins of the concept. The broadest formulation of the Rule of Law refers

K. Dionysiou, *CETA's Investment Chapter*, European Yearbook of International Economic Law 13, https://doi.org/10.1007/978-3-030-66992-8_3

to the notion that the law limits the sovereign, and its officials.[1] The roots of this notion date back to Ancient Greek and Roman thought. The first attempt to put together a formulation of the modern conception of the Rule of Law took place in Ancient Greece.[2] In the fifth century BC, Athens was the first Greek city-state governed, to a large extent, directly by its own citizens. Nevertheless, history demonstrates that a political system that is based on popular consent is as vulnerable to tyrannic rule as a monarchy.[3] In other words, if the law does not operate independently from politics, the latter might be utilised as a means through which the state conducts its affairs. The Rule of Law becomes redundant if it used as an instrument of unlimited state power, rather than becoming a tool that constrains political power.[4]

The substantial difference between Ancient Athens with the rest of the political regimes of that period was the subordination of popular sovereignty to the body of law.[5] In turn, for the sovereignty of laws to have an independent value, systems and standards were established in order to prevent arbitrary amendments and abusive revocations of the laws. In the words of Tamanaha, 'the faith they expressed in the Rule of Law was in contemplation of its stability and restraining effect.[6] In that sense, the Rule of law emerged to protect the people from the unlimited powers of the state. This feature in the political system of Ancient Athens, primitive in its application as it may have been, draws a bright line between the Rule *of* Law and Rule *by* Law. This was eloquently explained in the famous words of Aristotle when he said that man when separated from law and justice he is the worst animal of all and that the Rule of Law is preferred that of any individual.[7]

This historic passage further encapsulates a timeless problem that famously arose in Rome when Justinian became Emperor. Following Justinian's order, the *Corpus Iuris Civilis* was drafted which constituted a codification of the then civil code. The code pleaded, among others, that the law does not bind emperors, for they made the law.[8] In view of this, one of the great features of this period was the blur distinction between political power and law. Needless to say, history tells us that for the Rule of Law to work, the lawmaking power of the government should be reconciled with being subject to the law at the same time. In conclusion, the classical period illustrates that absolute political power is irreconcilable with the Rule of Law.

---

[1]Loughlin (2010), p. 324.

[2]*See generally* Miller (2010).

[3]*See generally* Hayek (2011), pp. 241–243.

[4]*See generally* Maravall (2003), pp. 264–265.

[5]Ostwald (1986), p. 497.

[6]Tamanaha (2004), p. 8.

[7]Aristotle (2008), pp. 29 & 140.

[8]Van Caenegem (1996), p. 73.

3.2.2 Medieval Period

Another milestone of historical importance for the Rule of Law can be traced back to the medieval period and, more specifically, in the Germanic customary law.[9] In that period, customary law required that legal change should be consented by those affected.[10] This legal tradition was important in order to protect the subjects to the law from arbitrary change. Along the same line, the monarchs and the state existed for the law and within the law. The importance of the law in the German customary law can be demonstrated from the 'the right of resistance', according to which the people could abandon their king if their king breached the law.[11] These features make clear, albeit certain deviations, that no one was above the law. The subsequent expansion of the Germanic lands across the European continent spread the Rule of Law in other parts of France and Spain.[12]

However, the most important development of that period was the signing of the Magna Carta in 1215, also known as the Great Charter. This document was a product of barons that forced the English King to limit his powers and prevent him from imposing further taxes that would have financed a war against France.[13] As famously stated in clause 39 of the Charter, no free man shall be imprisoned or sentenced except by the lawful judgment of his peers or by the law of the land.[14] This clause confirmed that the King's decisions were not to be arbitrary, but based upon the ordinary law of the land. The charter's historical importance lies in the fact that it 'represented and expressed a clear rejection of unbridled, unaccountable royal power, an assertion that even the supreme power in the state must be subject to certain overriding rules.'[15]

In addition to the subordination of the English King to the command of the law, Magna Carta became a symbol for the development of the modern notion of procedural fairness. This notion requires a minimum of legal procedures, including the right to be heard in front of an impartial judiciary, in the context of adjudication of legal disputes.[16] To this, clause 40 of the Charter states that 'to one we will sell, to no one deny or delay right or justice.'[17]

---

[9] On the German tradition and the Rule of Law ('Rechtsstaat') *See* Frandberg (2014).

[10] *ibid.*

[11] Tamanaha (2004), p. 24.

[12] Smithers (1902), pp. 689–690.

[13] Tamanaha (2004), p. 26.

[14] The Magna Carta, (The British Library).

[15] Bingham (2010), p. 12.

[16] Radin (1947), pp. 1060–1061.

[17] The Magna Carta, (The British Library).

3.2.3 Modern Period

In the previous sections it was demonstrated how the Rule of Law emerged as a concept in an effort to limit the powers of the state. Nowadays, the Rule of Law is understood and most widely used with reference to the liberal version of the concept. The Rule of Law is understood as a set of closely related principles that together aim to constrain governmental action and to protect human rights through the application of the law by independent judges.[18] The political developments in the US and France during the seventeenth and the eighteenth century constitute a crucial point in the history of the Rule of Law. The new conception of the Rule of Law viewed the individual independently of his social and political context and seen as a unitary subject with specific rights and freedoms.[19] The challenge of restraining political power acquired new impetus that called for a suitable constitutional structure to address the degenerative effects of politics over the law and the individual.

More specifically, both the French declaration and the American Bill of Rights set forth fundamental rights that a state should protect, including the protection of property and individual liberty.[20] Article VI of the Bill of Rights further states that an accused person should enjoy the right of an impartial tribunal.[21] The final milestone of the history of the Rule of Law is the Universal Declaration of Human Rights. Drawing inspiration from all the previous treaties and legal traditions, the declaration proclaimed that States should protect the fundamental rights of individuals, including the entitlement of procedural fairness.[22]

The liberal interpretation of the Rule of Law to some degree differs from the previous formulations as it emphasises individual liberty. Accordingly, the Rule of Law should enable individuals to predict the legal consequences of their actions might entail, thus allowing them to plan their affairs without interfering with the law. As Montesquieu once said, liberty is a right of doing whatever the law sanctions.[23] By the same token, it is also the freedom to do whatever one wishes if the law does not explicitly prohibit.

According to the liberal tradition, in order to uphold individual freedoms, state powers should be divided between the legislative, executive and the judiciary. The separation of powers prevents the accumulation of all the powers of the state to a single branch, thus enhancing the protection against potential abuses. This arrangement constitutes a paradigmatic shift in the history of the Rule of Law since for the first time a structural arrangement was established for the preservation of individual freedom.[24] In the same context, the judiciary should be entrusted with the application

[18]Allan (2000), ch. 3.

[19]Costa (2007), p. 78.

[20]Bingham (2010).

[21]Bill of Rights, Art. VI.

[22]Universal Declaration of Human Rights.

[23]Montesquieu (2007), p. 150.

[24]Tamanaha (2004), p. 36.

of the law and the adjudication of disputes. Most importantly, public authority should be controlled and restrained through judicial oversight to protect the fundamental rights of individuals from potential abuses.

Nowadays, the judiciary in most States has been tasked with subjecting political power to the law. For this reason, there is a widespread understanding that legal questions should be resolved by the application of the law and not the exercise of discretion. Therefore, any provision and legal system that confers excessive discretion on public authorities undermines the Rule of Law.[25] As will be discussed in the following sections, Rule of Law issues often arise in the context of statutory interpretation and judicial discretion as the judiciary is an integral part of the Rule of Law framework.[26]

To sum up, the historical trajectory of the Rule of Law reveals that it came about in an effort to limit the powers of the government. In its domestic articulation, the Rule of Law protects the subjects to the law from arbitrary change and aims to hold public authority accountable. An independent judiciary and the separation of powers enhance the application of the Rule of Law as it prevents the accumulation of power to the executive. For this purpose, it is of cardinal importance to have an independent and impartial judiciary that upholds individual freedom and fundamental rights. This brief historical overview of the Rule of Law invites a more detailed theoretical examination of the scope and content of the Rule of Law in order to extract the constitutive elements of the Rule of Law and its relevance in investment disputes.

3.3 Scope and Content

3.3.1 Procedural Aspect of the Rule of Law

Some scholars have suggested that the Rule of Law is 'an essentially contested concept.'[27] While it is not an easy task to provide a complete survey of the literature relating to the scope and content of the Rule of Law, it is worth attempting to clearly define the Rule of Law. The brief historical account has provided a basic understanding of how the notion of the Rule of Law emerged. Yet, it is necessary to explore in more detail the constituent elements of the Rule of Law and the way it is maintained in practice. Otherwise, it will not be possible to extract the relevance of the Rule of Law and discern its elements in the context of investment arbitration.

It is commonly understood that the Rule of Law has been given both a substantive and procedural meaning.[28] The procedural aspect of the Rule of Law seeks to

---

[25]Bingham (2010), ch. 4.

[26]Fallon (1997), p. 10. For the dichotomy between judicial discretion and the Rule of Law *See* Scalia (1989).

[27]Waldon (2002).

[28]*Stanford Encyclopedia of Philosophy*, 'The Rule of Law' (2016).

examine the manner in which the law was promulgated and focuses on whether the law was properly enacted by an authorised body. The procedural aspect further examines whether the law is sufficiently clear in order to effectively guide the behavior of those governed by the law. Nonetheless, the procedural aspect of the Rule of Law does not evaluate the substantive content of the law. Putting it differently, a procedural conception of the Rule of Law does not examine whether a law is 'good' or 'bad', provided that certain procedural formalities were met.[29]

Joseph Raz focused on the procedural aspect of the Rule of Law since, in his view, if it is taken to encompass substantive elements, it would lose any meaningful independent value in comparison with social philosophy.[30] For this reason, the moral correctness of law should be distinguished from the formal requirements comprising the Rule of Law.[31] However, this does not mean that Raz claimed that it is sufficient to promulgate a law in the correct procedural manner in order to fully meet the standards set by the Rule of Law. On the contrary, the law should also be able to guide the conduct of those subject to the law. This criterion led Raz to deduce certain attributes that the law should meet.

According to Raz, laws should be prospective, stable and clear.[32] If the law should guide people's conduct for long-term planning, they must be able to find out what is the relevant law. Further, there should be an independent judiciary to adjudicate legal disputes.[33] There should also be in a place open, impartial and fair hearings and the ability to review administrative and legislative acts.[34] For these reasons, Raz quite rightly noted that without independent adjudicators, 'people will only be able to be guided by their guesses as to what the courts are likely to do, but these guesses will not be based on the law but on other considerations.'[35] Therefore, the safeguards for the independence of the adjudicators are designed in order to ensure that adjudicators will be free from extraneous pressures and other potential influences. As was rightly observed, that judicial independence is a system in which disputes are resolved by a neutral third party.[36]

The above draw attention to *The Law of the Constitution*, published by Albert Dicey, and especially to the meaning of the Rule of Law given therein. According to Dicey, the Rule of Law is at odds with arbitrary or discretionary power.[37] In his monumental work, Dicey compares the then English system of law with other European systems and finds that *legality* is of paramount importance for individuals

[29]Craig (1997), p. 1.

[30]Raz (1979), p. 211.

[31]*ibid*, p. 211.

[32]*ibid*, p. 213.

[33]This requirement can be found in the Universal Declaration of Fundamental Human Rights, Art.10; European Convention on Human Rights, Art. 6.

[34]Raz (1979).

[35]*ibid*, p. 217.

[36]Cross (2008), p. 558.

[37]Dicey (1958), p. 202.

to avoid the caprices of some others. The latter being a sign of lawless power.[38] For this purpose, Dicey suggests for a system to avoid formal arbitrariness law should be textually clear and applied by an impartial judiciary.

Another prominent approach to the procedural aspect of the Rule of Law is Fuller's theory of the inner morality of law. According to Fuller, formal legality is indifferent toward the substantive content of the law and is ready to serve a variety of such substantive aims with the same efficiency.[39] Fuller's theory provides two key principles that could be used to assess the fairness of a process of adjudication. The first one is the requirement to 'hear the other side', referring to the need to provide notice and opportunity to reply. Most importantly, Fuller talks about the principle of that 'no one shall judge his own cause', referring to the requirement for unbiased decision-makers and adjudicators.[40] Nowadays, it is commonly understood that a constitution of a modern democracy, that respects the Rule of Law, guarantees the independence of the judiciary.

The importance of an independent judiciary is demonstrated by the concept of judicial security of tenure that is commonly found in domestic legal systems. The concept of the security of tenure dates back to England and the Glorious Revolution of 1688. The Act of Settlement of 1701 provided that no King's order could remove the judges, but only a joint approval of both the House of Lords and the House of Commons provided a good cause was established.[41] Currently, additional protection in the UK for judicial independence is provided through the Constitutional Reform Act 2005. The Act provides that everyone with responsibility for matters relating to the judiciary or otherwise to the administration of justice must uphold the continued independence of the judiciary.[42] This provision makes clear that members of the judiciary should maintain their independence from other branches of the government.

It would be an obvious threat to the independence of adjudicators if their remuneration or tenure of office were dependent on the acceptability of judgment by those affected by it. Therefore, the independence of the judiciary requires those making the decisions to remain independent from anything that could lead them to decide a case on the basis of anything other than the legal and factual merits of a case. Eventually, provisions for the security of tenure were incorporated into the US constitutional order[43] and of many other States as a prerequisite for the separation of

---

[38] *ibid*, p. 192.

[39] Fuller (1969), p. 153.

[40] *ibid*, ch. 2.

[41] Act of Settlement (1701).

[42] Constitutional Reform Act 2005, Art. 3.

[43] The Constitution of the United States guarantees US Federal Judges security of tenure. In specific Article 3 of the Constitution states that federal judges may hold their position during 'good behaviour' and provides that their compensation for their services shall not be diminished.

powers.[44] Further, fixed judicial salaries are considered a fundamental aspect of the Rule of Law as they ensure that adjudicators are not susceptible to economic pressure.[45]

Alexander Hamilton, one of the framers of the US Constitution, once famously wrote in *The Federalist Papers* that adhering to the Constitution, which is supposed to be indispensable in the courts, should not be expected from judges who are appointed by a temporary commission.[46] Such arrangements, however regulated, would be fatal to their necessary independence.[47] As he further argues, the idea of judicial independence is supported by the need to avoid a situation where people are governed by the caprices and unpredictable idiosyncrasies of others.[48] Without this element of financial independence, it is hard to argue that a system of law is consistent with the Rule of Law.

Indicatively, several international courts and tribunals have rules to ensure judicial independence. The relevant articles predominantly prohibit any conflict of interest and provide procedures for the disqualification of judges in those scenarios.[49] At the same time, they guarantee judicial tenure for a fixed term and a transparent method for allocation to specific cases. In turn, these safeguards provide an 'objectively verifiable capacity for fair decision-making.'[50] The rules and statutes of these bodies further stipulate that the hearings should be held in public, third party intervention is permitted in contentious cases and the annulment of judgments and awards is possible.[51]

The above brings about another feature of the Rule of Law, namely, legal certainty and predictability. As Friedrich Hayek puts it, the law should provide the subject to it the ability to foresee with fair certainty what their actions will entail and to plan one's affairs on the basis of this knowledge.[52] In other words, those subject to the law should be able to identify the legal consequences their actions might entail.[53]

---

[44]It is commonly accepted in all modern democracies that the selection of judges should be based upon legal qualifications. Moreover, the members of the judiciary should be provided with permanent or at least long-term appointments, sufficient remuneration and substantive and procedural protections against their removal from office. *See generally* United Nations - Office of the High Commissioner for Human Rights (2003), ch. 4.

[45]Gaukrodger (2017), p. 11.

[46]The Federalist Papers, No.78.

[47]*ibid.*

[48]*ibid.*

[49]*See* Code of Conduct for Members and Former Members of the CJEU, Art. 4-5; Rules of Court—ECHR, Art. 3-4; Rome Statute of the ICC, Art. 40-41; Statute of the ICTY, Art. 15.

[50]Van Harten (2010a), p. 642.

[51]For a detailed analysis *See* Brown (2010), p. 662.

[52]Hayek (2005), p. 75.

[53]The European Court of Human Rights gave an authoritative definition of 'legal certainty.' *See* Case *Maestri v Italy* Application No. 39748/98, para. 30. According to Court, the law should be accessible to the individuals concerned and formulated with sufficient clarity to enable them to foresee, to a reasonable degree, the consequences which a given action may entail.

Predictability provides a stable and safe basis for planning and increases one's ability to action. Legal uncertainty might also lead to frustrating legitimate expectations. Legal rules should, therefore, be relatively stable, adequately specific and, at the same time, drafted for general categories of behavior.

Unless the legal rules meet these requirements, those subject to the law cannot take the law into consideration before taking action. The more determinate a legal rule, the most difficult it is to justify disobedience. As Max Weber famously argued, the law helps to raise the probability that contemplated actions will take place and, thus, provides an ordered and functionally social interaction. For this reason, market transactions require legal rules that provide legal security and predictability.[54] Simplified, yet accurately, Lon Fuller describes the Rule of Law as 'dependable guideposts for self-directed action.'[55] For these reasons, everyone should have access to the law so that people can study it and realise what is required from them.

3.3.2 *Substantive Aspect of the Rule of Law*

The substantive aspect of the Rule of Law examines the content of the law through a moral lens. A morally empty account of the Rule of Law runs contrary to the historical purpose of this concept ofthe preventing of arbitrary rule and the protecting individuals freedoms and rights. Foran argues that within the Rule of Law lie restrictions on State powers and duties to protect the rights of legal subjects, which subsequently ensures that the Rule of Law is not content-neutral, a tool to be put to whatever objective politicians might wish.[56] In other words, if the law is whatever the state chooses it to be, then there will no visible to set limits on the state actions. The limits imposed by the Rule of Law are not merely procedural, therefore, but substantive as well.

In the same vein, it would be difficult to accept that a legal system respects the Rule of Law without considering human rights law.[57] Greater procedural fairness should therefore be advanced in parallel with doing justice. It is the extraordinary capacity of the Rule of Law to constrain political power that has been so crucial in developing human rights against potential arbitrariness.[58] As a matter of fact, the Rule of Law is characterised by the strong protection of human rights coupled with the ability to invoke these rights during judicial proceedings, even against the political prerogatives of a state. Ronald Dworkin has developed a prominent theory in favor of a 'thick' conception of the Rule of Law. According to Dworkin, this version of the Rule of Law assumes that individuals have rights and duties with

[54]For the theory of Weber *See* Weber (1978).

[55]Fuller (1969), p. 229.

[56]Foran (2019), p. 26.

[57]Arnold (1932), p. 618; Report by the Venice Commision on Human Rights (2011).

[58]Zolo (2007), p. 18. *See generally* McCorquodale (2016), pp. 296–303.

respect to one another, and rights against the State, which should be enforceable upon the demand of individuals through courts.[59] In the same vein, Dworkin adds that the Rule of Law requires, as a part of the ideal of law, that the rules in the rule book capture and enforce moral rights.[60]

Regardless of their widespread acceptance, human rights are not a coherent body of law. Therefore, in order to proceed to the next section it is of paramount importance to demarcate the term 'human rights'. As the study adopts a 'thick' version of the Rule of Law, the same should be done with respect to human rights law. The Office of the UN High Commissioner for Human Rights highlights the interdependence of human rights—civil, cultural, economic, political and social—which are essential tenets of international human rights law.[61] For example, the right to life, which is widely recognised, must include other rights that are essential to basic quality of life, such as healthcare and education.[62] Consequently, the term 'human rights' whenever mentioned in the monograph, refers to all kinds of international legal instruments designed to promote economic, social and cultural norms/rights on both international and regional level.

In summation, regardless of certain peripheral diversities found across legal traditions, it is possible to provide a functional definition of the Rule of Law. Both from a historical and theoretical point of view, the Rule of Law emerged in an effort to solve specific problems. These problems include the exercise of public authority in an arbitrary, unpredictable and discretionary manner. To combat this problem, the notion of the Rule of Law was developed to limit the exercise of public authority through substantial and procedural conditions. For this purpose, specific institutional means were used to address this challenge. This is the case with respect to a number of legal structures, which in substantially similar ways distinguish modern democracies from other political regimes. That is an independent, transparent and accessible judiciary that protects human rights and provides legal certainty.

Accordingly, the Rule of Law is a legal principle in which all institutions, especially those who are dealing with the exercise and control of public authority, are accountable to laws that are accessible to the public, independently adjudicated and which are consistent with international human rights standards.[63] The Rule of Law also requires measures to ensure accountability to the law, procedural fairness, participation in the decision-making and access to justice, legal certainty, avoidance of arbitrariness, and transparency.[64] In the second chapter, it was argued that investment tribunals resemble a public law system as their decisions affect the

[59]Dworkin (1985), p. 11.

[60]*ibid*, pp. 11–12.

[61]Office of the UN High Commissioner For Human Rights (2005), p. 4.

[62]*ibid.*

[63]In 2012, the Security Council of the UN issued a report on the Rule of Law placing it at the center of the UN's mission and, at the same time, providing an authoritative definition of the Rule of Law. *See* United Nations General Assembly (2012), para. 2.

[64]*ibid*, para. 2.

conduct of States and non-disputing parties. This begs the question as to how the notion of the Rule of Law can be applied in the context of investment arbitration. This will be explored in the following section.

3.4 The Rule of Law in the Context of Investment Treaty Arbitration

3.4.1 Preliminary Observations

Before reviewing the Rule of Law in the context of investment arbitration, certain general observations should be made. In the previous chapter, it was argued that the legitimacy crisis facing investment arbitration can be articulated through the vocabularies of the public law concept of the Rule of Law. As it was rightly stated by Van Harten, investment treaty arbitration is despicted as a fair, rules-based dispute settlement system that advances the rule of law.[65] This proposition is undermined, according to Van Harten, by aspects of this system that tend to favour States and other actors that wield power over appointing authorities or the system of investment arbitration as a whole.[66]

In this context, Montt supports the notion that investment tribunals function like state courts by being able to impose liability on States' governments.[67] Yet, Montt adds that investment tribunals suffer from a legitimacy deficit as from a Rule of Law perspective tribunals do not adhere to the same standards of openness, accountability, and independence.[68] Montt's findings echo to Sweet's argument regarding investment arbitration. Sweet argues that the gradual judicialization of investment arbitration should find both States and arbitrators developing methods to ensure procedural fairness, transparency and the protection of human rights principles.[69]

The Rule of Law emerged in the first place at the domestic level to place limits on the political power of States. Nevertheless, fundamental aspects of the Rule of Law fit well in the domain of investment arbitration.[70] Despite that investment tribunals

[65]Van Harten (2010a), p. 628.

[66]Van Harten (2010a), p. 628.

[67]Montt (2009), p. 139. In a recent report issued by the International Law Association it is claimed that one of the primary methods to identify domestic principles that could be used at the international level is through 'functionalism.' In accordance with, international institutions that have similar functions with domestic institutions could take advantage of certain practices and principles. *See* International Law Association- Study Group (2016), p. 56.

[68]*ibid.*

[69]*See generally* Sweet (2014), pp. 33–35.

[70]While several constituent 'elements' of the Rule of Law have been the subject of a number of studies and commentaries, a study that puts them all together and comprehensively addresses the Rule of Law in the context of investment arbitration is missing. For example, August Reinisch argues that the Rule of Law could be used as a yardstick for investment arbitration. Yet, his paper

are not part of the judicial branch of a local government, it can be considered that are part of the state apparatus to administer justice. Ultimately, the vertical relationship between a host state and a foreign investor, in combination with the public law function of tribunals, establish a new method of accountability at the international plane. It can therefore be argued that investment tribunals require proper safeguards in coherence with the Rule of Law. As will be argued in the next sub-section, various components of the Rule of Law represent answers to certain problems that are commonly found in the realm of investment arbitration.[71] Therefore, a well-grounded and concretised definition of the Rule of Law in the context of investment arbitration could inform a response to the legitimacy crisis in investment arbitration.

At this point, one must ask how does the concept of the Rule of Law fits within the context of investment arbitration. Using the Rule of Law as a framework, the following section will lay out the specific problems of investment arbitration, and will thereby reconstruct widespread, but often incomplete, critiques of this dispute settlement mechanism. In particular, the substantive and procedural aspects of the Rule of Law will be reviewed in order to identify the flaws with the current system and provide normative benchmarks for its reform.[72]

3.4.2 *Substantive Rule of Law*

3.4.2.1 *Human Rights Principles*

As was illustrated in the previous chapter, investment tribunals have been accused of favoring foreign investors' interests over the host States' interests and policy-making powers. It is suggested that these concerns emerged when foreign investors began to excessively challenge public measures aiming to protect human rights. Even though the UN urged States not to compromise human rights protection in the manner in which investment liberalization is done, investment arbitration has so far contributed little in the protection of human rights.[73] In practice, an investment tribunal is able to review a sovereign act that caused a dispute without taking into consideration a

adopts a narrow procedural aspect of this concept. *See* Reinisch (2016); For the same observation *See* Shokouh (2014), ch. 4; Schultz (2014); Schill (2015); Puig and Shaffer (2018); Tobias Stoll (2018); Allsop (2017); Schacherer (2018); Arcuri (2009); Pauwelyn (2015); Chase (2015); Ohler (2017); Hansen (2010). Finally, it is worth noting that the International Law Association has established a committee in order to develop a concept of the Rule of Law in the domain of international investment law. The committee is expected to deliver its final report in 2022. For a draft version of the report *See* International Law Association in Sydney (2018).

[71] Kanetake (2016), p. 10. *See generally* Collins (2019).

[72] Schill (2017), p. 10. *See generally* Hurd (2015). Also Lord Neuberger in a speech at the Chartered Institute of Arbitration explains the relevance of the Rule of Law in arbitration and how it fits within this context. *See* Lord Neuberger (2015).

[73] *See generally* United Nations Commision on Human Rights (2003).

human rights law objective behind such act.[74] This criticism raises legitimate concerns since the protection of human rights is a core element of the Rule of Law as demonstrated earlier in this chapter.

The reason behind the fact that human rights are regularly ignored by tribunals is due to the fact that they are is not an accepted method through which investment and non-investment obligations could be balanced in investment disputes. Another reason behind this concern is that IIAs don't include any provisions regulating the relationship between investment provisions and human rights.[75] Taking into consideration the absence of guidance regarding the way tribunals should interact with different branches of international law, Atanasova argues that promoting the coherence of international law is in line with the requirement of the Rule of Law and constitutes a legitimating factor for tribunals.[76] Ignoring other norms stemming from international law does not only hinder the formal aspect of the Rule of Law, as the law is incapable of guiding its subjects, but also risks undermining human rights protection which is the substantive aspect of this concept. This section will further expand on these issues.

In general terms, IIAs do not usually provide any guidance or any relevant provisions regarding the method through which human right obligations should be balanced against investment protection standards. The reluctance of investment tribunals to apply human rights in investment disputes is further attributed to the limited jurisdiction of tribunals. The consent of the States is usually given only for claims related to investments and cannot, therefore, be extended to human rights law concerns.[77] Consequently, a tension emerges between the substantive element of the Rule of Law and arbitral awards as it is not clear whether human rights should be taken into consideration and in what way they should be balanced with investment protection standards.[78]

For example, in the case of *Biloune v Ghana*, the tribunal held that it is not competent to deal with every human rights violation of the investor since such a decision would fall outside the scope of the investment dispute.[79] In the same vein, in the *Tecmed* case, the tribunal held that it finds no principle stating that regulatory measures, even if they are beneficial to the society as a whole, are excluded from the scope of the IIA.[80]

[74]Prislan (2012), p. 451.

[75]Among others these often include the UN Convention and the International Labor Organization Conventions. *See generally* Ulrich Petersmann (2009), pp. 523–526.

[76]Atanasova (2019), p. 366.

[77]Article 25 of the ICSID Convention limits the jurisdiction of the Centre to 'to any legal dispute arising directly out of an investment.'

[78]*See generally* Brabandere (2019).

[79]*Biloune and Marine Drive Complex Ltd v Ghana Investments Centre and the Government of Ghana* (UNCITRAL), Award on Jurisdiction and Liability, 27th October 1989, para. 203.

[80]*Técnicas Medioambientales Tecmed, S.A. v. The United Mexican States*, ICSID Case No. ARB (AF)/00/2, para. 121.

In the absence of any authoritative method through which human rights could be integrated in investment disputes, tribunals are neither obliged to resolve conflicts between competing obligations nor to take into account human rights when applying the law.[81] It is, therefore, argued that in the context of investment arbitration a 'bridge' should be developed in order to remedy the possible missing link between investment and human rights law. This implies that better drafting of IIAs is required to construe standards of treatment with better guidance as to how to deal with the interplay between investment and human rights principles. In the absence of such methods, it is doubtless whether investment tribunals will be able to reconcile human rights with investment protection.[82] The inclusion of general exceptions in IIAs will also serve as an important factor when tribunals are deciding upon investment disputes with human rights aspects.

Last, but not least, in the previous chapter it was argued that investment arbitration has been modeled after international commercial arbitration. In a commercial law setting, finality is prioritised at the expense of fairness. This bias towards finality has subsequently caused the lack of an effective appeal mechanism. Despite the fact that ICSID and non-ICSID arbitration permit annulment, it is very limited in its application.[83] For example, Article 52 of the ICSID Convention permit a party to apply for an annulment, yet the grounds for annulment do not include a review of substantive grounds or review on the merits of the award.[84] An appellate mechanism could be used as a mechanism to integrate investment and non-investment obligations.

In other words, a comprehensive appeal mechanism can provide a procedural safeguard when it comes to awards that ignored or misapplied human rights issues.[85] As Paulsson rightly points out, if arbitration simply bow to formal enactments without examining the lawfulness of their awards under more fundamental principles

[81]Waibel argues that tribunals often follow superficial treaty interpretation distorting the parties intentions and treaty bargain in a way that favors investment protection at the detriment of non-investment obligations. *See* Waibel (2011).

[82]For an analysis as to how human rights are invoked and used in the context of investment arbitration *See* Steininger (2018), pp. 45–46.

[83]In *CMS v Argentina* the annulment committee identified a series of errors and defects. However the Committee acknowledged that it exercises its jurisdiction under a limited mandate conferred by the ICSID Convention. According to the Committee, the scope of this mandate allows annulment as an option only when specific conditions exist and in those circumstances the Committee could not simply substitute its view of the law and its own appreciation of the facts for those of the panel. *See CMS Gas Transmission Company v. The Republic of Argentina*, ICSID Case No. ARB/01/8, Decision of the Ad Hoc Committee on the Application for Annulment of the Argentine Republic, para. 158.

[84]ICSID Convention, Art. 52.

[85]Butler and Musa (2018), p. 445.

they may just end up giving sectarian conflicts.[86] For this reason, it is of paramount importance to reconcile investment awards with other legal norms.[87]

The fact that investment arbitration has become an instrument of protection for foreign investors to the exclusion of other interests, such as human rights, raises a critical Rule of Law concern. The fact that several investment treaties focus almost exclusively upon the obligations of host States, without any substantial reference to obligations of investors towards the host state or third parties, has created a moral vacuum. Subsequently, morally empty investment awards run contrary to the historic purpose of the Rule of Law, which has been the protection of human rights through the law. This moral vacuum drives the current initiatives to reshape the substantive content of investment agreements in order to provide justice to all state and non-state actors of the international economic system.[88]

3.4.3 Procedural Rule of Law

3.4.3.1 Transparency and Access to Justice

The tension between investment disputes and the substantive aspect of the Rule of Law may be addressed by integrating human rights principles in investment disputes. In addition to the substantive aspect of the Rule of Law, the arbitral process requires a degree of transparency and institutional legitimacy. In the absence of legitimacy, the processes of adjudication and interpretation become arbitrary and illegitimate.[89] Simply put, in order to respect the Rule of Law a high degree of openness and publicity should be maintained. The need for greater transparency underscores the critical role the Rule of Law plays in keeping public authority, including judicial bodies controlling such authority, under constant scrutiny.

In addition to transparency, several problems have been noted with regard to access to justice in investment arbitration. Access to justice is a component of the Rule of Law that dictates that disputing parties should have 'the financial resources or the ability to acquire the financial resources needed to bring a claim or muster a defence in international arbitration.'[90] In the absence of access to justice, those concerned cannot access their rights or defend claims made against them. The high costs of investment disputes mean that financially weak parties cannot take

---

[86]Paulson (2013), p. 232.

[87]Recently a tribunal held that it enjoyed jurisdiction over a human rights counterclaim. *See Urbaser S.A. and Consorcio de Aguas Bilbao Bizkaia, Bilbao Biskaia Ur Partzuergoa v. The ArgentineRepublic*, ICSID Case No. ARB/07/26. In particular, the Tribunal held that accepts corporate social responsibility as a standard of crucial importance for companies. Furthermore, the panel accepted that this standard includes commitments to comply with human rights.

[88]*See generally* Desierto (2018).

[89]Calamita (2013), p. 170.

[90]O'Connor (2018).

up the burden of litigation. Both the principle of transparency and access to justice are essential prerequisities for upholding the Rule of Law and ensuring that anyone who is affected by the outcome of a dispute has access to the proceedings. For this reason, the section also looks on the high costs of investment disputes and the challenges to accessing justice for the parties to a dispute.

Transparency is broadly understood as 'unfettered access to timely and reliable information on decisions.'[91] This notion also includes making procedures accessible to the public, holding decision-makers accountable for their decisions and providing avenues for redress.[92] The lack of transparency is one of the most widely voiced criticisms against investment arbitration. In particular, investment arbitration is characterised by a lack of transparency at almost every stage of the arbitral process, including the decision-making process and outcomes. As it will be demonstrated in this section, this definition illustrates the fact that investment arbitration is in conflict with this Rule of Law requirement.[93]

In investment arbitration, usually, both the proceedings and arbitral awards are confidential. In addition, a considerable amount of arbitral venues do not allow non-disputing parties to attend the hearings nor to make submissions even in cases of public interest.[94] Without mutual consent from both parties, there is generally no requirement of public access to the proceedings or to the documents associated with it, or even the final award.[95] In fact, recent research indicates that the vast majority of IIAs signed between 2010 and 2013 did not address the issue of transparency.[96]

For example, neither the Stockholm nor the UNCITRAL Arbitration Rules address the publication of information while both institutions forbid public access to awards and hearings without the previous consent of the parties.[97] In a slightly more permissive manner, ICSID provides certain information to the public through the registrar of disputes.[98] In light of the above, it would be reasonable to assert that investment tribunals function in a non-transparent manner. Consequently, these features of investment arbitration are at odds with the requirement of transparent procedures and subsequently with the Rule of Law.

While this secretive approach may be accepted in a commercial arbitration context that primarily deals with private disputes, its transplantation into investment arbitration permits arbitrators to rule on the legality of the sovereign acts in secrecy.

[91]UN Economic and Social Council, para. 49.

[92]Schefer (2016), p. 535.

[93]As the OECD recognises, there is a problem in using a private dispute settlement mechanism for resolving disputes between private parties and States. *See* OECD (2005).

[94]For example, look at the relevant rules of the London Court of International Arbitration, the Stockholm Chamber of Commerce and the International Chamber of Commerce.

[95]For a case regarding a tribunal rejecting a request for additional information *See Biwater Gauff (Tanzania) Ltd. v. United Republic of Tanzania*, ICSID Case No. ARB/05/22.

[96]Nyegaard Mollestad (2014), p. 38.

[97]Arbitration Rules of the Arbitration Institute of the Stockholm Chamber of Commerce, Art. 3; UNCITRAL Arbitration Rules, Art. 34.

[98]ICSID Convention, Art. 11.

Transparency requires that arbitration proceedings take place in the public eye, subject to specific exceptions, and all the relevant documents are placed on the public record.[99] Therefore, enhancing transparency in investment arbitration has been viewed as a step to increase public confidence and address accountability concerns.[100] This view was articulated, in the *Suez and others v Argentina*, where the tribunal held that the legitimacy of investment arbitration is enhanced by increased openness, which has subsequently led to increased transparency in the proceedings of the World Trade Organization and the North American Free Trade Agreement.'[101]

As was demonstrated in the previous chapter, investment disputes involve issues that directly relate to the public interest and with a wide spectrum of interests. The guest for more transparency is a result of the paradigmatic shift that investment arbitration is facing as a dispute settlement method tasked to rule upon the legality of sovereign acts. This system of law, which is customarily based on private law, seeks to be in search of public legitimacy, which is anticipated to be obtained through an enhanced transparency framework.[102] This shift is associated with efforts to open the arbitral process through public hearings, to allow the participation of third parties and the publications of awards and other documents prepared in the course of the proceedings.[103] The subsequent public scrutiny of the arbitration process will eventually put pressure on arbitrators for well-reasoned awards and consistency on decision-making.

Furthermore, advocates of greater transparency claim that greater participation and access to arbitral proceedings might generate more informed decision-making by arbitrators.[104] More informed decision-making and greater adherence to the treaty prescriptions will make this system of law more acceptable by the public and responsive to a wide variety of interests.[105] Given the fact that through greater transparency third parties will gain a right to intervene in the arbitral process; it will also be possible to realise other principles associated with the Rule of Law, such as access to justice. In this way, investment arbitration will integrate the Rule of Law through well-established practices of broad deliberation, accountability, and, finally, transparency.

Access to justice is a basic principle of the Rule of Law, which is threatened by the high litigation costs of investment disputes as financially disadvantaged parties

[99] The complete subordination of transparency to rules of confidentiality is inappropriate. Trade secrets and other sensitive information of foreign investors should be excluded. This is discussed in Chap. 7.

[100] *See generally* United Nations Commision on International Trade Law (2010), pp. 9–10.

[101] *Suez, Sociedad General de Aguas de Barcelona, S.A.and Vivendi Universal, S.A. v. Argentine Republic*, ICSID Case No. ARB/03/19, Order in Response to a Petition for Transparency and Participation as Amicus Curiae, para. 22.

[102] Stern (2009), p. 347.

[103] Fortier (2009), p. 13.

[104] Shirlow (2017), p. 98.

[105] *ibid*, p. 98.

may not be able to access this system. On top of that, there is no universal approach on how investment tribunals should address costs. Critiques of high costs further claim that decisions on costs are usually arbitrary and unpredictable.[106] For this reason, Franck argues that disadvantaged stakeholders may, therefore, need more information about costs in investment arbitration to promote access to justice.[107]

Recent reforms have also sought to lower costs.[108] For instance, a standing tribunal could streamline the arbitration process and, subsequently, reduce the costs.[109] Other issues relating to high costs involve ways to discourage frivolous claims. Finally, certain rules could be introduced to guide tribunals how to assess the costs involved during the arbitration proceedings.[110] Promoting certainty and lower costs in investment disputes will help financially weak parties to access this system and will enhance the legitimacy of investment arbitration.[111]

3.4.3.2 Procedural Fairness

Adding to the absence of transparency, another criticism against investment arbitration relates to procedural fairness that lies at the heart of the Rule of Law. For the Rule of Law to properly function, judicial bodies must ensure the fair application of the law through certain procedural conditions.[112] That is to say, the observance of procedural constraints by investment tribunals enables the law to be correctly ascertained and applied. Procedural fairness means that adjudicators must be able to exercise their duties without being influenced by other inappropriate factors.

Given that judicial independence has been developed in the context of the separation of powers, a question arises regarding what arbitrators should be independent and impartial from in the context of investment arbitration. It was rightly claimed that the independence and impartiality of the judiciary should not only be guarded against executive and legislature pressures but also against business interests and corporate giants.[113] In essence, the judiciary should not be involved in situations that might affect or are likely to affect that independent exercise of judicial functions.[114] Independence and impartiality requirements prevent arbitrators from

[106]Franck (2011), p. 775; Salacuse (2007), p. 142.

[107]Franck (2011), p. 788.

[108]*ibid.*

[109]Rosert (2014), p. 15.

[110]*ibid.*

[111]Third-Party Funding will be discussed on the seventh chapter as a method through which financially weak parties may proceed with a claim. In short, the financialization of investment arbitration could undermine the assumption that investment arbitration is functioning as a credible and, most importantly, a fair legal system for dispute settlement.

[112]Allan (2000), ch. 5.

[113]Dieng (1997), p. 550.

[114]Sheetreen and Turenne (2013), p. 6.

taking extra-legal considerations into account. Procedural safeguards and professional ethics ensure a legal system's commitment to the Rule of Law.[115]

On this basis, for investment arbitration to comply with the notion of the Rule of Law, it is crucial to ensure that arbitrators are not affected by self-interest. The ethical standards of arbitrators are the alpha and omega of the legitimacy of the process. This is because; ethical standards attempt to ensure that adjudicators apply the law and not their own personal preferences.[116] Another critical factor is the arbitral institution's structure. This section suggests that, in spite of the need for arbitrators to exercise their duties in true independence, arbitrators are often subjected to pressures of various kinds that compromise their duties. This section looks on the lack of institutional independence and guarantees of impartiality as two key factors that put in jeopardy the fairness of the arbitral proceedings in investment disputes.

Individuals usually act as arbitrators in one proceeding and as counsel to a party in another case. This 'double-hatting' phenomenon has raised legitimate concerns about the lack of procedural fairness and impartiality of arbitrators.[117] The absence of security of tenure for arbitrators in investment arbitration raises further credible concerns about the lack of procedural fairness in the system.[118] Van Harten argues that investment arbitration proceedings are biased in favor of foreign investors who are the 'heavy consumers' of arbitration services.[119] He further argues that arbitrators favor those States that are powerful enough to appoint individuals in high places in arbitral venues.[120] His argument is based on the fact that only foreign investors are able to bring a claim against a state and not *vice versa*. These features, coupled with the fact that arbitrators are appointed on a case-by-case basis, creates legitimate concerns that the preservation of this system lies in the ability of foreign investors to bring successful claims against host States.[121]

Schneiderman points out that one should understand arbitrators as operating within a particular institutional environment that forces them to strike a balance

---

[115]Boies (2006), p. 62.

[116]Paulson (2013), p. 147.

[117]Philippe Sands, a well-known scholar and arbitrator, acknowledges the dangers of having individuals acting both as counsel and arbitrator. *See* Sands (2011).

[118]Scholars claim that judicial selection is highly politicised even in systems that provide tenure of appointment. According to this argument, judicial selection compromises judicial independence even in situations where adjudicators enjoy security of tenure. However, in systems that provide security of tenure, once appointed, the adjudicators decisions' are purely internal and are protected by outside illegitimate influences. Therefore, in legal systems where judicial appointments are done on a case-by-case basis, the appointing authority is in a stronger position to influence the workings of the tribunal. *See* Voete (2003); Crawford (2003).

[119]Van Harten (2010a), p. 643.

[120]*ibid.* An appointing state would put forward an arbitrator who shares the political values and inclinations of that state. Mackenzie and Sands (2003), pp. 278 & 284.

[121]For a paper explaining independence at the systemic level rather than a particular adjudicator *See* Caron (2011).

between several factors in addition to the legal issues in individual case.[122] This strategic attitude occasionally makes arbitrators advance a position that is associated with the appointing state and the institutional setting of the arbitral venue.[123] In a system of law that only allows foreign investors to bring claims, it is plausible to assume that arbitrators have an inclination to decide claims and interpret IIA in a way that will encourage more claims and, eventually, grow the business.[124]

Dezalay and Garth in their seminal work about arbitration explain how arbitrators' decisions affect their success and focus on the ways they seek to keep the customers satisfied in order to gain repeat business.[125] It is exactly these features that raise concerns about procedural fairness and independence since arbitrators are having personal interests and career considerations while deciding investment disputes. Independent arbitrators suggest that they should be independent of the claiming parties appearing before them. In investment arbitration, the independence and impartiality of arbitrations appear to be severely compromised.

In fact, a recent study drawing on a dataset of 542 claims indicates that investment treat arbitration appears to have been used as a weapon in the hands of the interests of foreign investors from rich States against governments of poorer States.[126] The same study adds that investment arbitration has also been used by foreign investors from rich States against other rich States.'[127] Finally, the study concludes that investment arbitration 'favours the 'haves' over the 'have-nots', allowing or making the international investment regime to be harder on poorer countries than in richer countries.'[128] For this reason, it is difficult to assume that these institutions are free from bias in favor of foreign investors.[129]

Last, but not least, the standards for disqualification in investment arbitration are too high making the disqualification process troublesome. A party wishing to disqualify an arbitrator under ICSID claiming lack of independence a *manifest lack of independence* must be established.[130] It is worth noting that it is practically

---

[122]Schneiderman (2010), p. 403.

[123]This phenomenon was illustrated in the *Loewen* case. In this case, the tribunal referred to the viability of NAFTA' and to the interests of the international investing community to reach a decision. *See Loewen Group, Inc. and Raymond L. Loewen v. United States of America*, ICSID Case No. ARB(AF)/98/3, para. 242.

[124]Corporate Europe Observatory (2012), ch. 2.

[125]Dezalay and Garth (1996), p. 194.

[126]Schultz and Dupont (2015), p. 1149.

[127]*ibid*, p. 1150.

[128]*ibid*, p. 1168.

[129]Van Harten (2010b), p. 443.

[130]ICSID Convention, Art. 57. Quiet illustratively, one tribunal held that the ICSID requirement that the lack of independence should be "manifest" necessitates that this lack of independence be objectively established. Accordingly, it is not sufficient to show an appearance of a lack of impartiality or independence. *See OPIC Karimum Corporation v. The Bolivarian Republic of Venezuela*, ICSID Case No. ARB/10/14, Decision on the Proposal to Disqualify Professor Philippe Sands Arbitrator, para. 45.

hard, if not impossible, to provide evidence on the state of mind of an arbitrator. The equivalent standard of proof in the majority of legal systems is whether the arbitrator demonstrates *apparent or credible* bias.[131] This standard is supported by the notion that even if adjudicators appear to be biased, the trust to a tribunal will be diminished.[132] In direct contrast, the standard set by ICSID, which stipulates that a challenging party should establish *manifest lack of impartiality*, is at odds with the *appearance of bias* standard and, subsequently, with the notion of the Rule of Law.

Against this background, there are compelling reasons to expect procedural fairness and independence of arbitrators in investment arbitration. Judge Buergenthal argues that it is of paramount importance to develop and adopt strict ethical standards applicable to adjudicators and counsels in the context of international arbitration in order to ensure that the rule of law is observed.[133]

The process of investment arbitration is compulsory and final with limited oversight by domestic courts or an appellate mechanism. Investment awards usually lead to state liability involving large sums of capital or even severe losses for foreign investors. These aspects of investment arbitration, namely its determinativeness and its function, demonstrate the need for procedural fairness and independence. Procedural fairness enhances the confidence of the public and those affected by arbitral awards and raise the legitimacy of investment tribunals.

In conclusion, concerns regarding the dangers posed by 'double-hatting' and the lack of tenure of appointment could be translated into concerns about the lack of procedural fairness in arbitration proceedings. In turn, the public perception of investment arbitration as a fair process of international dispute settlement would be enhanced with greater respect for procedural fairness. This could be achieved with the development of strict ethical standards, security of tenure for arbitrators as well as a robust mechanism for the disqualification of arbitrators. Such reforms would ultimately promote the Rule of Law in investment disputes.

3.4.3.3 Legal Certainty

As was illustrated in previous sections, the Rule of Law prescribes that those subject to the law should be able to rely on it. For this reason, the Rule of Law is considered as a tool to protect individuals from arbitrary rule through predictability. Without legal certainty, those subject to the law will not be able to assess whether their actions bear legal consequences. Accordingly, this section focuses on legal certainty and, more specifically, on the problems posed by the broad wording of IIAs, the lack

---

[131] *See generally* Judiciary of England and Wales (2013), chapters 2–3.

[132] The European Court of Human Rights took a strict view on judicial bias and impartiality. In particular, the Court held that even appearances may be of importance. What is at stake, according to the Court, is the confidence which the Courts in a democratic society must stimulate in the public. Accordingly, any judge in respect of whom there is a legitimate reason to fear a lack of impartiality must withdraw from the panel. *See Petur Thor v. Iceland*, App. No. 39731/98, Judgment, para. 37.

[133] Buergenthal (2006), p. 130.

of judicial restraints and the phenomenon of multiple proceedings. As will be shown in this section, the current regime of investment arbitration threatens predictability and the autonomy of those subject to the IIAs.

First and foremost, the vague and open-ended wording of the standards of treatment in IIAs has resulted in unpredictable results and to a great deal misinterpretation. The legal uncertainty has subsequently caused negative implication for the host States and, most importantly, their citizens as it undermines the ability of those subject to IIAs to understand what the standards of treatment entail.[134] Even the fear of a legal claim occasionally prevents States from enacting public policy measures that might excite claims by foreign investors. The same goes for foreign investors, as they cannot tell for sure whether they are protected under IIAs or not. In the absense of legal certainty, the Rule of Law is diminished.

The general remarks made by Alvarez fit perfectly well in the investment arbitration domain. In particular, he claims that whatever doubts one may have as to the existence of 'pre-existing' law in the context of domestic legal system, such doubts multiply in the context of the international legal system where gaps in the applicable law exist on every topic, and where a common task of judges is often to give meanging to vague or contradictory legal provisions.[135]

The Rule of Law is a broad concept that can incorporate many checks and restraints on judicial power.[136] Accordingly, the Rule of Law is violated when the arbitrators act on the basis of their own discretion rather than already existing laws. Vague standard of treatment, therefore, has raised Rule of Law concerns since arbitrators might use their own personal views to interpret the content of those standards. The assumption that personal preferences are taken into consideration in applying the standard of treatment frustrates a sense of judicial propriety.[137] A key factor therefore in the maintenance of the Rule of Law is the application of the law by the adjudicators independently from their personal beliefs.[138] A corollary to this is that judicial activism subverts the Rule of Law. Judicial activism occurs when adjudicators fail to apply the law within the constraints of the law and regardless of the outcome of a particular case. In those cases of judicial activism, arbitrators trade the notion of the Rule of Law for the rule of men.[139] The exercise of discretion violates the Rule of Law by co-opting individuals and States in the service of other considerations.[140]

---

[134]For this criticism *See* Gottwald (2007), pp. 259–260. Recent trends illustrate that States have taken steps to express with greater certainty the obligation of States under IIAs, including clarifications as to the content of 'expropriation' and the FET standard. For example *See* the Canadian and US model model BITs.

[135]Alvarez (2006), p. 523.

[136]For a discussion *See* Posner (1983). Also *See* Ekins and Forsyth (2015).

[137]Schill (2010), p. 157.

[138]Dyson (2004), p. 3.

[139]For a seminal book on judicial activism *See* Griffith (First Published 1977).

[140]John Locke claimed that one of the things individuals wish to avoid being subject to others incalculable decisions and opinions. *See* Locke (First Published 1689, 1956), p. 64.

As a matter of fact, in the case of *PSEG Global Inc et al v Turkey* the tribunal held that the FET standard changes on each case and it is not precise as would be desirable.[141] Yet, the standard 'clearly allows for *justice* to be done in the absence of the more traditional breaches of international law standards.'[142] In the case of *Sempra Energy International v Argentina* the tribunal held that even in situations where there is no clear justification for making a finding of expropriation, there is still a standard of treatment which serves the objective of *justice* and can of itself redress damage that is against the law.[143]

The reasoning followed by both tribunals, as well as the reference to 'justice'; raise serious concerns about arbitrators since they are able to use their personal inclinations to reach a decision. The more abstract or general the terms of a legal provision are, the greater the discretion to investment tribunals when interpreting them.[144] This variability of application invites the application of external political values by arbitrators in order to interpret IIAs as they are not self-defining.

The above are exemplified in the report undertaken by the United Nations Conference on Trade and Development which states that if the govertment of a State does not know in advance what type of actions constitute a breach of a treaty, then it that cannot organise its decision-making processes to ensure that the the FET standard is not violated.[145] This uncertainty may in turn produce negative effects such as 'regulatory chill' or positive discrimination against domestic investors and in favour of foreign investors.[146] Therefore, without a clear understanding of the specific obligations arising from each standard, States cannot implement public policy effectively. Limiting the discretion of adjudicators through more precise wording is of vital importance for the Rule of Law as it protects those subjected to the law from arbitrary and unpredictable decisions.

That said, one could counter-argue that different outcomes and arguments in legal disputes inevitably have diverse degrees of legal merit.[147] By the same token, Martti Koskenniemi quite famously argued that it is in the very nature of international law for one to be able to draw different conclusions from the same legal norm.[148] According to the above, legal uncertainty, judicial discretion and value judgments are inherent in the practice of law. Although this reasoning makes the Rule of Law appear like an unattainable goal, there is a way to ensure that judicial discretion is consistent with the Rule of Law.

---

[141] *PSEG Global Inc et al v Turkey*, ICSID Case No. ARB/02/05, para. 239.

[142] *ibid*, para 239.

[143] *Sempra Energy International v. The Argentine Republic*, ICSID Case No. ARB/02/16, para. 300.

[144] Sureda (2012), p. 9.

[145] United Nations Conference on Trade and Development (2012), p. 12.

[146] *ibid.*

[147] Lauterpacht (1958), p. 398.

[148] *See generally* Koskenniemi (1989), ch. 1.

In particular, the study does not share the view that is realistic, or even desirable, to reach a situation where legal interpretations are 'discretion-free'.[149] In order to preserve the integrity of the Rule of Law, guidelines are usually introduced as to how adjudicators should interpret the law while ensuring that discretion is properly framed and authorised.[150] Therefore, for the judiciary to uphold the Rule of Law certain limits should be imposed as to how the law should and could be interpreted and applied. States should also be able to accept why they lost a case instead of just passively accepting the outcomes of arbitral awards. A sophisticated set of interpretation techniques will allow States to predict with some accuracy how investment tribunals might engage a claim made against them, hence ensuring a higher degree of legal certainty. Ultimately, the monograph takes the view that, under certain conditions, judicial discretion in the context of investment disputes could peacefully coexist with the Rule of Law.

For instance, adjudicators are usually tasked to interpret legal provisions according to their plain meaning. Whenever this method is not enough, judges are looking for evidence of intention in an effort to identify the state of mind of the drafters and the purpose of the legal provision.[151] Moreover, judges often look at the systematic context that a specific legal provision was promulgated to shed light on potential indeterminacy. Subsequently, these interpretation rules obviate the risk of potential subjectivity and judicial creativity by the adjudicators.[152] After all, the notion of the Rule of Law prescribes that judicial bodies, such as investment tribunals, must exercise their powers conferred to them without exceeding the limits of such powers.

As was illustrated earlier, the concept of judicial discretion is not automatically irreconcilable with the Rule of Law, yet it does require that no discretion should be unconstrained and legally unfettered so as to be arbitrary. In the fitting words of Regis Lanneau, legal certainty is not synonymoys with inflexibility of law but refers to predictability, which depends on a judgment.[153] Even under this flexible definition, investment tribunals demonstrated that they could just move between different interpretative techniques.[154]

---

[149]For a critique on Legal Certainty *See* Popelier (2008). In the same manner, Relja Radovic supports the idea that 'total legalism' is unattainable in the context of investment arbitration and as such it is a reality that should be lived with because it stems from the foundations of the international legal order, and is inherent to the system of international treaty arbitration. *See* Radovic (2018), p. 183.

[150]Stanford Encyclopedia of Philosophy (2016).

[151]VCLT, Art. 31.

[152]Maxeiner (2007), p. 572. *See generally* Bianchi (2015).

[153]Lanneau (2013), p. 16.

[154]Kurtz (2014), p. 274. The misapplication of the rules of interpretation was also heavily criticised by Michael Reisman and Mahnoush Arsanjani noting that although the provisions of the Vienna Convention are routinely and briefly referred to, they are not always applied. *See* Arsanjani and Reisman (2010), p. 598.

Moreover, legal uncertainty is aggravated by the fact that the interpretation of IIAs is delegated to a diffused network of *ad hoc* investment tribunals in the absence of a central authoritative body that could resolve inconsistencies and textually restrain arbitral discretion.[155] Multiple proceedings and conflicting awards clearly undermine the predictability requirement of the Rule of Law as individual disputes are open to all kinds of competing views and analogies by different tribunals. As Zolo rightly observed, the differentiation of social subsystems creates 'law inflation', which entails normative instability.[156] For this reason, Blackaby argues that whenever in a legal system diametrically opposed decisions legally coexist, the sense of Rule of Law is shocked.[157] Developing methods to deal with these phenomena is of cardinal importance since they have raised great concerns about legal certainty.

Finally, in the context of investment arbitration there is no appeal mechanism or any other supervisory mechanism, thus States are largely unable to challenge effectively arbitral awards. In other words, the finality of an arbitral award is prioritised at the expense of correctness and the right to appeal an award. As Van Harten argues, the fact that 'private arbitrators are able [...] to redraw the boundaries of the regulatory sphere, without effective judicial supervision, is one of the more perilous aspects of the present system.'[158]

Legal certainty puts a premium on the way law facilitates reasoning and whether at the domestic or international level every subject to the law deserves this positive aspect of the Rule of Law. On this basis, the Rule of Law in investment arbitration proves to be a useful tool to protect both the States and their citizens from legal uncertainty and arbitrary rule. This could be done by clarifying the line between legitimate exercise of the right to regulate by host States and illegal exercise of sovereign power upon FDIs. Legal certainty can also prove useful for foreign investors as they could assume their rights under IIAs without the current great risk that is caused by uncertainty. In a nutshell, legal certainty improves the *ex ante* ability of those subject to the law to understand what their obligations are under IIAs.

The criticism against investment arbitration has given rise to proposals for the establishment of an appellate body, consolidating cases and the establishment of a permanent investment court to remedy this perceived situation. As a way to remedy poor hermeneutics certain stakeholders have proposed to include guidelines as to how investment tribunals should interpret the provisions of IIAs. These mechanisms would theoretically reduce legal uncertainty and could eventually contribute to the sustainability of investment arbitration as a method for international dispute settlement. Most importantly, the above measures, including the proposals for an appellate mechanism to correct legal errors, echo the basis on which the Rule of Law is

---

[155]In a similar fashion, Thomas Franck argued that harmonization in international investment law would contribute to greater fairness. *See also* Franck (1998), ch. 14.

[156]Zolo (2007), p. 44. Further on legal pluralism in international law and the threats to the Rule of Law *See* Monika and Theresa (2016) and Isiksel and Thies (2013).

[157]Nigel Blackaby quoted in Goldhaber (2004).

[158]Van Harten (2010a), p. 131.

built on, since such proposal aim to impose procedural features of public law systems upon investment tribunals.[159]

3.5 Conclusion

This chapter argues that the notion of the Rule of Law incorporates the idea that public authority should be accountable to an independent, transparent and accessible judicial body that fundamentally aims to guard human rights and provide legal certainty. On the basis of this framework, one can realise that the architects of investment arbitration failed to place the arbitral proceedings in a suitable legal framework. This shortcoming has resulted in arbitrary and purely discretionary awards taken in accordance with the arbitrators' preferences. However, adjudicative law-making based on vaguely construed standards in the absence of procedural fairness and transparency will inevitably exhaust any remaining traits of legitimacy.

Every legal system faces challenging transformations that provoke the normative foundations upon which the system was built on. Investment arbitration is at this critical moment as it faces a daunting challenge to identify ways to counter a legitimacy deficit. The critique in this chapter is not an attempt to reject this legal system, but to focus on precise failings of investment arbitration in order to develop a concrete theoretical framework that could address its legitimacy crisis. In that sense, the Rule of Law framework could form a horizon for reform aspirations to restructure investment arbitration. After all, legal stability and legal security lie at the heart of IIAs, while taking investment disputes from the realm of politics to the realm of law goes to the very essence of investment arbitration.

A dispute settlement mechanism in order to be consistent with the Rule of Law must, therefore, have certain attributes. Principally, the Rule of Law can influence the way investment arbitration procedures take place. In this way, it will be possible to make arbitrators accountable and the proceedings transparent. As proposed by the EU, accountability could be achieved through an appellate mechanism. Further clarifications could also be made regarding the content and interpretation of the standards of treatment in an effort to enhance legal certainty.

Additionally, the possibility of third parties to participate reflects the Rule of Law notion that those who are affected should be allowed to speak during the decision-making. Subsequently, in order for arbitrators to respect the Rule of Law, they should act in an impartial and independent manner. The latter could be achieved through a comprehensive code of conduct for all the parties involved in the proceedings. Most importantly, for the Rule of Law to work, the parties to a dispute should be able to access investment arbitration. In this spirit, certain rules should be introduced to reduce the high costs associated with investment disputes. The supremacy of the Rule of Law over the power of arbitrators and the systemic

[159] Dunoff and Trachtman (2009), p. 13.

shortcomings of investment arbitration impedes any misuse of power. The purpose of the Rule of Law is to remove both the injustice and the sense of injustice.

To conclude, this chapter argues that the Rule of Law framework constitutes the normative assumption based on which the criticism against investment arbitration is made. As a result of this realisation, the question arises whether CETA's Investment Chapter is consistent with the Rule of Law. Answering this question will ultimately provide a convincing account as to whether CETA's Investment Chapter constitutes a decisive attempt to address the legitimacy crisis facing investment arbitration. The following chapters will attempt to give an answer to this question.

References

Allan TRS (2000) Constitutional justice: a liberal theory of the rule of law. Oxford University Press, Oxford

Allsop J (2017) International arbitration and conformity with international standards of due process and the rule of law. In: Menaker A (ed) International arbitration and the rule of law: contribution and conformity. Kluwer Law International, Alphen aan den Rijn

Alvarez JE (2006) International organizations as law-makers. Oxford University Press, Oxford, p 523

Arcuri A (2009) The great asymmetry and the rule of law in international investment arbitration. In: Sachs L et al (eds) Yearbook of international investment law and policy 2018. Oxford University Press, Oxford

Aristotle (2008) Politics: books 1 & 3. Cosimo Classics, New York, p 29 & 140

Arnold TW (1932) The role of substantive law and procedure in the legal process. Harv Law Rev 45 (617):618

Arsanjani M, Reisman M (2010) Interpreting treaties for the benefit of third parties: the "Salvors Doctrine" and the use of legislative history in investment treaties. Am J Int Law 104(597):598

Atanasova D (2019) A rule of law view on the relations of international courts and tribunals. Temple Int Comp Law J 33(2):366

Bianchi A et al (2015) Interpretation in international law. Oxford University Press, Oxford

Bingham T (2010) The rule of law. Penguin Books, London, p 12

Boies D (2006) Judicial independence and the rule of law. Wash Univ J Law Policy 2(57):62

Brabandere E (2019) Human rights and foreign direct investment. In: Krajewski M, Hoffmann R (eds) Research handbook on foreign direct investment. Edward Elgar Publications, Cheltenham

Brown C (2010) Procedure in investment treaty arbitration and the relevance of comparative public law. In: Schill S (ed) International investment law and comparative public law. Oxford University Press, Oxford, p 662

Buergenthal T (2006) The proliferation of disputes, dispute settlement procedures and respect for the rule of law. ICSID Rev Foreign Invest Law J 21(1):130

Butler N, Musa S (2018) Systemizing human rights within investment arbitration. Am Rev Int Arbitr 28(4):445

Calamita J (2013) International human rights and the interpretation of international investment treaties-constitutional considerations. In: Baetens F (ed) The interaction of international investment law with other fields of public international law. Cambridge University Press, Cambridge, p 170

Caron D (2011) The independence and impartiality of legal systems. World Arbitr Mediation Rev 5:3

Chase P (2015) TTIP, investor-state dispute settlement and the rule of law. Eur View 14:2

Collins R (2019) Two Idea(l)s of the international rule of law. Global Constitutionalism 8:2

Costa P (2007) The rule of law: a historical introduction. In: Costa P, Zolo D (eds) The rule of law: history, theory and criticism. Springer Publications, New York, p 78
Craig P (1997) Formal and substantive conception of the rule of law: an analytical framework. West Law Public Law 467:1
Crawford J (2003) International law and the rule of law. Adelaide Law Rev 24:3
Cross F (2008) Judicial independence. In: Whittington K et al (eds) The Oxford handbook of law and politics. Oxford University Press, Oxford, p 558
Desierto D (2018) Shifting sands in the international economic system: 'arbitrage' in international economic law and international human rights. Georgetown J Int Law 49:3
Dezalay Y, Garth BG (1996) Dealing in virtue: international commercial arbitration and the construction of a transnational legal order. The University of Chicago Press, Chicago, p 194
Dicey AV (1958) Introduction to the study of the law of the constitution, 10th edn. Liberty Fund Publications, Carmel, p 202
Dieng A (1997) Role of judges and lawyers in defending the rule of law. Fordham Int Law J 21 (2):550
Dunoff J, Trachtman J (2009) A functional approach to international constitutionalization. In: Dunnoff J, Trachtman J (eds) Ruling the World? Constitutionalism, international law and global governance. Cambridge University Press, Cambridge, p 13
Dworkin R (1985) A matter of principle. Harvard University Press, Cambridge, p 11
Dyson H (2004) Judicial activism and the rule of law. Otago Law Rev 10(493):3
Ekins R, Forsyth C (2015) Judging the public interest: the rule of law Vs the rule of courts. Judicial Power Project. judicialpowerproject.org.uk/wp-content/uploads/2016/10/judging-the-public-interest-.pdf. Accessed 1 May 2020
Fallon R (1997) The rule of law as a concept in constitutional discourse. Columb Law Rev 97(1):10
Foran M (2019) The rule of good law: form, substance and fundamental rights. Camb Law J 78 (3):570–595, p. 26
Fortier LY (2009) Investment protection and the rule of law: change or decline?. ICCA Database, p 13. www.arbitration-icca.org/media/4/54271857323013/media0123927854601400732_001.pdf
Franck T (1998) Fairness in international law and institutions. Oxford University Press, Oxford, ch. 14
Franck S (2011) Rationalizing costs in investment treaty arbitration. Wash Univ Law Rev 88(4):775
Frandberg A (2014) From rechtsstaat to universal law - state: an essay in philosophical jurisprudence. Springer Publications, New York
Fuller L (1969) The morality of law. Yale University Press, London, p 153
Gaukrodger D (2017) Adjudicator compensation systems and investor-state dispute settlement. OECD Working Papers, p 11
Goldhaber MD (2004) Wanted: a world investment court, The American Lawyer
Gottwald E (2007) Leveling the playing field: is it time for a legal assistance center for developing countries in investment treaty arbitration. Am Univ Law Rev 22(2):259–260
Griffith JAG (1977) The politics of the judiciary, 5th edn. Fontana Press, London
Hansen R (2010) Parallel proceedings in investor – state treaty arbitration: responses for treaty – drafters, arbitrators and parties. Modern Law Rev 73:4
Hayek FA (2005) The road to serfdom. First Published 1944. Routledge Publications, Abingdon, p 75
Hayek F (2011) The constitution of liberty. First Published 1960. The University of Chicago Press, Chicago, pp 241–243
Hurd I (2015) The international rule of law and the domestic analogy. Global Const 14
International Law Association- Study Group (2016) The use of domestic principles in the development of international law. Johannesburg Conference, p 56
International Law Association in Sydney (2018) Draft report on the 'Rule of Law and International Investment Law' delivered at the annual conference of the International Law Association in Sydney

Isiksel T, Thies A (2013) Changing subjects: rights, remedies and responsibilities of individuals under global legal pluralism. Global Const 2:2
Judiciary of England and Wales (2013) Guide to judicial conduct, ch. 2–3
Kanetake M (2016) The interfaces between the national and international rule of law: a framework paper. In: Kanetake M, Nollkaemper A (eds) The rule of law at the national and international levels: contestations and deference. Hart Publishing, Oxford, p 10
Koskenniemi M (1989) From apology to Utopia: the structure of international legal argument. Cambridge University Press, Cambridge. ch. 1
Kurtz J (2014) Building legitimacy through interpretation in investor-state arbitration: on consistency, coherence and the identification of applicable law. In: Douglas Z et al (eds) The foundation of international investment law: bringing theory into practice. Oxford University Press, Oxford, p 274
Lanneau R (2013) What is legal certainty? A theoretical essay. SSRN Database, p. 16. papers.ssrn.com/sol3/papers.cfm?abstract_id=2361630
Lauterpacht H (1958) Development of international law by the international court, being revised edition of the development of international law by the permanent court of international justice. Stevens, p 398
Locke J (1956) Two treatises of government and a letter concerning toleration. First Published 1689. Dover Publications, New York, p 64
Lord Neuberger (2015) Arbitration and the rule of law. Speech at the Chartered Institute of Arbitrators. www.supremecourt.uk/docs/speech-150320.pdf
Loughlin M (2010) Foundations of public law. Oxford University Press, Oxford, p 324
Mackenzie R, Sands P (2003) International courts and tribunals and the independence of the international judge. Harv Int Law J 44:278 & 284
Maravall J (2003) Democracy and the rule of law. In: Maravall JM, Przeworski A (eds) Democracy and the rule of law. Cambridge University Press, Cambridge, pp 264–265
Maxeiner J (2007) Legal certainty and legal methods: a european alternative to American legal indeterminacy? Univ Baltimore Law:572
McCorquodale R (2016) Defining the international rule of law: defying gravity? Int Comp Law Q 65:296–303
Miller F (2010) The rule of law in ancient Greek thought. In: Sellers M, Tomaszewski T (eds) The rule of law in comparative perspective. Springer Publications, New York
Monika H, Theresa R (2016) The rule of law in global governance. Palgrave Publications, London
Montesquieu B (2007) Spirit of laws, p 150
Montt S (2009) State liability and investment treaty arbitration: global constitutional and administrative law in the BIT generation. Hart Publishing, New York
Nyegaard Mollestad C (2014) See no Evil? Procedural transparency in international investment law and dispute settlement. PluriCourts Research Paper No. 14–20, p 38
O'Connor S (2018) Defining access to justice in international arbitration. Oxford Online. oxia.ouplaw.com/page/defining-access-to-justice
OECD Investment Committee (2005) Transparency and third party participation in investor-state dispute settlement procedure. OECD Investment Division
Office of the UN High Commissioner For Human Rights (2005) In: Office of the UN High Commissioner For Human Rights (ed) Economic, social and cultural rights: a handbook for national human rights institutions. UNDP, New York, p 4
Ohler C (2017) Democratic legitimacy and the rule of law in investor-state dispute settlement under CETA. In: Bungenberg M et al (eds) European yearbook of international economic law 2017. Springer Publications, New York
Ostwald M (1986) From popular sovereignty to the sovereignty of law: law, society and politics in fifth-century athens. University of California Press, Berkeley, p 497
Paulson (2013) The idea of arbitration. Oxford University Press, Oxford, p 232
Pauwelyn J (2015) The rule of law without the rule of lawyers? Why investment arbitrators are from mars, trade adjudicators are from venus. Am J Int Law 109:761–805

Popelier P (2008) Five paradoxes on legal certainty. Legisprudence 2:47–66
Posner RA (1983) The meaning of judicial self- restraint. Indiana Law J 59:1
Prislan V (2012) Non-investment obligations in investment treaty arbitration - toward a greater role for states. In: Baetens F (ed) Investment law within international law: an internationalist perspective. Cambridge University Press, Cambridge, p 451
Puig S, Shaffer G (2018) Imperfect alternatives: institutional choice and the reform in investment law. Am J Int Law 112:361
Radin M (1947) The Myth of the Magna Carta. Harv Law Rev 60(7):1060–1061
Radovic R (2018) Inherently unneutral investment treaty arbitration: the formation of decisive arguments in jurisdictional determinations. J Disp Resol 1:183
Raz J (1979) The s. Oxford University Press, Oxford, p 211
Reinisch A (2016) The rule of law in international investment arbitration. In: Papartzis P et al (eds) Reconceptualizing the rule of law in global governance, resources, investment and trade. Hart Publishing, Oxford
Report by the Venice Commision on Human Rights (2011) www.venice.coe.int/webforms/documents/default.aspx?pdffile=CDL-AD(2011)003rev-e. Accessed 10 May 2020
Rosert D (2014) The stakes are high: a review of the financial costs of investment treaty arbitration. International Institute for Sustainable Development, Winnipeg, p 15
Salacuse J (2007) Is there is a better way? Alternative methods for treaty-based investor-state dispute resolution. Fordham Int Law J 31(138):142
Sands P (2011) Conflict and conflicts in investment treaty arbitration: ethical standards for counsel. In: Rovine A (ed.) Contemporary issues in international arbitration and mediation: the fordham papers
Scalia A (1989) The rule of law as a law of rules. Univ Chicago Law Rev 56:4
Schacherer S (2018) Independence and impartiality of arbitrators: a rule of law analysis. University of Geneva Working Papers
Schefer K (2016) International investment law: text, cases and materials, 2nd edn. Elgar Publications, Camberley
Schill S (2010) Fair and equitable treatment, the rule of law and comparative public law. In: Schill S (ed) International investment law and comparative public law. Oxford University Press, Oxford, p 157
Schill S (2015) International investment law and the rule of law. In: Lowell J et al (eds) Rule of law symposium 2014: the importance of the rule of law in promoting development. Singapore Academy Publishing, Singapore
Schill S (2017) Reforming investor - state dispute settlement: a (comparative and international) constitutional law framework. J Int Econ Law:10
Schneiderman D (2010) Judicial politics and international investment law: seeking an explanation of conflicting outcomes. Northwest J Int Law Bus 30(383):403
Schultz T (2014) Against consistency in investment arbitration. In: Douglas Z et al (eds) The foundations of international investment law: bringing theory into practice. Oxford University Press, Oxford
Schultz T, Dupont C (2015) Investment arbitration: promoting the rule of law or over-empowering investors? A quantitative empirical study. Eur J Int Law 25(4):1149
Sheetreen S, Turenne S (2013) Judges on trial: the independence and accountability of the English judiciary, 2nd edn. Cambridge University Press, Cambridge, p 6
Shirlow E (2017) Three manifestations of transparency in international investment law: a story of sources, stakeholders and structures. Goettingen J Int Law 8:98
Shokouh H (2014) Power in investor-state arbitration. King's College London Thesis Repository, ch. 4
Smithers W (1902) The German Civil Code. The American law register. University of Pennsylvania, Pennsylvania, pp 689–690
Stanford Encyclopedia of Philosophy (2016) The rule of law. plato.stanford.edu/entries/rule-of-law/. Accessed 1 May 2020

Steininger S (2018) What's human rights got to do with it? An empirical analysis of human rights references in investment arbitration. Leiden J Int Law 31:45–46
Stern B (2009) Civil society's voice in the settlement of international economic disputes. ICSID Rev 22(2):347
Sureda AR (2012) Investment treaty arbitration: judging under uncertainty. Hersch Lauterpacht Memorial Lectures. Cambridge University Press, Cambridge, p 9
Sweet AS (2014) The evolution of international arbitration: delegation, judicialization, governance. In: Mattli W, Dietz T (eds) International arbitration and global governance: contending theory and evidence. Oxford University Press, Oxford, pp 33–35
Tamanaha BZ (2004) On the rule of law: history, politics, theory. Cambridge University Press, Cambridge, p 8
The Magna Carta, (The British Library). www.bl.uk/magna-carta/articles/magna-carta-an-introduction
Tobias Stoll P (2018) International investment law and the rule of law. Goettingen J Int Law 9:1
Ulrich Petersmann E (2009) International rule of law and constitutional justice in international investment law and arbitration. Indiana J Global Legal Stud 16(2):523–526
UN Economic and Social Council, Definition of basic concepts in governance and public administration, E/C.16/2006/4 (2006), para. 49
United Nations - Office of the High Commissioner for Human Rights (2003) Human rights in the administration of justice: a manual on human rights for judges, prosecutors and judges, ch. 4
United Nations Commision on Human Rights (2003) Human rights, trade and investment, U.N. Doc E/CN.4/Sub.2/2003/9 documents-dds-ny.un.org/doc/UNDOC/GEN/G03/148/47/PDF/G0314847.pdf?OpenElement. Accessed 20 Apr 2020
United Nations Commision on International Trade Law (2010) Report of Working Group II (Arbitration and Conciliation) A/CN.9/712, pp 9–10
United Nations Conference on Trade and Development (2012) Fair and equitable treatment: a series, series on issues in international investment agreements II, p 12
United Nations General Assembly (2012) Delivering justice: programme of action to strengthen the rule of law at the national and international levels (Report of the Secretary-General, A/66/749), para. 2
Van Caenegem RC (1996) An historical introduction to private law. Cambridge University Press, Cambridge, p 73
Van Harten G (2010a) Investment treaty arbitration, procedural fairness, and the rule of law. In: Schill S (ed) International investment law and comparative public law. Oxford University Press, Oxford, p 628
Van Harten G (2010b) Perceived bias in investment treaty arbitration. In: Waibel M et al (eds) The backlash against investment arbitration: perceptions and reality. Kluwer Law International, Alphen aan den Rijn, p 443
Voete E (2003) The politics of international judicial appointments. Chicago J Int Law 9:2
Waibel M (2011) International investment law and treaty interpretation. In: Hofmann R, Tams C (eds) International investment law and general international law-from clinical isolation to systematic integration. Nomos Publications, Baden-Baden
Waldon J (2002) Is the rule of law an essentially contested concept (in Florida)? Law Philos 21:137
Weber M (1978) Economy and society: an outline of interpretive sociology. University of California Press, Berkeley
Zolo D (2007) The rule of law: a critical reappraisal. In: Costa P, Zolo D (eds) The rule of law: history, theory and criticism. Springer Publications, New York, p 18

Chapter 4
Legal Certainty and CETA: The Fallacy of a Single Treaty As a Solution

4.1 Introduction

Investment arbitration must fulfil the expectations of a wider audience and its demands for legal certainty, which is a sub-element of the Rule of Law. In particular, the Rule of Law prescribes that the law must be predictable and clearly defined in order for those subject to the law to be able to rely on it. Without legal certainty, those subject to the law will only be able to be guided by their guesses as to what the tribunal is likely to do, but these guesses will not be based on the law but on other considerations. Hence, the Rule of Law is considered as a means to protect those subject to the law from arbitrary rule and unpredictability by enhancing legal certainty. Against this background, this chapter analyses whether the provisions introduced in CETA's Investment Chapter further legal certainty in the context of investment arbitration. In particular, this chapters goes through the drafting of the investment standards in CETA, the binding interpretative rules, the joint interpretative declarations, the provisions aiming to address the phenomenon of conflicting awards and multiple proceedings, including the appellate mechanism attached to the ISDS mechanism in CETA. The chapter finally argues that CETA's Investment Chapter largely provides legal certainty, but stresses possible shortcomings and open questions.

4.2 Investment Protection Provisions

4.2.1 Fair and Equitable Treatment

A major concern of States when it comes to signing IIAs is their regulatory powers. This concern is also one of the major drivers behind the legitimacy crisis in investment arbitration. As argued in the previous chapter, more imprecise norms

K. Dionysiou, *CETA's Investment Chapter*, European Yearbook of International Economic Law 13, https://doi.org/10.1007/978-3-030-66992-8_4

provide greater discretion on arbitrators to make evaluative judgments. The resulting legal uncertainty regarding the standards of treatments has a negative impact on the regulatory power of States. For this reason, in a press statement about CETA, the European Commission claimed that investors will not be able to use the arbitration mechanism against States simply because their profits are negatively affected but they will only be permitted to bring a claim in a limited number of well-defined cases, so there will be no room for the members of the tribunal to interpret CETA's provisions freely.'[1]

This part examines whether the standards of treatment included in CETA provide substantive clarity in regard to their scope. Without a doubt, the Fair and Equitable Treatment (FET) standard is the most invoked standard in investment arbitration.[2] As explained in the previous chapters, the vague wording of the FET standard in various IIAs creates legal uncertainty for both investors and States. Therefore, the first section examines the extent to which the FET standard limits the discretion of tribunals.

Paragraph 2 of article 8.10 contains a negative list of acts that constitute a breach of the FET standard.[3] Consequently, the tribunal cannot consider any acts or omissions by host States that are not listed as breaches of the FET standard. At the same time, the FET standard is not linked with customary international law or any other autonomous standard of international law.[4] As will be argued in this sub-section, the fact that the FET standard is neither linked with customary international law nor with an open-ended autonomous standard of international law makes it a brave attempt towards greater legal certainty. As a matter of fact, CETA adopts an exhaustive, closed text and relatively well-defined version of the FET standard.

CETA follows the paradigm of other IIAs, which attempt to limit the tribunals' interpretive discretion by clarifying the type of conduct that would violate the FET standard.[5] By injecting explicit clarifications regarding the content of the FET standard, CETA attempts to improve predictability.[6] In this way, CETA substantially limits any arbitrary discretion by the investment tribunal in its interpretation of this standard and, at the same time, attempts to enhance legal certainty.

---

[1]European Commision (2004).

[2]Klager (2011) and Tudor (2008).

[3]These measures include: (a) denial of justice in criminal, civil or administrative proceedings (b) fundamental breach of due process, including a fundamental breach of transparency, in judicial and administrative proceedings (c) manifest arbitrariness (d) targeted discrimination on manifestly wrongful grounds, such as gender, race or religious belief (e) abusive treatment of investors, such as coercion, duress and harassment.

[4]OECD indicates that many governments attempted to circumscribe the scope of the FET standard by either linking it to customary international law or to an autonomous self-contained treaty standard. *See* OECD (2004a, b).

[5]Unuvar (2016), p. 36.

[6]This method reflects Ortino's suggestion that standards of treatment should operate as 'rules' rather than 'standards' to ensure predictability. In this context, rules have a higher degree of predictability. *See* Ortino (2013).

Turning to certain observations, several States have attempted to restrict the interpretation of the FET standard by linking the standard to customary international law, which gives a minimum standard of treatment to foreign investors. This particular version of the FET standard is understood as one of the elements of customary international law and, consequently, arbitral tribunals are tasked to assess the content of the customary norm.[7] In the famous *Neer* case, the tribunal set out the elements and the threshold for acts constituting a violation of customary international law. In particular, the tribunal held that 'the treatment of an alien, in order to constitute an international delinquency, should amount to an outrage, to bad faith, to wilful neglect of duty, or to an insufficiency of governmental action so far short of international standards that every reasonable and impartial man would readily recognise its insufficiency.'[8]

Regardless of the *Neer* award, the reference to customary international law was not successful so far to harmonise the interpretation of the FET standard with the threshold set out by the award.[9] As to this point, in the *ADF v United States*, the tribunal held that the customary international law standard is not "frozen in time" but evolves through time.[10] In the same manner, the tribunal in *Merrill & Ring* has clearly distanced itself from the *Neer* award. In specific, the tribunal held that the minimum standard of treatment is found in customary international law and that nowdays is broader than that defined in the Neer case.[11]

In a nutshell, the *Neer* award has been unable to circumscribe the scope of the FET standard. Another approach that has been used is to detach the FET standard from customary international law and adopt an autonomous approach. This approach conceives that FET standard as a self-contained standard that should be interpreted on the basis of its own general definition.[12] Accordingly, a state should treat foreign investors in a 'fair' and 'equitable' manner, without any further clarifications. Yet, this open-ended obligation does not usually refer to any guidance as to what fair and equitable means and from where this obligation originates. As a result of this ambiguity, tribunals have been interpreting the FET standard in different, often diverging, ways.

The most comprehensive definition of the 'autonomous' FET standard was set out in *Tecmed*. In specific, the tribunal held that the foreign investor expects the State to act in a consistent, transparent and unambiquous manner in its conduct with the

---

[7]De Brabandere (2016), p. 267.

[8]*L. F. H. Neer and Pauline Neer (U.S.A.) v. United Mexican States*, Reports of International Arbitral Awards (15th October 1926), p. 61.

[9]In *Cargill* the tribunal, when discussing about the FET standard in NAFTA, held that 'that these words are imprecise and thus leave a measure of discretion to tribunals. But this is not unusual.'*See Cargill, Incorporated v. United Mexican States*, ICSID Case No. ARB(AF)/05/2, para. 285. For the same observation *See Mondev International Ltd. v. United States of America*, ICSID Case No. ARB (AF)/99/2.

[10]*ADF Group Inc. v. United States of America*, ICSID Case No. ARB (AF)/00/1, para. 179.

[11]*Merrill and Ring Forestry L.P. v. Canada*, ICSID Case No. UNCT/07/1, para. 213.

[12]Klein Bronfman (2006), p. 672.

foreign investor, so that the foreign investor may know beforehand all the applicable rules, as well as the objectives of the relevant regulations, to be able to plan its conduct and comply with such regulations.'[13] The tribunal added further that the foreign investor expects the State to act without arbitrarily taking back any decisions or licenses issued by the State that were relied upon by the foreign investor to plan its investment activities.[14]

Yet, another tribunal, interpreting an autonomous FET standard, added that host States should act proactively in favor of foreign investors. In particular, the tribunal held that the FET standard should be understood to include pro-active statements—"to promote", "to create", "to stimulate"—rather than prescriptions for a passive behavior on behalf of the State.[15]

Therefore, despite the States' attempts to circumscribe the scope of the FET standard, neither of the above approaches has been able so far to effectively delimit the FET standard and provide legal certainty to States and foreign investors. As a matter of fact, it is also possible for different standards, either linked to customary international law or an autonomous provision, to produce the same outcome. Martins Paparinskis argues that it seems permissible in arbitral practice to assume that the ordinary meaning of the FET standard refers to customary international law.[16] Consequently, the borderline between customary international law and an autonomous notion of the FET standard appears to be blurred.

A number of arbitral awards support this statement. For example, in the case of *Waste Management v Mexico,* the tribunal held that the FET standard in NAFTA, which is linked to customary international law, is violated if the conduct the State is arbitrary, grossly unfair, unjust or idiosyncratic, or involves a lack of due process leading to an outcome which offends judicial propriety, or a complete lack of transparency and candor an administrative process.[17] At the same time, the tribunal in *Saluka v Czech Republic*, interpreting an autonomous FET standard, did not hesitate to borrow the reasoning of the *Waste Management* case, which had to do with a qualified FET standard.[18] Most importantly, the tribunal in *Saluka* case elaborating on the difference between customary international law and an autonomous FET standard held that the difference between the standard laid down in the investment treaty and the customary minimum standard may well be more apparent than real.[19]

[13]*Técnicas Medioambientales Tecmed, S.A. v. The United Mexican States*, ICSID Case No. ARB (AF)/00/2, para. 154.

[14]*ibid,* para 154.

[15]*MTD Equity Sdn. Bhd. and MTD Chile S.A. v. Republic of Chile*, ICSID Case No. ARB/01/7, para. 113.

[16]*See generally* Paparinskis (2013), pp. 160–166.

[17]*Waste Management, Inc. v. United Mexican States*, ICSID Case No. ARB(AF)/00/3, para. 98.

[18]*Saluka Investments B.V. v. The Czech Republic*, UNCITRAL, paras. 288 & 303.

[19]*ibid*, para. 291.

The cases above illustrate that neither formulation of the FET standard has been able to effectively delimit the scope of this controversial standard of protection. This is due to the fact that customary international law is as imprecise as the autonomous notion of the FET standard. Additionally, as was suggested in previous chapters, it is possible for the same vague standard of treatment to produce diverging interpretation. Ultimately, linking the FET with either customary international law or an autonomous standard hasn't brought greater legal certainty.

In accordance with the above, the exhaustive list of the FET elements in CETA constitutes of a brave attempt to avoid expansive interpretations by tribunals. A tribunal would not be able to expand the scope of the FET standard by broadly interpreting how customary international law or the autonomous notion of the standard has evolved in recent years.[20] Additionally, article 8.9 of the investment chapter reaffirms that the parties have the right to regulate for the protection of public health and the environment. The same articles further stipulate that 'the mere fact that a party regulates [...] in a manner which negatively affects an investment or interferes with an investor's expectations, including its expectations of profits, does not amount to a breach of an obligation.'[21]

Another controversial aspect of the FET standard is the so-called doctrine of legitimate expectations as tribunals often apply it inconsistently.[22] Scholars further argue that the doctrine of legitimate expectations has been applied primarily in the interest of the foreign investor.[23] Very broadly, legitimate expectation gives the right to a foreign investor to seek legal protection from harm caused as a result of a public authority departing from a previously stated position.[24] Turning to CETA, the text stipulates that:

> a Tribunal may take into account whether a Party made a specific representation to an investor to induce a covered investment, that created a legitimate expectation, and upon which the investor relied in deciding to make or maintain the covered investment, but that the Party subsequently frustrated.[25]

Despite different views on this point,[26] the drafters of CETA could have given a more concise and clear definition of the notion of legitimate expectation. Simply

---

[20]One could argue that tribunals maintain the ability to interpret the FET standard in a broad manner. However, CETA has an appellate mechanism, a roster of arbitrators, and a mechanism for States to issue joint interpretative declarations. These mechanisms will ensure continuity in decision-making, thereby ensuring consistency, as well as maintaing that States control on the scope and content of investment provisions.

[21]CETA, Art. 8. 9 (2).

[22]For an overview *See* Potesta (2013).

[23]For this argument *See* Ngangjoh-Hodu and Ajibo (2018).

[24]*ibid.* pp. 93–94.

[25]CETA, Art. 8.10 (4).

[26]Unuvar argues that when it comes to the FET standard, which includes the concept of legitimate expectations, the parties have successfully articulated its elements and delimited its scope. *See* Unuvar (2007), p. 17. For the same argument about CETA and legitimate expectations *See* Nyer (2015), p. 703.

frustrating investors' expectations should not automatically qualify for a valid legitimate expectation argument in the context of an investment dispute. On the contrary, for an expectation to qualify as 'legitimate', a specific representation must be made to the investor upon which the investor relied. For example, in *Charanne v Spain*, the tribunal held that in the absence of specific representation a legitimate expectation could not be created.[27] In the tribunal's view, any other ruling would have unduly constrained the regulatory power of Spain.[28]

CETA's wording can be deceiving given that CETA limits legitimate expectations only to 'specific representations' made by the host state. With a closer look, the notion of legitimate expectation remains subject to expansive interpretation by investment tribunals. This is because; the wording contemplated remains unclear and vague. The treaty text does not specify in what form the representation has to be made. In addition, Article 8.10 grants to tribunals a significant margin of appreciation with regard to whether or not legitimate expectations should be taken into account in the context of investment disputes. As a consequence, a tribunal is granted wide discretion regarding the nature of the representation that could give rise to legitimate expectations.[29]

The formulation of the notion of legitimate expectation in the agreement between the EU and Singapore would have been a better example to avoid potential pitfalls. According to article 9 of the agreement, 'a specific and clearly spelled out commitment in a contractual written obligation towards a covered investor'[30] would give rise to legitimate expectations. In addition, that obligation should indicate that a home state 'shall not frustrate or undermine the said commitment through the exercise of its governmental authority either deliberately' or 'in a way which substantially alters the balance of rights and obligations in the contractual written obligation.'[31] With CETA's less precise wording, there is a greater risk that state commitments, broadly construed, would fall under the scope of the provision.

4.2.2 Expropriation

In addition to the FET standard, the expropriation provisions of IIAs have been the subjects of debate as they gave rise to tensions between public policy and investors' rights.[32] This is due to the fact that numerous expropriation provisions contain

[27] *Charanne and Construction Investments v. Spain*, SCC Case No. V 062/2012, para. 499. Also *See EDF (Services) Limited v. Romania*, ICSID Case No. ARB/05/13, para. 217.

[28] *ibid*, para. 493.

[29] The dangers posed by the vague scope of the concept of 'legitimate expectations' in CETA is highlighted by other commentators as well. *See* Dumberry (2018), p. 109.

[30] EU-Singapore FTA, Chapter 2, Art. 2.4.

[31] *ibid*, Art. 2.4.

[32] For an overview of the debate *See* OECD (2004a, b) and Reinisch (2008).

open-ended obligations with no substantial guidance regarding their scope, therefore, giving wide discretion to arbitrators. In addition, the broad wording makes it difficult to predict whether a state will be held liable to compensate an investor.

Compensating a foreign investor for every regulatory measure taken would impair the sovereign power of States. At the same time, not every sovereign act should automatically lead to the conclusion that no expropriation has occurred. Whilst there has been a lot of discussion regarding the scope of the expropriation clause, there is no accepted approach that defines when foreign investors should be compensated or not. This is particularly so where foreign investment is indirectly expropriated by a sovereign act. In the case of indirect expropriation, the foreign investor maintains legal ownership of the property but loses the ability to exercise the economic benefits arising therefrom.[33] As the center of attention of expropriation is indirect expropriation, this section will focus on this aspect of the expropriation clause and the clarifications made in CETA.

Article 8.12 of CETA does not prohibit expropriation *per se*. On the contrary, the article lays down certain requirements that a state measure should fulfill to constitute lawful expropriation.[34] In specific, expropriation should only be done for (a) public purpose (b) under due process of law (c) in a non-discriminatory manner and (d) on payment of prompt, adequate and effective compensation.[35] Such wording is a classic example of a vaguely construed expropriation clause. This is because; it fails to provide a concrete definition of expropriation or what constitutes an indirect expropriation. At least in terms of the basic elements of what constitutes an expropriation, CETA does not introduce any major re-elaboration of this provision by making a reference to both direct and indirect expropriation and to 'measures having equivalent effect.'[36] In addition to this standard provision, the drafters of CETA have established an interpretative link to Annex 8.12. As will be shown in this sub-section, the annex attached to CETA enhances legal certainty. This is because; CETA includes a precise list, accompanied with important clarifications and a proportionality test, that should be taken into account by tribunals to identify an indirect expropriation.

Annex 8.12 stipulates 'that indirect expropriation occurs if a measure or series of measures of a Party has an effect equivalent to direct expropriation, in that it substantially deprives the investor of the fundamental attributes of property in its investment [...] without formal transfer of title or outright seizure.'[37] Firstly, the reference to a 'series of measures' attempts to clarify that indirect expropriation may

[33]Kriebaum (2015), p. 971. In a similar fashion, the tribunal in *CME v Czech* held that de facto or indirect expropriation are subject to expropriation claims, a proposition which is undisputed under international law. *CME Czech Republic BVv The Czech Republic*, UNCITRAL Award 9/2001, para. 604.

[34]CETA, Art. 8.12.

[35]*ibid*, Art. 8. 12.

[36]*ibid.*

[37]CETA, Annex 8-A (1b).

occur in a gradual or growing form and not only through a sole and unique action.[38] This wording is a direct response to the controversial issues as regards to when an indirect expropriation materialises and whether an indirect expropriation may occur in a gradual form.

Secondly, the 'substantial deprivation' requirement indicates that a foreign investor should demonstrate that he was deprived of fundamental rights to be able to claim compensation. Thus, it all comes down to the question of whether an investor's property is destroyed or the investor no longer has control over it. This provision further suggests that as far as the investor can still use and enjoy his property, no expropriation can be concluded.[39] As was argued by Ortino, such a codification settles the controversy surrounding the required level of deprivation, because certain panels set the bar just below 'total' deprivation', while some other panels adopt an approach requiring a higher level of deprivation.[40]

The same annex states further that the determination of whether a measure constitutes an indirect expropriation 'requires a case-by-case, fact-based inquiry' that takes into account a list of considerations.[41] These considerations include the economic impact of the measure, although such an adverse effect will not automatically establish indirect expropriation.[42] Other factors are listed as well, including the duration of the measure, the expectations of the investors and the object and intent of a measure.[43] For the purpose of establishing indirect expropriation, it is one thing to say that a state measure aimed to protect environmental pollution, and another to claim that it aims at expropriating a foreign investor's property.

In addition to the delineation of the clause, according to Shirlow a tribunal having to take into account both the effect and purpose of a sovereign act will eventually develop 'state conscious.'[44] This would lead the tribunals to be more considerate with the regulatory power of States. In other words, a host state will not incur liability provided the measure was adopted for a genuine regulatory purpose and not with the intention to expropriate the property of a foreign investor.

Most importantly, the annex attached to CETA carves out vital regulatory measures from the scope of the expropriation clause. As to this, the final paragraph states that:

---

[38]*Supra* note 155, *LG&E*, para. 188. In *Biloune*, the tribunal held that: 'Expropriation may occur in the absence of a single decisive act that implies a taking of property. it could result from a series of acts and/or omissions that, in sum, result in a deprivation of property rights' *Biloune and Marine Drive Complex Ltd v Ghana Investments Centre and the Government of Ghana* (UNCITRAL), para. 209.

[39]De Naunteil (2018), p. 133.

[40]Ortino (2016), p. 355.

[41]CETA, Annex 8-A (2).

[42]*ibid,*Annex 8-A (2).

[43]*ibid*, Annex 8-A (2).

[44]Shirlow (2014), p. 607.

> except in the rare circumstance when the impact of a measure or series of measures is so severe in light of its purpose that it appears manifestly excessive, non-discriminatory measures of a Party that are designed and applied to protect legitimate public welfare objectives, such as health, safety and the environment, do not constitute indirect expropriations.[45]

As evidenced by the paragraph, a regulatory measure, provided that it's not discriminatory and serves a legitimate public purpose, will not fall under the scope of the expropriation clause in CETA. The 'except in rare circumstances' and 'manifestly excessive' requirements suggest that the parties intended to narrow the scope of indirect expropriation. Moreover, the list of legitimate objectives in the paragraph is not exhaustive, thus, leaving open the possibility for future extensions.

In essence, CETA's expropriation clause builds upon the experience of previous treaties that were drafted in a similar way. The case of *Railroad Development Corporation v Guatemala,*[46] a dispute held under the Central American Free Trade Agreement (CAFTA) that has a similar expropriation clause with CETA, proves this assertion. The tribunal, in its elaboration about the legality of indirect expropriation, held that it will firstly 'proceed to analyse the nature [of the measure] and its public purpose.[47] The tribunal added further that it would evaluate 'whether the Government interfered with reasonable investment-backed expectations and their economic impact on the claimant's investment.'[48] According to this reasoning, a tribunal constituted under CETA is obliged to consider both the purpose and the intent behind an expropriation.[49] Absent such clarification, a tribunal is not obliged to take into consideration the rationale behind a sovereign act.

Additionally, the reference to the severeness of a measure involves a proportionality test, thus implicitly requiring a certain degree of balancing. This requirement adds a European touch, common in the case-law of the Court of Justice of the European Union (CJEU), to the regulations exceptions.[50] This test could indeed be helpful in an effort to adopt a balanced approach in the interpretation of CETA by taking into account both the foreign investors' interests and the regulatory power of States. When it comes to legal certainty, it has been argued that the adoption of proportionality in the context of investment disputes 'would inject a measure of analytic, or procedural, determinacy to the balancing exercise'[51] by means of elucidating 'the bargain inherent in every IIA to reconcile conflicting interests.'[52]

[45]CETA, Annex 8-A (3).

[46]*Railroad Development Corporation v. Republic of Guatemala*, ICSID Case No. ARB/07/23.

[47]*ibid*, para. 81.

[48]*ibid.*

[49]Perkams argues that a variety of jurisdictions recognise a certain margin of appreciation to public institutions when they adopt regulations in the public interest. In this way, it is possible to build a more reliable and balanced foundation for the interpretation of expropriation provisions in an effort to avoid contradicting interpretations. *See* Perkams (2010).

[50]Kriebaum (2014), p. 467.

[51]Stone Sweet (2010), p. 63.

[52]*See generally* Bucheler (2015), ch. 9.

In that sense, the annex attached to CETA attempts to avoid a tribunal following the sole effects doctrine.[53] Tribunals who disregard the purpose behind a regulatory measure and instead focus on the effect of a measure to determine whether an expropriation occurred use the sole effects doctrine.[54] In contrast, CETA follows the so-called radical police approach, where only arbitrary and discriminatory regulatory measures will be considered expropriations for the purpose of an investment dispute.[55] In comparison with previous practices,[56] the text of CETA clearly offers more guidance to tribunals than other IIAs, which left the task of interpreting the details of the expropriation clause to tribunals. CETA therefore attempts to enhance legal certainty by drawing a bright line between lawful regulatory measures and indirect expropriation.

4.2.3 Most-Favored-Nation Clause

A Most-Favored-Nation treatment (MFN) clause is usually invoked to prevent host States from treating foreign investors of one nationality better than investors of another nationality. As shown in the second chapter, the MFN clause has attracted controversy since most IIAs do not make clear what kind of treatment a foreign investor may import from another investment treaty. According to Schill, MFN provisions 'lock States into the most favorable level of investment protection reached at one point in time',[57] thus become instruments of multilateralization. On this basis, it is argued that MFN clauses limit the ability of States to conclude different IIAs with other States and, subsequently, make it difficult for them to predict their scope of potential liability.[58]

As most MFN clauses do not make clear whether 'treatment' includes both procedural and substantive rights conferred by other IIAs, it has fallen to tribunals to decide this issue.[59] In particular, the tribunal in *Renta v Russia* held that there is

---

[53]Hoffmann (2020), pp. 156–158.

[54]Bonnitcha et al. (2017), p. 106. In *Tecmed*, the tribunal held that:'The government's intention is less important than the effects of the measures on the owner of the assets or on the benefits arising from such assets affected by the measures; and the form of the deprivation measure is less important than its actual effects.' *Técnicas Medioambientales Tecmed, S.A. v. The United Mexican States*, ICSID Case No. ARB (AF)/00/2, para.116.

[55]*ibid.* Also *See Chemtura Corporation v. Government of Canada*, UNCITRAL (formerly Crompton Corporation v. Government of Canada), para. 266.

[56]*See generally* The Energy Charter Treaty, Art. 13; NAFTA, Art. 1110; Chinese Model BIT (2003), Art. 4; German Model Treaty (2008), Art. 4; UK Model BIT (2005), Art. 5.

[57]Schill (2009), p. 196.

[58]Batifort and Benton Heath (2017), p. 875.

[59]For a general overview *See* Ziegler (2008).

not a dominant view regarding the jurisdictional implications of the MFN clause.[60] More specifically, some tribunals have been interpreting MFN clauses in a way that allows them to import standards of treatment from different IIAs unless persuaded that the parties to the IIA actively intended to exclude such option.[61] Tribunals reaching the opposite ruling have tended to restrict the scope of the MFN clause unless persuaded that the parties specifically intended to include such option.[62]

CETA stipulates that the clause 'does not includes procedures for the resolution of investment disputes between investors and States.'[63] The same article further stipulates that it does not apply to 'substantive obligations in other international investment treaties and other trade agreements'[64] and, therefore, cannot give rise to claims by foreign investors. CETA further clarifies that 'substantive obligations in other international investment treaties and other trade agreements do not in themselves constitute "treatment", and thus cannot give rise to a breach of this article.'[65]

It is clear that CETA adopts a restrictive approach. Under such a formulation, therefore, the foreign investor will have to establish that another investment from a third state, in similar circumstances, is receiving or has received different treatment to invoke this clause.[66] In *Ickale v Turkmenistan*, the tribunal was called to examine whether the claimant could invoke certain standards of treatment contained in another IIA for the purposes of his claim. After careful examination of the wording of the MFN clause, the tribunal held that given the limitation of the scope of application of the MFN clause to "similar situations," it cannot be interpreted to refer to standards of treatment included in other investment treaties.[67]

The tribunal based this reasoning on the treaty text, which limits the clause's application to situations in which at least two foreign investors of differing nationality were in 'similar situations'. Further, the treaty's text limits the clause's application to differences in actual treatment, rather than mere differences in different IIAs. The clear restrictions on the scope of the MFN clause in CETA will prove useful for the purposes of greater legal certainty regarding the circumstances a foreign investor could invoke this clause.

Lastly, article 28 (3) of CETA provides for general grounds of justification for discriminatory treatment listing, among others, the protection of public security,

---

[60]*Renta 4 S.V.S.A, Ahorro Corporación Emergentes F.I., Ahorro Corporación Eurofondo F.I., Rovime Inversiones SICAV S.A., Quasar de Valors SICAV S.A., Orgor de Valores SICAV S.A., GBI 9000 SICAV S.A. v. The Russian Federation*, SCC No. 24/2007 (Award on Preliminary Objections), para. 94.

[61]Maupin (2011), p. 179. For an illustration *See* Reinisch (2015).

[62]*ibid.*

[63]CETA, Art. 8.7.

[64]*ibid.*

[65]*ibid.* Art, 8.7 (4).

[66]*ibid.*

[67]*İçkale İnşaat Limited Şirketi v. Turkmenistan*, ICSID Case No. ARB/10/24, para. 329.

health and safety.[68] In this way, CETA clarifies that States are permitted to provide different treatment to foreign investors if it serves certain objectives. All in all, the MFN clause in CETA makes clear in what ways and under what conditions it could be invoked. The evolution of the MFN clause in CETA shows an attempt to bring legal certainty in the context of investment arbitration.

To sum up, in an effort to enhance legal certainty, CETA has attempted to introduce certain standards of treatment with greater precision. To a great extent, the provisions relating to the FET standard constitute a brave attempt towards greater legal certainty. Though there could be some improvements relating to the legitimate expectations, the introduction of the list and the removal of the reference to an autonomous standard or customary international law brings greater precision. In addition, the expropriation clause in CETA draws a bright line between indirect expropriation and lawful regulatory measure by means of an annex attached to the text of CETA. The same goes for the MFN clause where a foreign investor will have to clearly establish ongoing discrimination by the host state to be able to invoke the protection provided by this provision.

4.3 Interpretation of Investment Protection Provisions

4.3.1 Vienna Convention on the Law of Treaties

In addition to the vague wording of the standards of treatment, another source of legal uncertainty is the lack of precise guidance on the proper method the standards of treatments should be interpreted. As argued in the previous chapter, investment tribunals are able to move between different interpretative techniques. Despite that CETA provides more tangible guidelines as to the scope of the standards of treatment, the manner in which these guidelines are used is left to tribunals. Such discretion, subsequently, gives rise to Rule of Law concerns since arbitrators act on the basis of their own discretion rather than already existing laws. A corollary to this is that judicial activism subverts the Rule of Law. Judicial activism occurs when adjudicators fail to apply the law within the constraints of the law.

Limiting the discretion of arbitrators, therefore, is of vital importance for the Rule of Law as it protects those subjected to the law from arbitrary and unpredictable decisions through checks and restraints on judicial power. CETA stipulates that its text should be interpreted 'in accordance with the Vienna Convention on the Law of Treaties (VCLT), and other rules and principles of international law applicable between the Parties.'[69] Regardless of the inherent flexibility of the VCLT rules of interpretation, this part argues that the explicit reference to these rules in the text of CETA will most likely reduce legal uncertainty.

---

[68]CETA, Art. 28 (3) (2).

[69]CETA, Art. 8.31.

Article 31 of the VCLT stipulates that a treaty *shall* be interpreted 'in good faith in accordance with the ordinary meaning to be given to the terms of the treaty in their context and in the light of its object and purpose.'[70] The grammatical centrality of this provision is made clear from the beginning. According to the International Law Commission (ILC), the 'starting point of interpretation is the elucidation of the meaning of the text, not an investigation *ab initio* into the intentions of the parties.'[71] A tribunal acknowledged that 'the duty of the tribunal is to discover and not to create meaning.'[72] The centrality of interpretation to the text of CETA is the first step towards greater legal certainty.

Nonetheless, it would be too narrow to restrict the interpretation of provisions to a simple examination of terminology. As the article further stipulates, an adjudicative body should interpret a provision by taking into account both the object and the purpose of the text.[73] For example, the legal uncertainty regarding the scope of application of the standards of treatment can be eliminated through an unequivocal translation of the common intention of the parties to CETA. This interpretative operation aims to extract from the text of the treaty the balance, which the parties agreed to achieve. The objective and purpose of an IIA are normally expressed in the preamble.

The importance of the purpose of an IIA has been emphasised from the standpoint of interpretation in the case of *Hamadi Al Tamimi v Oman.* The tribunal held that the parties to the US-OMAN FTA expressed in its preamble the need to 'strengthen the development and enforcement of environmental laws and policies, promote sustainable development, and implement this agreement in a manner consistent with the objectives of environmental protection and conservation."[74] According to the tribunal, this provision amounted to 'clear indication by the State parties that the Treaty is to be interpreted to give effect to the objectives of environmental protection and conservation.'[75]

In the same spirit, the tribunal in *Tokios v Ukraine* accepted that diverging interpretations were plausible, yet agreed with the respondent that 'the use of the control-test to define the nationality of the corporation to restrict the jurisdiction of the Centre would be inconsistent with the object and purpose'[76] of the treaty. Consequently, even in cases where two or more diverging interpretations are plausible, the VCLT is meant to give effect rather than depart from the intention of the

[70]VCLT, Art. 31.

[71]Draft Articles on the Law of Treaties with commentaries (1966), p. 220.

[72]*Renta 4 S.V.S.A, Ahorro Corporación Emergentes F.I., Ahorro Corporación Eurofondo F.I., Rovime Inversiones SICAV S.A., Quasar de Valors SICAV S.A., Orgor de Valores SICAV S.A., GBI 9000 SICAV S.A. v. The Russian Federation*, SCC No. 24/2007, para. 93.

[73]VCLT, Art. 31 (1).

[74]*Adel A Hamadi Al Tamimi v. Sultanate of Oman*, ICSID Case No. ARB/11/33, para. 389.

[75]*ibid.*

[76]*Tokios Tokelés v. Ukraine*, ICSID Case No. ARB/02/18, Decision on Jurisdiction, 29 Apr 2004 para. 46.

parties. When the VCLT rules of interpretation are followed, evolutionary interpretation is firmly anchored to the state parties' intentions.[77] In the words of Hai Yen, the VCLT rules of interpretation have the potential to 'prevent misleading and liberal employment of interpretative aids.'[78]

Consequently, particular attention should be paid to the preamble of CETA with regard to identifying the objective and purpose of CETA. A clearly defined objective and purpose in the preamble could facilitate greater certainty when it comes to interpreting the agreement. The preamble of CETA recognises 'the right of the Parties to regulate within their territories and the Parties' flexibility to achieve legitimate policy objectives, such as public health, safety, environment, public morals and the promotion and protection of cultural diversity.'[79] The above may draw positive consequences on the interpretation of CETA's provisions, notably when a state's measure is taken to adapt to new public policy challenges.[80]

Further, recourse to supplementary means of interpretation would also assist in determining the content of CETA's provisions if deemed necessary and, consequently, contribute to greater legal certainty. As article 32 of the VCLT stipulates, tribunals may choose to take into consideration 'the preparatory work of the treaty and the circumstances of its conclusion, in order to confirm the meaning resulting from the application of article 31.'[81] Tribunals may also take into consideration article 32 to determine the meaning of a provision when the interpretation according to article 31 leaves ambiguities or leads to absurd or unreasonable results.[82] It should be highlighted, nonetheless, that article 32 is somewhat auxiliary to article 31 and not an autonomous means of legal interpretation. The tribunal in *Methanex v United States* held that the text of the treaty is deemed to be the authentic expression of the intentions of the parties and that pursuant to Article 32, recourse may be had to supplementary means of interpretation only in limited circumstances.[83]

Arbitrators, therefore, could refer to the preparatory work of CETA in order to strengthen the authoritative value of an award.[84] The tribunal in *Camuzzi v*

---

[77] *See generally* Gazzini (2016), pp. 105–108.

[78] Hai Yen (2014), p. 116.

[79] CETA, Preamble.

[80] The formulation of the preamble of CETA avoids prioritising investment protection over the regulatory power of States. In the opposite case, the tribunal in *Siemens v Argentina,* following a teleological approach, held that it shall be guided by the purpose of the Treaty as expressed in its title and preamble. The treaty's objective is "to protect" and "to promote" investments. Furthermore, according to the tribunal, the preamble provides that the parties have agreed to the provisions of the Treaty for the purpose of creating favorable conditions for the investments of nationals or companies of one of the two States in the territory of the other State. *See Siemens A.G. v. The Argentine Republic*, ICSID Case No. ARB/02/8 (Decision on Jurisdiction), para. 81.

[81] VCLT, Art. 32.

[82] *ibid,* Art. 32.

[83] *Methanex Corporation v United States of America*, UNCITRAL 2005, para. 22.

[84] The confirmation of meaning through supplementary means can take different forms. For example, the preparatory works could provide the arbitrators with arguments that directly support

Argentina held that it is unnecessary to resort to supplementary means.[85] Yet, the same tribunal stated that the history of the particular agreement does not show the existence of a common intent that would contradict the conclusion reached through the application of Article 31.[86] At the same time, article 32 can play a determinative role in the interpretation only in very limited circumstances. The tribunal in *Veteran Petroleum v Russia,* discussing the hierarchical structure of the VCLT rules, observed that although tribunals may consider the *travaux préparatoires* whenever the text is ambiguous or leads to a absurd or unreasonable results.[87]

In conclusion, the VCLT rules of interpretation have been occasionally excluded, misapplied or partially used by tribunals.[88] This section does not deny that the VCLT rules are far from perfect.[89] In fact, throughout the interpretative process, tribunals may have to make choices, balance contradictory arguments or even create meaning when a legal provision is vague.[90] Hence, the VCLT can hardly be held responsible for the legal uncertainty that still characterises the standards of treatment in IIAs.

Nonetheless, the direct reference to the VCLT in CETA for the entire interpretative process has the potential to reduce the scope for differing application and conflicting awards. After all, the VCLT rules of interpretation aim to establish predictable and sustainable practices to arrive at a consistent meaning of treaty provisions. As Ascensio rightly argues, the rules of interpretation in the VCLT would frame interpreters' discretion, reduce legal uncertainty and enhance systemic consistency.[91]

4.3.2 *Joint Interpretative Declarations*

Despite that certain provisions in CETA could have been drafted in a better way, the parties have retained their ability to revise the content of the standards of treatment through joint interpretative declarations. The necessity for *ex-post* interpretative declarations stems from the vague wording of the standards of treatment, and the

the interpretation at hand. Furthermore, the preparatory work might confirm an interpretation if it appears that its content does not contradict the meaning resulting from Article 31. *See* Mbengue (2016), pp. 405–406.

[85] *Camuzzi International S.A. v. The Argentine Republic*, ICSID Case No. ARB/03/2, para. 134.

[86] *ibid*, para. 134.

[87] *Veteran Petroleum Limited (Cyprus) v. The Russian Federation*, UNCITRAL, PCA Case No. AA 228 (Interim Award on Jurisdiction and Admissibility), para. 268.

[88] Saldarriaga (2013), p. 204; Also *See* Kristian Fauchald (2008).

[89] For a paper explaining how tribunals may use other techniques to reach a decision *See* Pauwelyn and Elsig (2012).

[90] Bonnitcha (2014), pp. 357–360. To this point, it has been suggested that arbitrators are not generally activists but they are merely conferred with broad authority. *See generally* Bjorklund (2018).

[91] Ascensio (2016), p. 366. For the same argument *See* Boisson de Chazournes (2015).

expansive interpretation of their scope by tribunals. By the same token, regardless of the improvements made in CETA, tribunals will always have some discretion when interpreting the standards of treatment. Take for example the various measures a host state could take that might threaten the interest of foreign investors. It is not hard to imagine a case in which a tribunal could argue that a state violated its obligations under CETA, even if the treaty text is not clear about it.[92]

Considering the above, the possibility of revising the text of the treaty illustrates the will of States to retain control of the interpretation of CETA's provision and, subsequently, to provide legal certainty if deemed necessary.[93] Furthermore, the interpretation of a standard of treatment by the CETA's Joint Committee may also have some *de facto* precedential value. Technically speaking, interpretative declarations are intended to serve as an additional consideration when interpreting CETA that shall be taken into account together with the ordinary meaning of the text, including the object and purpose of the treaty.[94] However, as this section explains, in addition to achieving greater legal certainty, the manner in which the state parties issue these declarations could threaten the Rule of Law.

Starting with some positive remarks, the provisions on the joint interpretative declarations can be found in the section dealing with the applicable law.[95] According to the relevant article, the Joint Committee may adopt binding declarations concerning the interpretation of CETA's provisions where 'serious concerns' arise as regards matters of interpretation.[96] CETA borrows from the example of NAFTA's FTC, which is entitled to issue binding interpretations on the standards of treatment. The tribunal in *Methanex* held that the FTC interpretative declaration constitutes a 'subsequent agreement' for the purposes of the VCLT, thus being binding to the tribunal.[97] As was illustrated in the second chapter, the FTC's note in 2001 showed the weight of interpretative declarations in the context of investment disputes.[98] Similarly, the ability of the CJEU to interpret EU law provisions, at the request of a

[92] For an illustration *See* Ishikawa (2014).

[93] *See generally* Gordon and Pohl (2015), pp. 25–28.

[94] According to Article 31 (3) (a) of the VCLT, a tribunal should apply and interpret a treaty in accordance with any subsequent agreement or practice between the parties of a dispute. A 'subsequent agreement' is 'an agreement between the parties, reached after the conclusion of a treaty, regarding the interpretation of the treaty or the application of its provisions.' This provision is a manifestation of the intention of sovereign States to keep the interpretation of international treaties anchored to their intentions.

[95] CETA, Art. 8.31.

[96] *ibid,* Art. 8.31.

[97] *Methanex Corporation v United States of America,* UNCITRAL Award 8/2005, paras. 20–21.

[98] A report indicates that 22% of NAFTA cases (decided between 2001 and 2010) had a positive outcome for investors on their FET claims. In non-NAFTA cases where an investor alleged an FET breach, tribunals found that the state violated the standard in 62% of the cases. *See* UNCTAD (2012), p. 61.

member state, through binding interpretative declarations has clearly enhanced legal certainty.[99]

A problematic aspect of these declarations, however, is that the Joint Committee may decide that an interpretation shall have binding effect from a specific date.[100] Since past dates are not excluded, the parties to CETA are in a position to adopt interpretative declarations retroactively. This possibility raises legitimate concerns since the state parties could issue an interpretative declaration in a way that interrupts an ongoing dispute by determining the outcome of the proceedings. Such action could undermine the Rule of Law in a number of ways. Put differently, the manner in which CETA's Joint Committee exercise its right to issue interpretative declaration will eventually determine whether this practice will either undermine or promote the Rule of Law.

In particular, scholars have criticised the exercise of these interpretive powers by States as being a violation of the Rule of Law principle of procedural fairness.[101] For example, a binding interpretation issued by the States and potential disputing parties might jeopardise procedural fairness since no one may be the judge of its own cause.[102] Other scholars argue, however, that a joint interpretative declaration should not be considered *ab initio* as incompatible with the Rule of law. According to this reasoning, States acting in their public international law capacity have the right to interpret the treaty they have entered into.[103] Failing to appreciate the interpretative interests of the States is particularly problematic.[104] At the same time, by consenting to investment arbitration, States accept to act as respondents in investment disputes.

Scholars further argue that interpretative declarations should not be explicitly excluded simply because a state party to CETA has the capacity to influence the drafting of an interpretative declaration while acting as a respondent state in investment disputes. This is because; the respondent state cannot issue an interpretation on its own. Instead, another party, which is not a party to the dispute, must also consent to the interpretative declaration. It's not unreasonable to assume that the non-disputing state has the interest to keep the interpretation of the agreement as balanced as possible. As was pointed by Chow and Losari, in that scenario the

---

[99]TEU Article 19 (3).

[100]CETA, Art. 31.

[101]Kaufmann-Kohler (2011). p. 188. *See generally* Polanco (2018), ch. 4.

[102]Ecuador's attempt to secure a joint interpretation of the 'effective means' provision was questioned by the US as an attempt to interfere with a pending dispute. *See Republic of Ecuador v. United States of America* (PCA Case No. 2012-5).

[103]Castro de Figueiredo (2015), p. 529.

[104]For a paper illustrating the dual role of States in the context of investment disputes *See* Roberts (2010). In support of interpretative declarations, the tribunal in the *Methanex* held that if a legislature, having enacted a statute, feels that the courts implementing it have misinterpreted the legislature's intention, it is proper for the legislature to clarify its intention. In a democratic system in which legislation expresses the will of the nation, legislative clarification in this sort of case would appear to be mandatory. The Tribunal further stated that it sees no reason why the same analysis should not apply to international law. *See Supra* note 90, Methanex, para. 22.

non-disputing party will have to act both as a capital importing and capital-exporting state, thus, alarming that state to ensure the correct interpretation of an IIA.[105]

Against this reasoning, this chapter argues that the critical issue is whether a declaration of this kind will influence the outcome of a *pending* investment dispute. The point in time where a binding interpretation will take effect is crucial in determining whether an interpretative declaration will eventually serve the Rule of Law.[106] For example, there might be a situation where an interpretation in the context of a *pending* investment dispute influences the outcome of that arbitration. Accordingly, if the responding state attempts to issue a favorable interpretative declaration *after* a particular dispute has been initiated, that state practice would compromise the fairness of the arbitral process. In that case, the interpretation would fail the test for procedural fairness.[107] In other words, the fact that CETA's Joint Committee may decide the date at which the interpretation becomes binding to the tribunal may pose a threat to the Rule of Law.[108]

In addition to procedural fairness, a joint declaration could touch upon the principle of non-retroactivity and, subsequently, to legal certainty by influencing the outcome of arbitral proceedings. According to this criticism, if an interpretative declaration is adopted while a relevant investment dispute takes place, the expectations of the foreign investors as to the applicable law might be frustrated. For example, Brower noted that States might choose to amend an IIA through an interpretative declaration in an effort to avoid liability in a pending case.[109]

Before expanding on this argument any further, a distinction should be made between a treaty amendment and treaty interpretation. This distinction is of vital importance since a retroactive treaty amendment will violate the principle of legal certainty, while a treaty interpretation that is made through an interpretative declaration will not.[110] According to the prevailing view, an interpretative declaration, that merely attempts to interpret a treaty, would not violate the principle of non-retroactivity because the content of a standard of treatment is clarified, not changed. According to the ICJ, a treaty interpretation is a testimony to the original intent of the contracting States.[111]

The conceptual difference between a treaty interpretation, which is made through an interpretative declaration, and a treaty amendment is also reflected in the different procedures that have to be followed respectively. Namely, a treaty interpretation in

---

105 Ewing-Chow and Losari (2014), p. 14.

106 Gaukrodger (2016), p. 14.

107 Roberts (2010), p. 212.

108 It is interesting to note that during the CETA negotiations, the European Commission rejected a proposal that would have prohibited the possibility of issuing retroactive interpretative declarations. *See* Lavranos, (2016), p. 314.

109 *See* Brower (2003), p. 75.

110 The difference between an interpretation and an amendment arose in *Pope & Talbot*. The tribunal considered an interpretative declaration to be an amendment to the treaty than an interpretation. *Pope & Talbot v. Canada* UNCITRAL.

111 *Kasikili/Sedudu Island, Botswana v Namibia*, Judgment, Merits, [1999] ICJ Rep 1045, para. 49.

the form of a 'subsequent agreement' usually does not have to go through the same burdensome process as a treaty amendment. The varying procedural requirements are very important in light of concerns that parties might choose to 'disguise' a treaty amendment as an interpretation in order to circumvent the formal requirements of the former.[112] Failing to abide by the formal requirements of a treaty amendment would compromise the Rule of Law since these amendments will create legal uncertainty.

In an effort to avoid this, some scholars claim that it is possible to draw a bright line between an interpretation and an amendment. For example, Szilagyi argues that an interpretative declaration that details an existing provision on CETA should be considered as a treaty interpretation.[113] In contrast, a declaration that creates new rights and obligations would amount to a treaty amendment or even the creation of a new agreement.[114] In the former case, an interpretative declaration of the Joint Committee should be considered as a clarification, not a creation of new law, therefore, in line with the principles of non-retroactivity and legal certainty.[115]

However, in practice, the distinction between interpretation and amendment can be blurry and difficult to define.[116] This is mostly due to the vague wording of many provisions in IIAs. In particular, it is unclear as to how one may draw a bright line between a clarification, which would amount to an interpretation, and the creation of new rights, which would amount to an amendment, in a situation where the provisions of an IIA are too vague and broad. The more vague a provision is, the more difficult it is to make this kind of distinction.

Moreover, a number of tribunals were reluctant so far to make this distinction in order to protect investors from arbitrary amendments issued under the guise of interpretative declarations. For example, the tribunal in *ADF v United States* refused to determine whether the FTC interpretations were, in fact, interpretations or amendments since such a decision would degrade the binding character of the FTC interpretations.'[117] Lastly, when it comes to procedural differences, CETA provides that Joint Committees' amendments of protocols and annexes should be done through a very simple procedure that merely requires a decision of the Joint Committee, in a similar way to treaty interpretations.[118] Therefore, the procedural differences between a treaty interpretation and a treaty amendment for the purposes of CETA are hardly distinguishable.

---

[112]Lavranos (2016).

[113]Gaspar-Szilagyi (2017), p. 115.

[114]*ibid*, p. 115.

[115]*See generally* Methymaki and Tzanakopoulosa (2016), pp. 178–180.

[116]For a discussion *See* Brower (2006). Bonnitcha goes one step further by arguing that since it's not a simple task to distinguish an interpretation from an amendment, it's preferable to present an interpretative declaration as a prospective 'amendment' clarifying the level of protection provided by investment treaties than as a retrospective 'interpretation.' *See* Bonnitcha (2014), p. 350.

[117]*ADF Group Inc. v. United States of America*, ICSID Case No. ARB (AF)/00/1, para. 177.

[118]CETA, Art. 30.2.

Considering the above, although it might be possible for foreign investors to challenge the application of an interpretative declaration on the basis that they perceive it as an amendment, it is preferable to avoid interpretative declaration having retroactive effect. As was rightly argued by Roberts 'the earlier and more reasonable the interpretation, the more likely it is to be consistent with or have molded reasonable investor expectations; the later and less reasonable the interpretation, the more likely it is to have undermined reasonable investor expectations, resulting in detrimental reliance.'[119]

In a nutshell, whether an interpretative declaration will violate the Rule of Law or not will depend on the timing. If the interpretative declaration is delivered after the award, no real issue arises with regard to the Rule of Law. In other words, skepticism over interpretative declarations arises over concerns that one of the disputing parties has the potential to influence the outcome of *ongoing* arbitral proceedings. On the contrary, joint interpretative declarations, which do not interfere with pending investment disputes, have the potential to enhance legal certainty by providing guidance to tribunals on how to interpret certain CETA provisions. At the same time, interpretative declarations that do not have retrospective effect, will not put in jeopardy the fairness of the arbitral proceedings by allowing a disputing party to influence the outcome of the award. These types of Rule of Law considerations must be taken into serious consideration in order to meet the normative expectations arising from the public law function of investment tribunals.

4.4 Multiple Proceedings and Conflicting Awards

4.4.1 Conflicting Awards

Another source of legal uncertainty is the phenomenon of multiple proceedings and conflicting awards. This phenomenon clearly undermines the predictability requirement of the Rule of Law, as individual disputes are open to all kinds of competing, and often conflicting, interpretations by different tribunals. This section looks at the phenomenon of conflicting awards. As illustrated in the second chapter, the Lauder/CME and SGS cases constitute blatant examples how tribunals can reach different decision even though the facts of the cases and the identities of the disputing parties remain essentially the same. Inconsistent awards are particularly challenging in a system that has very limited ways to rectify errors given the narrowness of review by the current annulment procedures.

CETA purports to override the implicit prohibition on appeals in investment arbitration by allowing a substantial review of error of law and fact. This mechanism was largely inspired by the WTO Appellate mechanism, which has been applauded

[119]Roberts (2010), pp. 220–221.

for bringing more legal certainty.[120] In such circumstances, an appellate mechanism would normally provide a way through which it would be possible to correct legal errors and, subsequently, provide legal certainty.[121] In addition to rectifying errors, an appeal mechanism would sustain finality.

The appellate mechanism in CETA is empowered to modify or reverse first instance arbitral awards, as opposed to simply annulling an award in whole or in part.[122] Further, the scope of remedial power is much expanded, allowing the appeal tribunal to intervene on issues of merit. In particular, an appeal tribunal constituted under CETA will have the power to modify or reverse an award based on (a) errors in the application or interpretation of applicable law (b) manifest errors in the appreciation of the facts, including the appreciation of relevant domestic law (c) the grounds set out in Article 52 (1) (a) through (e) of the ICSID Convention, in so far as they are not covered by paragraphs (a) and (b).[123]

Furthermore, CETA's appellate mechanism allows for errors to be corrected without the disputing parties to have to resubmit the dispute to another tribunal following a successful appeal. On the contrary, the appellate mechanism in CETA shall apply its own findings to the facts of the dispute and render a final decision. The appellate mechanism would make sure more control is being exercised over a decision of the tribunal and would improve its decision-making.[124] Awards that are inconsistent would be removed, hence, creating a coherent body of law.[125]

At this stage, it is not possible to know for sure to what extent the appellate mechanism in CETA will deal with the phenomenon of conflicting. Yet, the very existence of a standing tribunal and an appellate mechanism in CETA will provide 'personal and institutional continuity',[126] which is generally considered to be beneficial for more consistency. As CETA states, a group of the same adjudicators will decide disputes and will remain in the roster for a fixed period of time.[127] Both the institutional continuity and the appellate mechanism also have the potential to better guarantee legal certainty through a quasi *stare decisis*. For example, in a situation where a tribunal does not follow previous cases in its decision-making, the losing party can appeal the award on that basis.

Nonetheless, an additional layer of arbitration proceedings in CETA would not completely solve the inconsistencies arising out of the phenomenon of conflicting

---

[120]According to the WTO's Dispute Settlement Understanding, the dispute settlement mechanism should 'clarify the existing provisions of those agreements in accordance with customary rules of interpretation of public international law.'

[121]Jojo Sushama (2014). Gal-Or argues that an appeal mechanism serves one main purpose, namely countering the risk of legal uncertainty arising from conflicting awards and, thus, serving the Rule of Law. *See* Gal-Or (2008), p. 45.

[122]CETA, Art. 8.28.

[123]*ibid*, Art. 8.28 (2).

[124]Sardinha (2017), p. 515.

[125]*ibid.*

[126]Mbengue and Schacherer (2018), p. 643.

[127]CETA, Art, 8. 27.

awards. An appellate mechanism attached to CETA might be able to enhance legal certainty in the agreement's legal biotope. The same appellate mechanism, however, will do little to promote legal certainty in the international investment regime in general.[128] This is because; another tribunal constituted on the basis of a different agreement has no obligation to follow the reasoning of a tribunal constituted under CETA dealing with a similar legal and/or factual scenario.

The appellate mechanism in CETA will do little in fostering coherent interpretation of basic investment protection rules and principles across this field of law. After all, international investment law consists of a body of thousands of IIAs with no central authority available to bring coherence across this entire field of law.[129] The ICSID cases brought against Argentina reveal the potential risk of conflicting awards. Regardless of the fact that Argentina faced more than forty identical claims in relation to the same measure, the awards rendered by the various tribunals often conflicted.

The above observation is particularly topical, given that an attempt is currently underway by the EU and Canada regarding the establishment of a multilateral investment court.[130] Such a court could be placed on top of international investment law in order to ensure consistency. Yet, it remains to be seen how many States are willing to join this court.[131] Depending on the number of States that are willing to join, such a multilateral court could either create more fragments in international investment law or further enhance legal certainty.

4.4.2 Multiple Proceedings

As illustrated in the second chapter, there are situations where investors are able to sue a host state for the same dispute in different forums to increase their chances to receive compensation. Multiple proceedings have further the risk of producing contradictory decisions regarding the same state measure. As a result of this situation, tribunals often face the question of what to do when another dispute is pending, either before domestic courts or before another international tribunal. A similar question arises when a decision has already been rendered on the same or related subject matter. As a response to this, CETA seeks to prohibit multiple proceedings and, subsequently, enhance legal certainty by limiting foreign investors' options to seek multiple remedies in different forums. This section, therefore, asks whether CETA could succeed in limiting the undue proliferation of proceedings.

[128] *See generally* Laura Marceddu (2016), pp. 56–58.

[129] This has been identified as the 'challenge of decentralization'. Hansen (2010), p. 534. Butler and Subedi have proposed the establishment of a multilateral investment organization in order to address inconsistency in international investment law. *See* Butler and Subedi (2017).

[130] CETA. Art. 8. 29.

[131] For a discussion *See* Legum (2008).

4.4.2.1 *Consolidation Mechanism*

The first situation where the phenomenon of multiple proceedings could occur is where two disputes, dealing with the same or related subject matter, are brought separately under CETA. As a response to this risk, CETA provides that, where two or more claims submitted separately to CETA's ISDS mechanism have a question of law or fact in common and arise out of the same events or circumstances, a disputing party may submit a request for consolidation.[132] The consolidation division should also take into account whether consolidation would best serve the interests of fair and efficient resolution of the claims, including the interest of consistency of awards.'[133] If all the conditions are satisfied, the consolidation division may assume jurisdiction over some or all of the claims.[134] In that case, the consolidation division will stay or adjourn, as appropriate, the relevant proceedings.[135] Most importantly, the fact that the consolidating division does not have to ensure the consent of every disputing party to proceed with the consolidation makes this mechanism an effective tool for consistent decision-making. To date, consolidation of two or more claims under the ICSID Convention and UNCITRAL rules has been done consensually.[136]

Nevertheless, consolidation under CETA is a challenging task since a tribunal will still have to assess whether two or more proceedings are similar enough to allow consolidation. Another problematic aspect of the consolidation proceedings is the lack of any provision regarding the possibility for cross-treaty consolidation or consolidation of proceedings brought to international and domestic forums simultaneously. In such a case, it would have been possible to avoid simultaneous parallel proceedings under different instruments from taking place. Nevertheless, it would be realistically impossible to contemplate consolidation of disputes, brought under different legal instruments, unless the same law and procedural rules govern the related disputes and the proceedings are by agreement to take place in the same state.[137]

---

[132]CETA, Art. 8.43.

[133]*ibid,* Art. 8. 43 (8).

[134]*ibid,* Art. 8. 43 (8).

[135]*ibid,* Art. 8. 43 (10).

[136]Dugan et al. (2008), pp. 26–33, pp. 186–190.

[137]Kaufmann Kohler et al. (2006), p. 89. Multinational enterprises are able to take advantage of the protection of several IIAs due to the fact that they hold several legal personalities across many jurisdictions. In this way, different subsidiaries or multiple shareholders of the same company may bring simultaneous claims in different proceedings against the same respondent. As Shookman argues, bilateralism, non-exclusivity and multiple investor claims are some of the reasons behind the phenomenon of multiple proceedings. *See* Shookman (2010), p. 365.

4.4.2.2 *Other Related Mechanisms*

Despite the absence of a robust consolidation mechanism, CETA includes a number of other related mechanisms to deal with the phenomenon of multiple proceedings. A novel approach in CETA is the inclusion of an express 'abuse of process' clause. Article 8.18 (3) of CETA stipulates that 'an investor may not submit a claim to arbitration under this section where the investment has been made through fraudulent misrepresentation, concealment, corruption, or conduct amounting to an abuse of process.'[138] The inclusion of this clause is a useful tool, especially when a multinational company has been incorporated in a foreign jurisdiction solely to gain access to favorable investment protection treaties.[139] This clause could also be invoked to prevent an investor from relitigating issues if their behavior is seen as abusive.[140] As Wehland argues, the applicability of this clause to situations of multiple proceedings is beyond doubt.[141]

CETA further limits the scope of protected investors to legal entities that have actual and substantial business operation in their country of incorporation.[142] CETA also denies the benefits of its provisions to a company if it's owned or controlled by an investor of a third country.[143] Overall, these requirements were introduced in an effort to exclude shell and mailbox companies from protection and, as such, to address treaty shopping and the phenomenon of multiple proceedings.[144]

Secondly, in an attempt to limit multiple proceedings under different legal instruments, CETA limits the ability of foreign investors and its subsidiaries to bring parallel proceedings, either internationally or domestically, alongside a claim under CETA.[145] In particular, CETA requires the investor to withdraw or discontinue, and waive the right to initiate, from any existing proceedings before another tribunal or court under domestic or international law with respect to the measure alleged to constitute a breach referred in its claim.[146] Further, as the provision clearly stipulates, the aim of this prohibition is to avoid overlapping compensations and conflicting awards.[147] The same provision requires a tribunal to stay its proceedings or otherwise ensure that it takes into consideration the existence of a parallel claim

[138] CETA, Art. 8 (18) (3).

[139] For further discussion *See* Wehland (2016) and Watson and Brebner (2018).

[140] Wehland (2013), p. 219.

[141] *ibid,* p. 219.

[142] CETA, Art. 8.1 (iii) (a-b).

[143] *ibid*, Art. 8 (16).

[144] As Baumgartner argues, IIAs which accord protection on purely formal basis, letting suffice incorporation, they can be considered as inherently treaty-shopping friendly. On the contrary, States that prescribe additional substantive criteria in BITs, the more difficult it will become for an investor to create and use a corporate vehicle for the sole purpose of bringing a claim as an eligible investor under a given investment treaty. *See* Baumgartner (2016), ch. 8.

[145] CETA, Art. 8.24.

[146] *ibid,* Art. 8.22 (f-g).

[147] *ibid*, Art. 8. 24 (a-b).

(*wait and see*).[148] Failing to fulfil this procedural requirement will prompt the tribunal to decline jurisdiction. Last, but not least, in an effort to prevent parallel proceedings between investment treaty and investment contract claims, CETA does not include an umbrella clause.[149]

Regardless of CETA's laudable attempt to restrict multiple proceedings, it is still unclear whether the above provisions will deliver results. It is doubtful whether another adjudicative body, dealing with the same or similar dispute, is going to stay proceedings due to a previous arbitral award rendered under CETA. This is largely due to the lack of hierarchical order between different tribunals and/or domestic courts.[150] For example, it is uncertain whether a different forum will refuse to assume jurisdiction because of the fact that CETA's tribunal adjudicated a similar dispute. The awards rendered in the *Lauder/CME* cases illustrate how the same investor is able to initiate multiple proceedings for the same state measures based on two different IIAs and win.

Additionally, when it comes to domestic forums, article 27 of the VCLT stipulates that 'a party may not invoke the provisions of its internal as justification for its failure to perform a treaty.'[151] Similarly, the ILC's Draft Articles on the responsibility of States provides that 'the characterization of an act of a State as internationally wrongful is governed by international law. Such characterization is not affected by the characterization of the same act as lawful by internal law.'[152] This clear separation between the spheres of domestic and international law makes it even more difficult to address the phenomenon of multiple proceedings since neither international tribunals nor domestic courts have an obligation to follow each other's decisions.[153]

---

[148] *ibid*, Art. 8. 24 (a-b).

[149] The total rejection of an umbrella clause by the drafters of CETA constitutes a decisive attempt to address multiple proceedings. Umbrella clauses usually permit an investor to include a contractual undertaking under the 'umbrella' of protection of an IIA. Consequently, an investor is able to hold a host state accountable for a contractual commitment in the same way as breaches of investment protection standards. As a result of this possibility, the distinction between a treaty claim and contractual claim is disturbed by the inclusion of an umbrella clause. Through an umbrella clause, therefore, an investor can initiate multiple procedings on the basis of different legal instruments. It is no surprise that the jurisdictional uncertainty caused by umbrella clauses has occasionally resulted in overlapping claims. Although that it has been attempted to limit the scope of the umbrella clause in an attempt to address multiple proceedings, such attempts have been unsuccesfull. *See* Pereira De Souza Fleury (2015), p. 688.

[150] Dugan (2008), p. 377. The lack of hierarchical order between different courts and tribunals is the reason why Wehland argues that the role of both *lis pendens* and *res judicata* principle is more limited than frequently assumed. Wehland (2013), p. 228.

[151] VCLT, Art. 27.

[152] Draft articles on Responsibility of States for Internationally Wrongful Acts, with commentaries 2001, Art. 3.

[153] In support of this, the tribunal in *GAMI* held that each jurisdiction is responsible for the application of the law under which it exercises its mandate. According to the tribunal, it was for the Mexican judiciary to determine whether the expropriation was legitimate under domestic law. Lastly, it was held that it is for the present Tribunal to determine whether there have been breaches

Even if that was possible, for different tribunals to stay proceedings they usually require the identity of parties, object and the cause of action. The task of identifying common identity, therefore, is of paramount importance in an effort to address multiple proceedings in the domain of investment arbitration. In practice, however, the application of this test has proven to be unsuccessful. A recent study demonstrates that most attempts by States to prevent multiple proceedings by invoking prohibitory clauses failed because either the fundamental basis was found to be different or because tribunals held that there was insufficient identity between the claiming parties.[154] Tribunals have also been unable to reach a consistent approach as to what constitutes the identity of parties for the purposes of addressing multiple proceedings.[155]

In addition to the above, investment tribunals have also accepted that they have the *discretion* to stay a parallel claim. As to this point, the tribunal in *SPP v Egypt* held that 'when the jurisdictions of two unrelated and independent tribunals extend to the same dispute, there is no rule of international law which prevents either tribunal from exercising its jurisdiction.'[156]

To sum up, the appellate mechanism's ability to modify or reverse first instance arbitral awards, as opposed to simply annulling an award, would make sure that more control is exercised over tribunals and would improve their decision-making. In this way, awards that are inconsistent would be removed, hence, creating a coherent body of law. Further, the institutional continuity provided in CETA's tribunal has also the potential to better guarantee legal certainty through a quasi *stare decisis.*

When it comes to multiple proceedings, CETA forbids parallel proceedings, provides a mandatory mechanism for the consolidation of claims and limits the scope of eligible legal entities that could initiate claims in order to prevent treaty shopping. Regardless of the fact that CETA constitutes a bold attempt in an effort to deal with the phenomenon of multiple proceedings and conflicting awards, it is unlikely that it will completely eradicate this phenomenon. More treaty-shopping restrictive language is an appropriate way to rein in treaty shopping, yet it is limited in its application. The lack of a hierarchy of norms and the absence of a common coordinating mechanism in international investment law is a reality that set limitations from the outset to any individual attempt for the furtherance of the Rule of Law. Hence, the ability of those subject to CETA to predict their liability is clearly undermined as investors might find loopholes in the system to initiate multiple proceedings.

---

of international law by any agency of the Mexican government. *Gami Investments, Inc. v. The Government of the United Mexican States,* UNCITRAL, para. 41.

[154] McLachlan et al. (2017), p. 23. Also *See* Reinisch (2010), p. 121.

[155] McLachlan et al. (2017) p. 125. Also *See* Lee (2015), pp. 365–368.

[156] *Southern Pacific Properties (Middle East) Limited v. Arab Republic of Egypt*, Decision on Jurisdiction, ICSID Case No. ARB/84/3, para. 129.

4.5 Conclusion

This chapter attempted to examine the extent to which the parties to CETA have succeeded in enhancing legal certainty in the context of investment disputes. Answering this question is of paramount importance for the purposes of answering the core research question, since there needs to be legal certainty to promote the Rule of Law. Without legal certainty, those subject to the law will not be able to assess whether their actions bear legal consequences. In such a situation, those subject to CETA will only be able to be guided by their guesses as to what the tribunal is likely to do, but these guesses will not be based on the law but on other considerations. This chapter argues that CETA provisions largely provide legal certainty, yet certain shortcomings and open questions are also identified.

The attempt to adopt a text containing watertight investment protection standards can be seen as an effort to promote the Rule of Law. CETA provides an exhaustive and watertight list containing the sub-elements of the FET standard. Most importantly, the investment chapter of CETA removed any reference to customary international law. The removal of a definition by reference and the adoption of an exhaustive list will guide and constrain tribunals when interpreting this provision. There is, however, room for further clarification for legitimate expectations in terms of the character and the form that a representation must take. Further, there is no reference to the circumstances in which it would be permissible for a host state to frustrate the legitimate expectations of a foreign investor.

In addition, the annex attached to CETA explicitly carves-out legitimate public measures from the scope of the expropriation clause. When it comes to the MFN clause, the text clarifies that an investor will have to establish that another investment is receiving or has received different treatment in order to take advantage of the protection provided by the clause. Instead of leaving the interpretation of this provision to tribunals, the drafters have managed to make clear under what circumstances investors might invoke it and have also laid down clear exemptions. It appears that the parties to CETA have developed a consciousness with regard to the public function of tribunals and the negative implications of the vague wording of the standards of treatment. For this reason, the attempt made in CETA to further delineate the scope of the standard of treatment and clarify their drafting is a solid step towards greater legal certainty and the Rule of Law.

In any case, the interpretation of the standards of treatment will retain subjective elements and discretion. The latest clarifications in CETA, compounded with binding rules of interpretation, illustrate the determination of the state parties to keep the interpretation of CETA anchored to their intentions. In addition, the binding rules of interpretation and the introduction of the appellate mechanism will likely establish a quasi *stare decisis,* which are thus likely to enhance legal certainty and predictability in decision- making by rectifying legal errors.

CETA further provides the possibility of introducing joint interpretative declarations, while the parties might decide that an interpretation shall have binding effect from a specific date. Setting such a date may be either an efficient way to enhance legal certainty through a simple clarification or an arbitrary and retrospective amendment under the disguise of an interpretative declaration. This concern can actually be dealt by avoiding interpretative declaration having retrospective effect. If the parties alter the meaning of the provisions of CETA *after* an investment dispute is brought to a tribunal, such action will potentially undermine legal certainty and the investor's rights to due process.

When it comes to the last part of this chapter, multiple proceedings in investment arbitration occur because of decentralised jurisdiction and the multiple sources of applicable law. In instances where there are multiple claims under CETA instituted by the same or different parties, the treaty text provides a mechanism for consolidation. On such an occasion, there is a high possibility that conflicting awards may be avoided through the consolidation mechanism. Nonetheless, in the scenario in which the same parties initiate parallel claims under the different legal, it might be not so possible to consolidate or adjourn proceedings given that different jurisdictions are involved.

Lastly, when multiple proceedings arise between a claim under CETA and another legal instrument that involve different parties, albeit the same measure, a party may seek to stay the proceedings to avoid a conflicting result. While CETA requires an investor to initiate a claim, relating to the same investment and state measure, under one treaty alone, it's still debatable whether a different tribunal or domestic court, dealing with the same or similar dispute, is going to stay proceedings due to a previous award rendered under CETA. In a nutshell, the complexity of the phenomenon of multiple proceedings complicates the execution of responses to it. Regardless of the fact that CETA provides several mechanisms to address multiple proceedings and conflicting awards within its legal biotope, the chaotic network of IIAs, as well as the lack of hierarchical order, make this challenge even more difficult to address.

As a general remark, CETA represents a step forward towards the furtherance of legal certainty in the context of investment arbitration. Yet, it is doubtful whether CETA will completely address the legal uncertainty associated with investment arbitration. This is mostly because the shortcomings identified in this chapter highlight deeper, unsolved questions regarding international investment law. In particular, the lack of hierarchical order and a common coordinating mechanism in the international investment law network sets limitations from the outset to any individual attempt for the furtherance of the Rule of Law. A single treaty is not enough to deal with this problem.

In addition to legal certainty, investment tribunals should also take into account human rights law to maintain the Rule of Law. For this reason, the following chapter will evaluate to what extent various provisions in the investment chapter of CETA live up to their goal for greater protection of human rights in the domain of investment disputes.

References

Ascensio H (2016) Article 31 of the Vienna convention on the law of treaties and international investment law. ICSID Rev 31(2):366

Batifort S, Benton Heath J (2017) The new debate on the interpretation of MFN clauses in investment treaties: putting the brakes on multilateralization. Am J Int Law 111(4):875

Baumgartner J (2016) Treaty shopping in international investment law. Oxford University Press, Oxford, ch. 8

Bjorklund A (2018) Are arbitrators (judicial) activists? Law Pract Int Courts Tribunals 17:49–60

Boisson de Chazournes L (2015) Rules of interpretation and investment arbitration - CEMEC v. Venezuela, ICSID Case No. ARB/08/15. In: Kinnear M et al (eds) Building international investment law: the first 50 years of ICSID. Kluwer Law International, Alphen aan den Rijn

Bonnitcha J (2014) Substantive protection under investment treaties: a legal and economic analysis. Cambridge University Press, Cambridge, p 350

Bonnitcha J et al (2017) The political economy of the investment treaty regime. Oxford University Press, Oxford

Brower CII (2003) Structure, legitimacy and NAFTA's investment chapter. Va J Transnational Law 36(37):75

Brower C (2006) Why the FTC notes of interpretation constitute a partial amendment of NAFTA Article 1105. Va J Int Law 46:347

Bucheler G (2015) Proportionality in investor-state arbitration. Oxford University Press, Oxford, ch. 9

Butler N, Subedi S (2017) The future of international investment regulation: towards a World Investment Organization? Netherlands Int Law Rev 64:1

Castro de Figueiredo R (2015) Fragmentation and harmonization in the ICSID decision-making process. In: Kalicki J, Joubin-Bret A (eds) Reshaping the investor-state dispute settlement: journeys for the 21st century. Brill Publications, Leiden, p 529

De Brabandere E (2016) States' reassertion of control over international investment law - (Re)-Defining 'Fair and Equitable Treatment' and 'Indirect Expropriation'. In: Kulick A (ed) States' reassertion of control over international investment agreements and international investment treaty dispute settlement. Cambridge University Press, Cambridge, p 267

De Naunteil A (2018) Expropriation. In: Mbengue M, Schacherer S (eds) Foreign investment under the Comprehensive Economic Trade Agreement (CETA). Springer Publications, New York, p 133

Dugan C et al (2008) Investor - state arbitration. Oxford University Press, Oxford, pp 26–33

Dumberry P (2018) Fair and equitable treatment. In: Mbengue M, Schacherer S (eds) Foreign investment under the Comprehensive Economic Trade Agreement (CETA). Springer Publications, New York, p 109

European Commision (2004) EU-Canada Agree to boost trade and investment. europa.eu/rapid/press-release_MEMO-14-542_en.htm

Ewing-Chow M, Losari J (2014) Which is to be the master?: extra-arbitral interpretive procedures for IIAs. Transnational Dispute Manag 11(1):14

Gal-Or N (2008) The concept of appeal in international dispute settlement. Eur J Int Law 19(1):45

Gaspar-Szilagyi S (2017) Binding committee interpretations in the EU's new free trade and investment agreements. In: Mistelis L, Lavranos N (eds) European investment law and arbitration review 2. Brill Publications, Leiden, p 115

Gaukrodger D (2016) The legal framework applicable to joint interpretative agreements of investment treaties. OECD Working Papers on International Investment 2016/01, p. 14

Gazzini T (2016) Interpretation of international investment treaties. Hart Publishing

Gordon K, Pohl J (2015) Investment treaties over time-treaty practice and interpretation in a changing world. OECD Working Papers on International Investment 2015/02, pp. 25–28

Hai Yen T (2014) The interpretation of investment treaties. Brill Publications, Leiden, p 116

Hansen R (2010) Parallel proceedings in investor – state treaty arbitration: responses for treaty – drafters, arbitrators and parties. Modern Law Rev 73(4):524
Hoffmann AK (2020) Indirect expropriation. In: Reinisch A (ed) Standards of investment protection. Oxford University Press, Oxford, pp 156–158
Ishikawa T (2014) Keeping interpretation in investment treaty arbitration 'on track': the role of state parties. Transnational Disp Manag 11:1
Jojo Sushama D (2014) Appellate structure and need for legal certainty in investment arbitration. Kluwer Arbitration Blog. arbitrationblog.kluwerarbitration.com/2014/05/01/appellate-structure-and-need-for-legal-certainty-in-investment-arbitration/
Kaufmann Kohler G et al (2006) Consolidation of proceedings in investment arbitration: how can multiple proceedings arising from the same or related situations be handled efficiently?: final report on the geneva colloquium held on 22 April 2006. ICSID Rev 21(1):89
Kaufmann-Kohler G (2011) Interpretative powers of the free trade commission and the rule of law. In: Gaillard E, Bachand F (eds) Fifteen years of NAFTA Chapter 11 arbitration. JurisNet, Huntington, p 188
Klager R (2011) Fair and equitable treatment' in international investment law. Cambridge University Press, Cambridge
Klein Bronfman M (2006) Fair and equitable standard: an evolving standard. Max Planck Yearb United Nations Law 10:672
Kriebaum U (2014) FET and expropriation in the (Invisible) EU model BIT. J World Invest Trade 15:467
Kriebaum U (2015) Expropriation. In: Bungenberg M et al (eds) International investment law: a handbook. Nomos Publications, Baden-Baden, p 971
Kristian Fauchald O (2008) The legal reasoning of ICSID tribunals-an empirical analysis. Eur J Int Law 19:2
Laura Marceddu M (2016) The EU dispute settlement: towards legal certainty in an uneven international investment system? In: Mistelis L, Lavranos N (eds) European investment law arbitration review. Brill Publications, Leiden, pp 56–58
Lavranos N (2016) How the European Commission and the EU member states are reasserting their control over their investment treaties and ISDS rules. In: Kulick A (ed) Reassertion of control over the investment treaty regime. Cambridge University Press, Cambridge, p 314
Lee J (2015) Resolving concerns of treaty shopping in international investment arbitration. J Int Disp Settlement 6(2):365–368
Legum B (2008) Options to establish an appellate mechanism for investment disputes. In: Sauvant Karl P (ed) Appeals mechanism in international investment disputes. Oxford University Press, Oxford
Maupin JA (2011) MFN-bases jurisdiction in investor-state arbitration: Is there any hope for a consistent approach? J Int Econ Law 14(1):179
Mbengue M, Schacherer S (2018) Foreign investment under the Comprehensive Economic Trade Agreement (CETA). Springer Publications, New York, p 643
McLachlan C et al (2017) International investment arbitration - substantive principles, 2nd edn. Oxford University Press, Oxford, p 23
Methymaki E, Tzanakopoulosa A (2016) Master of Puppets? Reassertion of control through joint investment treaty interpretation. In: Kulick A (ed) Reassertion of control over the investment treaty regime. Cambridge University Press, Cambridge, pp 178–180
Moïse Mbengue M (2016) Rules of interpretation (Article 32 of the Vienna Convention on the Law of Treaties). ICSID Rev 31(2):405–406
Ngangjoh-Hodu Y, Ajibo C (2018) Legitimate expectations in investor-state arbitration: re-contextualizing a controversial concept from a developing country perspective. Manch J Int Econ Law 15:1
Nyer D (2015) The investment chapter of the EU-Canada comprehensive economic and trade agreement. J Int Arbitr 6(32):703

OECD (2004a) Fair and equitable treatment standard in international investment law. OECD Working Papers on International Investment 2004/03
OECD (2004b) Working papers on international investment. OECD Publishing, Paris
Ortino F (2013) Refining the content and role of investment 'rules and 'standards': a new approach to international investment treaty-making. ICSID Rev Foreign Invest Law J 28:1
Ortino F (2016) Defining indirect expropriation: the transatlantic trade and investment partnership and the (elusive) search for 'Greater Certainty'. Legal Iss Econ Integr 43(4):355
Paparinskis M (2013) The international minimum standard and fair and equitable treatment. Oxford University Press, Oxford, pp 160–166
Pauwelyn J, Elsig M (2012) The politics of treaty interpretation: variations and explanations across international tribunals. In: Dunoff JL, Pollack MA (eds) Interdisciplinary perspectives on international law and international relations. Cambridge University Press, Cambridge
Pereira De Souza Fleury R (2015) Umbrella Clauses: a trends towards its eliminations. Arbitr Int 31:688
Perkams M (2010) The concept of indirect expropriation in comparative public law - searching for light in the dark. In: Schill S (ed) International investment law and comparative public law. Oxford University Press, Oxford
Polanco R (2018) The return of the home state to investor-state disputes: brining back diplomatic protection? Cambridge University Press, Cambridge, ch. 4
Potesta M (2013) Legitimate Expectations in investment treaty law: understanding the roots and limits of a controversial concept. ICSID Rev 28:1
Reinisch A (2008) Legality of expropriations. In: Reinisch A (ed) Standards of investment protection. Oxford University Press, Oxford
Reinisch A (2010) Part II Chapter 5: the issues raised by parallel proceedings and possible solutions. In: Waibel M et al (eds) The backlash against investment arbitration: perception and reality. Kluwer Law International, Alphen aan den Rijn, p 121
Reinisch A (2015) The interpretation of international investment agreements. In: Bungenberg M et al (eds) International investment law: a handbook. Nomos Publications, Baden-Baden
Roberts A (2010) Power and persuasion in investment treaty interpretation: the dual role of states. Am J Int Law 104:2
Saldarriaga A (2013) Investment awards and the rules of interpretation of the Vienna Convention: making room for improvement. ICSID Rev Foreign Invest Law J 28(1):204
Sardinha E (2017) The Impetus for the creation of an appellate mechanism. ICSID Rev 32(3):515
Schill S (2009) The multilateralization of international investment law. Cambridge University Press, Cambridge
Shirlow E (2014) Deference and indirect expropriation analysis in international investment law: observations on current approaches and frameworks for future analysis. ICSID Rev Foreign Invest Law J 29(3):607
Shookman J (2010) Too many forums for investment disputes - ICSID illustrations of parallel proceedings and analysis. J Int Arbitr 27(361):365
Stone Sweet A (2010) Investor-state arbitration: proportionality's new frontier. Law Ethics Human Rights 4(1):63
Tudor I (2008) The fair and equitable treatment standard in international foreign investment law. Oxford University Press, Oxford
UNCTAD Series on Issues in International Investment Agreements II (2012) Report on the FET (New York and Geneva, p. 61
Unuvar G (2007) Is CETA the promised breakthrough? Interpretation and evolution of fair and equitable treatment and (indirect) expropriation provisions. iCourts Working Paper Series No, 97, p. 17
Unuvar G (2016) Protecting regulatory autonomy through greater precision in investment treaties: the TPP, CETA and TTIP. J Int Econ Law 19:36
Watson D, Brebner T (2018) Nationality planning and abuse of process: a coherent framework. ICSID Rev 33:1

Wehland H (2013) The coordination of multiple proceedings in investment treaty arbitration. Oxford University Press, Oxford, p 219

Wehland H (2016) The regulation of parallel proceedings in investor-state disputes. ICSID Rev 31:3

Ziegler A (2008) Most-Favoured-Nation (MFN) treatment. In: Reinisch A (ed) Standards of investment protection. Oxford University Press, Oxford

Chapter 5
Human Rights Protection in CETA: More Artificial Than Substantial

5.1 Introduction

Investment awards occasionally adversely impact on the human rights situation of host States. The legal issue that arises in these circumstances is how to deal with a situation where human rights-motivated measures interfere with the rights of foreign investors. Human rights based on international law are likely to appear as defenses invoked by a host state or a non-disputing party. Further, human rights might be invoked in an effort to prevent a foreign investor from seeking protection under an IIA. In these situations, the question arises as to the possible avenues and methods through which a tribunal could consider human rights arguments in the context of an investment dispute. Despite this interplay between investment obligations and human rights, there is no widely accepted methodology as to how to react to argumentation based on human rights law. From a Rule of Law perspective, neverheless, ignoring or misapplying human rights law is problematic. The chapter aims to examine whether CETA better integrates human rights law with international investment law. In particular, this chapters examines the effectiveness of the traditional 'toolbox' that is used to integrate human rights and investment obligations, such as the jurisdictional and the applicable law clause, as well as the novel provisions in CETA, such as the *amicus curiae* mechanism and the appelate mechanism. This chapter utlimately argues that CETA is unlikely to ease the tension between human rights law and international investment law.

5.2 Jurisdictional Stage

As most IIAs are silent on human rights issues, arbitrators are usually expected to deal with this gap by following common interpretative techniques within the limits of their mandate. The primary aim of the following two parts, therefore, is to

K. Dionysiou, *CETA's Investment Chapter*, European Yearbook of International Economic Law 13, https://doi.org/10.1007/978-3-030-66992-8_5

examine the effectiveness of the traditional 'toolbox' used by tribunals to integrate human rights law within investment protection.[1] In particular, human rights may be integrated into investment arbitration at the jurisdictional stage and as part of the applicable law. Starting with the former, the first stage in which human rights could be invoked is at the jurisdictional phase of an investment dispute. The first question that arises, therefore, is whether an investment tribunal has the power to accept non-investment obligations based arguments in the context of an investment dispute.

Traditionally, tribunals are constituted on an *ad hoc* basis, while the agreement to arbitrate contained in an IIA defines the tribunal's jurisdiction. The jurisdiction of investment tribunals is 'based on the consent of the parties and is confined to the extent accepted by them.'[2] Before elaborating on CETA, the *Grand River v United States* should be mentioned. In an effort to expand the jurisdictional scope of NAFTA, the claimant's main argument was that the 'minimum standard of treatment' includes the rights of indigenous people under customary international law. Although these rights were not explicitly included in the relevant IIA, the claimants argued that these rights have been violated by the host state. Responding to this argument, the tribunal held that it does not understand this obligation to provide permittion to import legal elements from other treaties, or to alter the interpretation established through the standard interpretive processes of the Vienna Convention.[3]

This ruling illustrates that the obligation in the VCLT to 'take into account' other rules of international law cannot be instrumentalised to expand the jurisdictional limit of an IIA[4] or to modify its content.[5] In other words, the available causes of action for an ISDS claim are limited to violations of the substantive standards included in IIAs. After all, a different situation 'would amount to a general license to override the treaty terms that would be incompatible with the general spirit of the Vienna Convention as a whole.'[6]

Having said that, CETA stipulates that an investor may bring a claim relating to non-discriminatory measures and investment protection standards.[7] Violations of any other provisions of CETA or claims relating to purely contractual claims are not eligible for resolution under the investment chapter.[8] Accordingly, CETA limits access to investment arbitration only for breaches of the seven protections standards

---

[1]For an overview *See* Radi (2011) and Dumberry and Dumas-Aubin (2012).

[2]*Armed Activities on the Territory of the Congo (New Application: 2002) (Democratic Republic of the Congo v. Rwanda)*, para. 88. This limitation in international adjudication has been identified as a factor in the fragmentation of international law. *See generally* Mclachlan (2005).

[3]*Grand River Enterprises Six Nations, Ltd., et al. v. United States of America*, UNCITRAL, para. 71.

[4]For the same conclusion *See Chevron Corporation and Texaco Petroleum Corporation v. The Republic of Ecuador*, UNCITRAL, paras. 202–203.

[5]Simma and Kill (2009), p. 694.

[6]*RosInvestCo UK Ltd. v. The Russian Federation*, SCC Case No. V079/2005. Award on Jurisdiction, para. 39.

[7]CETA, Art. 8. 18.

[8]*ibid.* Art. 8.18 (3).

in the treaty and only if an investor has incurred loss or damage.[9] Traditionally, both the jurisdictional limit as well as the absence of human rights provisions in IIAs made it easier for tribunals to deny competence to deal with separate non-investment claims.

Despite these jurisdictional limitations, human rights law might become relevant at the jurisdictional phase of an investment dispute. In particular, CETA contains provisions that aim to prevent foreign investors from seeking compensation when there is evidence that the investment is not going to be made in accordance with the applicable law of the host state.[10]

This standard provision, also known as 'clean hands doctrine', has been defined as 'an important principle of international law that has to be taken into account whenever there is evidence that an applicant state has not acted in good faith and that it has come to court with unclean hands.'[11] This standard provision forced tribunals to discuss whether their jurisdiction is limited to lawful investments, given that most IIAs contain a clause stipulating that foreign investment shall enjoy protection if it is made in accordance with the laws of the host state.[12] This doctrine has the potential to operate as a procedural human rights law defense for host States in situations where an investor has violated, for instance, labour standards. The tribunal in *Salini* explained that an 'in accordance with the host state law' clause seeks to prevent a tribunal from protecting an investment that should not be protected, in particular, because it would be illegal.[13]

In *Fraport v Philippines*, for example, the tribunal rejected jurisdiction, as the investment was not made in accordance with the host state's laws.[14] By the same token, in *Phoenix Action v Czech Republic* it was held that ICSID protection should not be granted to investments made in violation of fundamental rules of protection of human rights.[15] If this reasoning is followed, an investment that violates applicable human rights should fall outside the jurisdiction of the investment chapter of CETA. In other words, the practical effect of the 'clean hands doctrine' is to prevent a foreign investor, operating an investment not in accordance with the host state's law, from seeking legal protection.

---

[9] *ibid.* Art. 8. 18 (2).

[10] CETA, Art. 8. 1. *See generally* Balcerzak (2017), pp. 134–146.

[11] ILC, 57th session, para. 236.

[12] In *Salini* the tribunal held that such provisions seek to prevent the IIA from protecting investments that should not be protected because they would be illegal. *See Salini Costruttori S.p.a and Italstrade S.p.A v Hashemite Kingdom of Jordan*, ICSID Case No.. ARB/02/13), para 46.

[13] *ibid.*

[14] *Fraport AG Frankfurt Airport Services Worldwide v. The Republic of the Philippines*, ICSID Case No. ARB/03/25, para. 40-1. Also *See Hesham T. M. Al Warraq v. Republic of Indonesia*, UNCITRAL.

[15] *Phoenix Action, Ltd. v. The Czech Republic*, ICSID Case No. ARB/06/5, para. 78. Also *See Inceysa Vallisoletana S.L. v. Republic of El Salvador*, ICSID Case No. ARB/03/26 ; *Gustav F W Hamester GmbH & Co KG v. Republic of Ghana,* ICSID Case No. ARB/07/24.

Nevertheless, there are two limitations in relation to this clause. Firstly, the investor's illegal conduct must have occurred prior to the commencement of the investment. As noted in *Hamester v Ghana*, the legality of the creation of a foreign investment is a jurisdictional issue, but the legality of the foreign investor's conduct during the life of the investment is a merits issue.[16] On this basis, human rights violations will have to be associated with the introduction of the investment to invoke this clause. As Newcombe argues, experience so far suggests that using jurisdiction, as the 'control mechanism' for addressing investor misconduct is a blunt tool for this purpose.[17]

Secondly, if a host state has failed to adopt certain international obligations into its domestic law, that state will not be able to invoke this clause on the basis of those obligations. Therefore, only in cases where a state has incorporated the terms of international human rights law into its domestic legal regime the 'in accordance with the host state law' clause may be invoked for the purpose of raising international human rights concerns. In a nutshell, a tribunal constituted under CETA will have to decline jurisdiction over a claim when the said investment has not been made in accordance with a binding international obligation.

5.3 Applicable Law

5.3.1 General Observations

As illustrated in the second chapter, the negative impact of investment awards on human rights has been attributed, among others, to the monothematic commercial nature of IIAs. Reference to non-investment considerations in IIAs has been almost entirely unknown with no agreement between the parties on how to deal with human rights law.[18] For these reasons, tribunals prefer to dismiss arguments based on human rights law for procedural reasons, instead of engaging with the substance of these arguments. This attitude is often associated with the idea that investment treaty arbitration is a self-contained legal regime that prohibits tribunals from adopting into the applicable law of an investment dispute another set of legal rules.

Following this reasoning, tribunals have relied on applicable law restrictions to refuse the application of certain human rights in investment disputes. For example, in *Pezold v Zimbabwe* the tribunal rejected the rights of indigenous people on grounds of non-applicability. In particular, the tribunal held that such rules of general

[16]*Gustav F W Hamester GmbH & Co KG v. Republic of Ghana*, ICSID Case No. ARB/07/24, Award, 18 June 2010, para. 127.

[17]Newcombe (2011), p. 199.

[18]Jacob (2010), p. 11.

international law as may be applicable in the IIAs does not incorporate the universe of international law into the IIAs or into disputes arising under the IIAs.'[19]

Despite the above, there is much room to support that human rights may become applicable in the context of investment disputes, even in the absence of express provisions.[20] As rightly pointed out in the report of the ILC on the fragmentation of international law, treaties cannot be interpreted in a vacuum as they all belong to the same legal order, namely the international legal order.[21] In this spirit, tribunals have developed various techniques in order to accept non-investment obligations, which are not explicitly covered by an IIA, as part of the applicable law.[22]

The reasoning of the ILC provides the rationale for the customary rule of treaty interpretation codified in the VCLT. Article 8.31 of the investment chapter stipulates that the tribunal must interpret CETA in accordance with the VCLT while any *relevant* rules of international law *applicable* in the relations between the parties should be taken into account. This provision is also known as the 'principle of integration', in accordance with which treaties should not be considered in isolation of public international law. The parties would not have wanted an IIA to violate the existing rules of international law. In this spirit, the standards of treatment in CETA should be read in coherence with applicable human rights protection and other international treaties.[23] This presumption has been articulated in the context of investment arbitration in *Micula v Romania*. In particular, the tribunal in this case held it will interpret each of the treaties having due regard to the other treaties, assuming that the signatory parties entered into each of those treaties fully aware of their legal obligations under all of them.[24]

Against this backdrop, the causes of action for an ISDS claim are limited to violations of investment protection standards, yet the applicable law may include legal obligations that are not explicitly covered in an IIA. In other words, while human rights cannot form the basis of investment claims,[25] human rights may be part

[19] *Bernhard von Pezold and Others v. Republic of Zimbabwe*, ICSID Case No. ARB/10/15, para. 57.

[20] *See generally* Gonzalez Garcia (2013), p. 30; Marie Dupuy and Vinuales (2015); Elisabeth Kjos (2013), ch.3; Adeleke (2018), ch. 5.

[21] ILC Report (2005), p. 12. *See generally* Fry (2007); *Asian Agricultural Products Ltd. v. Republic of Sri Lanka*, ICSID Case No. ARB/87/3, para. 21. Lang argues that the recent attempts to defragment international economic law with human rights law forms part of a wider attempt to bring greater balance between competing obligations and, subsequently, to enhance the legitimacy of international economic governance. *See* Lang (2011), ch. 4.

[22] *See generally* Hirsch (2008), pp. 163–172.

[23] *Right of Passage over Indian Territory, Portugal v India, Merits, Judgment*, [1960] ICJ Rep 6, ICGJ 174 (ICJ 1960), 12th April 1960. On page 142, the court held that: 'It is a rule of interpretation that a text emanating from a Government must, in principle, be interpreted as producing and as intended to produce effects m accordance with existing law and not in violation of it.'

[24] *Ioan Micula, Viorel Micula, S.C. European Food S.A, S.C. Starmill S.R.L. and S.C. Multipack S.R.L. v.Romania,* ICSID Case No. ARB/05/20, para. 326.

[25] These observations were also reaffirmed in *Biloune*, where the tribunal held that it lacks jurisdiction to adjudicate a human rights claim as an independent cause of action. *Biloune and*

of the applicable law in investment disputes.[26] For example, in *SPP v Egypt,* the tribunal declined to award future lost profits to the claimants on the reasoning that they could not be compensated for activities that violate international law and, in particular, the UNESCO Convention.[27]

In the case of *Suez v. Argentina,* a consortium of multinational companies issued proceedings against Argentina due to its government's decision to freeze the water-prices charged to consumers. In particular, Argentina argued that the IIA should be construed in a manner, which does not negatively affect other international obligations and, in particular, the human right to water of the inhabitants of the country.[28] The same argument was put forward by an NGO that stressed that the international obligation to supply water forms part of the applicable law.[29]

In addition, the same NGO argued that international obligations should be used as a 'lens' through which IIAs should be interpreted and applied.[30] Despite the tribunal's reluctance to accept that the measures imposed were the only way for Argentina to protect its citizens, it was held that the right to water was an essential interest of the state that could be accepted as a valid defense.[31]

In the same context, a number of investment tribunals dealt with disputes concerning public protests and a host state's obligation to provide protection and security to foreign investors. For example, in *Noble Venture v Romania*, a case about the balance between investor's security and the right of protest or assembly, the tribunal dismissed the claim by the investors since the protests 'were conducted in an orderly manner and after notice had been given.'[32] The important aspect of this case, however, is the fact that the right of protest or assembly was not dismissed as inapplicable by the tribunal. In light of the above, the question that arises is which human rights could form part of the applicable law in the context of an investment dispute under CETA.

Marine Drive Complex Ltd v Ghana Investments Centre and the Government of Ghana (UNCITRAL), p. 203.

[26]Eric Peterson (2009), p. 22.

[27]*Southern Pacific Properties (Middle East) Limited v. Arab Republic of Egypt, Decision on Jurisdiction, ICSID Case No. ARB/84/3,* para. 190–191.

[28]*Suez, Sociedad General de Aguas de Barcelona, S.A.and Vivendi Universal, S.A. v. Argentine Republic, ICSID Case No. ARB/03/19*, para. 252.

[29]*ibid*, Amicus curiae Brief, para. 252.

[30]*ibid.*

[31]*ibid.*, para. 260.

[32]*Noble Ventures, Inc. v. Romania, Award. 12 Oct 2005. Noble Ventures, Inc. v. Romania,* ICSID Case No. ARB/01/11, para. 163.

5.3.2 *CETA*

The key question this section asks is which human rights principles could form part of the applicable law of investment disputes under CETA.[33] This question is critical for the purpose of answering whether the CETA tribunal will function in accordance with the Rule of Law by better integrating human rights law.[34] Generally speaking, this question could be answered by identifying the international obligations of the parties to an IIA. These obligations ordinarily include human rights treaties, binding customary international law, and other international treaties that the parties are parties to. Moreover, for a rule of international law to be applicable, it must be relevant to the particular investment dispute.

Considering the above, referring to non-investment obligations in the preamble to an IIA would have a positive impact in the context of an investment dispute. According to Article 31 (1) of the VCLT, a treaty should be interpreted in light of the treaty's context, object, and purpose. Since a preamble forms part of an IIAs context, a reference to human rights could color an IIAs object and purpose, as well as encouraging a tribunal to take into account the relevant human rights law applicable between the parties.[35] In *S.D Myers,* the tribunal interpreted the provisions of NAFTA by reference to its legal context, which according to the tribunal the parties to NAFTA have the right to establish high levels of environmental protection in a way that economic developtment and enviromental protection can and should be mutually supportive.[36]

The preamble to CETA recognises 'the right of the Parties to regulate within their territories and the Parties' flexibility to achieve legitimate policy objectives, such as public health, safety, environment, public morals and the promotion and protection

[33]The focus on different branches of international law in this chapter does not suggest that domestic law has no role to play in integrating investment law with human rights. However, the application of domestic law to an investment dispute will be limited compared with international law. This is because; investment tribunals are primarily concerned with establishing the international responsibility of a host state according to international law. By the same token, international law overrides domestic law when these areas of law conflict since a state cannot invoke the provisions of its domestic law as justification for its failure to perform an international obligation. In addition to the above, CETA expressly prohibits tribunals to determine the legality of a measure, alleged to constitute a breach of its provisions, under the domestic law of the disputing parties. Even if that was possible under CETA, human rights, which are based on domestic law, are usually invoked under the cloak of the public policy exception. For this reason, it's not easy to identify them and assess their impact on investment disputes. *See* Kulick (2012), ch. 2. For the rationale behind this prohibition in CETA *See Slowakische Republik v Achmea BV* (Case C-284/16), 6 March 2018.

[34]In a key policy paper on investment policy, the EU assumed the responsibility to draft investment agreements in consistency with the protection of the environment, decent work, health and safety at work, consumer protection, cultural diversity, development policy and competition policy. *See* European Commission (2010), p. 9.

[35]*See generally* Dumberry and Dumas-Aubin (2014).

[36]*S.D. Myers, Inc. v. Government of Canada,* UNCITRAL, Partial Award (13 November 2000), para. 468.

of cultural diversity.'[37] The text of the provision clearly reveals the partie's willingness to ensure that investors are not given a 'blank check', through which they could indefinitely prevent States from protecting human rights. The inclusion of non-investment considerations in the preamble will certainly have a positive impact on the outcome of investment awards. It would most likely lead tribunals to adopt a more balanced interpretation of IIA provisions. Yet, there is a more promising avenue for the protection of human rights in the context of investment disputes.

As stated by the tribunal in *ADF v United States*, provisions stating the object and purpose of a treaty may cast light on a specific interpretive issue, but should not be regarded as overriding and superseding to the text.[38] Such a preambular wording, therefore, does not have the same weight to substantive provisions when it comes to drawing a balance between investment and non-investment obligations. References in the preamble may be relevant for matters of treaty interpretation, but will not create any substantive rights or obligations. An explicit reference by the parties is perhaps the most straightforward way that human rights law may come into play in the context of investment disputes.

In parallel with signing CETA, Canada, and the EU have concluded a strategic partnership agreement (SPA), which is a side agreement to CETA, in an effort to upgrade the current framework of cooperation between them. The SPA enshrines both parties' shared democratic values and core public law principles. Article 2 (1) of the SPA states that both parties have agreed to:

> Respect for democratic principles, human rights and fundamental freedoms, as laid down in the Universal Declaration of Human Rights and existing international human rights treaties and other legally binding instruments to which the Union or the Member States and Canada are party, underpins the Parties' respective national and international policies and constitutes an essential element of this Agreement.[39]

The reference to the UN Declaration contains obligations covering political, civil, social and cultural rights. The potential scope of Article 2 (1) of the SPA is therefore extensive. This clause may be invoked in order to terminate CETA if a serious and substantial violation of human rights is taking place in one of the parties.[40] Despite that such a clause has been described of entirely political value,[41] its inclusion reaffirms the parties' commitments to protect human rights. This clause also bears interpretative value when it comes to incorporating human rights within international investment law as it reaffirms the parties' intentions to respect non-investment considerations. In addition to the SPA, the parties have agreed to a Joint Interpretative Instrument. This instrument adds some clarifications of material legal value. The instrument stipulates that:

[37]CETA, Preamble.

[38]*ADF Group Inc. v. United States of America, ICSID Case No. ARB (AF)/00/1*, para. 147.

[39]Strategic Partnership Agreement between the European Union and its Member States, on the one part, and Canada, of the other part., Art. 2 (1).

[40]*ibid*, Art. 28 (7).

[41]Bartels (2017), p. 210.

> CETA preserves the ability of the European Union and its Member States and Canada to adopt and apply their own laws and regulations that regulate economic activity in the public interest, to achieve legitimate public policy objectives such as the protection and promotion of public health, social services, public education, safety, the environment, public morals, social or consumer protection, privacy and data protection and the promotion and protection of cultural diversity.[42]

A table at the end of the instrument specifies that this paragraph is to assist in the interpretation of a list of provisions, including the right of States to regulate and the general exceptions.[43] These legal instruments will eventually direct the tribunal to accept the normative order as specified by the parties. In other words, both the SPA and the interpretative instrument may be instrumentalised in an effort to apply human rights, stemming from other international treaties, in the context of an investment dispute. This technique may be described as a sort of gravitational pull on a treaty rule that will result in an IIA interpretation that more closely coheres with other branches of international law.[44]

Without underestimating the significance of such provisions, upon closer examination, a possible problem that might arise, if an investment protection standard conflicts with a non-investment obligation, is the lack of formal hierarchy among different sources of international law. The lack of hierarchy means that international law does not provide any substantial guidance as to how conflicts between its different branches should be resolved and, in particular, which and under what circumstances a rule should prevail over another. As will be explained, in the absence of formal rules of hierarchy the temporal relations between different norms and the level of specialty are used to determine hierarchical relations in international law. Yet, this approach is not promising for the greater integration of human rights in investment disputes.

Hierarchical relations are based on other considerations such as the temporal relations between two conflicting norms (*lex posterior derogat anteriori*) and the level of specialty (*lex specialis derogat generali*), which are taken as presumptions of the intent of the parties.[45] The latter principles rest on the idea that special law adapts better to a specific dispute than any other general law, while the former stipulates that later norms should in principle supersede earlier ones. Thus, several difficulties may arise when prior agreements of a treaty party are broadly and vaguely drafted. This relative indeterminacy may put a serious obstacle to the greater integration of human rights with investment protection.[46] As Kulick observes, a number of awards indicate that in situations where tribunals give voice to human rights concerns they do not really know how to handle them.[47]

---

[42]Joint Interpretative Instrument on the Comprehensive Economic and Trade Agreement (CETA) between Canada and the European Union and its Member States (2016), para.2.

[43]*ibid.*

[44]*See generally* Wandahl Mouyal (2016), pp. 59–65.

[45]VCLT, 30 (2).

[46]*See generally* Kriebaum (2007), pp. 172–177.

[47]Kulick (2012), p. 267.

For example, the lack of clarity in regard to the scope and content of several non-investment obligations creates an unsatisfactory situation for the purpose of integrating these norms with investment protection. Lorenzo Cotula argues that generally, international investment law provides stronger legal protection, in terms of both substantive provisions and remedies, in comparison with regional human rights conventions.[48] Hence, concrete precedent cannot be used as a guideline for future cases.

For instance, the Kyoto Protocol provides that 'the Parties [...] shall, individually or jointly, ensure that their aggregate anthropogenic carbon dioxide equivalent emissions of the greenhouse gases [...] do not exceed their assigned amounts.'[49] In this case, although the Kyoto Protocol lays down a specific objective for the contracting States, the means to achieve this objective are left to the States. Therefore, it would be unclear whether a measure adopted by a state in furtherance of its obligations could be characterised as strictly required by international environmental law.[50] By the same token, irrespective of the fact that the right to water has been mentioned in various awards, there is currently no comprehensive and legally binding instrument in international law that addresses this norm.[51] Thus, the right to water remains ambiguous.

In the same context, in the case of *Spyridon Roussalis v Romania*, the tribunal observed that a host state might have applicable human rights obligations in parallel with the investment protection obligations.[52] Yet, it was also held that relevant human rights obligations had no specific effect in the present case since the IIA offered higher and more specific protection.[53] Further, in the case of *Hesham Talaat v Indonesia*, the claimant asked the tribunal to apply the principle of systemic integration to interpret the term 'basic rights' in article 10 (1) of the Organization of the Islamic Conference (OIC) as including the right to a fair trial.[54] Regardless of the claimant's request, the tribunal held that the term 'basic rights' as contained in OIC is not a general reference to civil and political rights and, thus, cannot be relied upon by the claimant.[55]

Considering the above, vaguely construed provisions make it even more difficult to argue that an act aimed to protect human rights is rooted in an international norm. As was rightly observed, tribunals could use this line of reasoning to avoid dealing with a conflict between non-investment obligations and investment protection.[56] In a

[48]Cotula (2012), p. 78.

[49]Kyoto Protocol, Art. 3 (1).

[50]*See generally* Vinuales (2012), pp. 34–38.

[51]Thielborger (2009), p. 488.

[52]*Spyridon Roussalis v. Romania*, ICSID Case No. ARB/06/1, para. 312.

[53]*ibid.*

[54]*Hesham T. M. Al Warraq v. Republic of Indonesia*, Final Award, UNCITRAL, 15 December 2014, para. 178.

[55]*ibid*, para. 521.

[56]Cali et al. (2017), p. 18.

situation where a human rights norm is vaguely construed, therefore, a tribunal would most likely give priority to the investment protection provisions of an IIA.

In addition to the difficulties that might arise in relation to the lack of hierarchy in international law and the vague scope of human rights, CETA is missing specific conflict rules to supplement the operation of the general ones.[57] Specific conflict rules are of paramount importance for this purpose since the general rules cannot solve every conflict of norms. First of all, it is not self-evident to assume that an investment obligation and a human rights obligation that stems from another international instrument can be considered as relating to the 'same subject matter', as required by Article 30 of the VCLT.[58] Furthermore, the VCLT does not offer an adequate solution to a conflict when the parties to the treaty are not the same. In addition to these difficulties, is not easy to determine which international rule constitutes the 'general' and the 'specific' rule in an effort to determine which one should prevail.

In contrast with CETA, there are certain agreements that have made better attempts to integrate human rights with investment protection.[59] For example, NAFTA contains specific provisions on the relationship between international investment law and international environmental law. Article 104 of the NAFTA states that, in the event of any inconsistency between NAFTA and the obligations set out in a list of international environmental treaties, including the Montreal Protocol and the Basel Convention, such environmental obligations shall prevail.In particular, such obligations shall prevail to the extent of the inconsistency, provided that where a party has a choice among equally effective and reasonably available means of complying with such obligations, the party chooses the alternative that is the least inconsistent with the other provisions of NAFTA.[60] This provision guided the reasoning of the tribunal in *S.D Myers v Canada* with respect to the relations between the Basel Convention and NAFTA.[61]

In addition to the above, in a number of other treaties, the concept of mutual supportiveness has been used to prevent conflicts between economic and non-economic considerations.[62] The so-called 'principle of mutual supportiveness'

[57]The ILC suggests that when States enter into a treaty that might conflict with another treaty, they should aim to settle the relationship between such treaties through conflict clauses. ILC Report (2005), p.182. The need for a mechanism for resolving conflicts between investment provisions and human rights law was reiterated in the discussions for the establishment of a multilateral framework for investment protection. *See generally* Zia-Zarifi (2007).

[58]As Simma and Kill have pointed out, 'relevant' is a term that lends itself to extremes of gradation and substantive lack of clarity, which means that arbitrators are given a significant amount of flexibility. As cited in Mota (2018), p. 221.

[59]On recent attempts to promote sustainable development through IIAs *See* Anthony VanDuzer (2016).

[60]NAFTA, Art. 104.

[61]*S.D. Myers, Inc. v. Government of Canada, UNCITRAL*, paras. 255–266.

[62]Vinuales (2012), pp. 148–149.

seeks to achieve harmony between environmental and trade agreements.[63] For example, a protocol attached to the Convention on Biological Diversity stipulates that the provisions of the protocol shall not affect that rights and obligations stemming from any other existing international agreement except where the exercise of those rights would cause serious damage or threat to biological diversity.[64] At the same time, the protocol states that the convention shall be implemented in a mutually supportive manner with other international treaties and due regard should be paid to work and practices of different treaties, provided that they do not run counter to the objectives of the Convention.[65]

The above provisions are quite instructive when it comes to solving conflicts between different branches of international law since they carve out space for the incorporation of human rights into this field of law. These provisions illustrate that the mere attempt to 'defragment' and, subsequently, unify international law through the VCLT is of little value when it comes to protecting human rights.[66] As has been rightly argued, normative conflicts between different branches of international law do not arise as 'technical mistakes' that could be 'avoided' by a more sophisticated way of legal reasoning.[67] In order for tribunals to respond to human rights law arguments, the drafters of IIAs require a legislative response, not a legal-technical.[68] The analysis in this part suggests that it is of paramount importance to include detailed provisions and specific conflict rules, addressing the relationship between investment protection and human rights, in order to successfully integrate human rights law with investment obligations.[69]

In summation, human rights can be invoked, under certain conditions, at the jurisdictional stage of an investment dispute. Nevertheless, the difficulties that exist regarding the delimitation of human rights raise serious problems regarding the possibility to successfully invoke them at the merits stage. Further, the limitation of the general conflict rules coupled with the absence of specific conflict rules in CETA raises further doubts as to the ability of tribunals to integrate non-investment considerations into international investment law.

The inclusion of explicit provisions and specific conflict rules, regarding the protection of human rights, would have been instructive in situations where tribunals had to strike a balance between competing considerations. This is of paramount importance, taking into consideration that States have been having difficulties to

---

[63]*ibid.*

[64]Nagoya Protocol on Access to Genetic Resources and the Fair and Equitable Sharing the Benefits arising from their Utilization to the Convention on Biological Diversity, October 2010, Art. 4(1).

[65]*ibid,* Art. 4 (4).

[66]Vadi argues that a balance between investment and non-investment norms could be achieved through the standard interpretative techniques enshrined in the VCLT. *See* Vadi (2012), pp. 187–188.

[67]Amado et al. (2018), p. 109.

[68]*ibid*, p.109. *See generally* Fahner and Happold (2019), Yotova (2017) and Acconci (2014).

[69]For some examples *See* Anthony Van Duzer et al. (2012) and Gehring et al. (2017).

establish a clear link between a state measure and a human rights commitment due to their vague phrasing.

5.4 *Amicus Curiae* Briefs

Non-disputing parties and host state populations are unable to hold foreign investors responsible before a tribunal since the proceedings are taking place between an investor and a state. Hence, tribunals cannot hear and decide upon claims originating from host state populations. As affected groups do not have the right to participate as parties in investment disputes, the inclusion of a mechanism for non-disputing party interventions in CETA is expected to better integrate human rights into investment disputes. This part examines to what extent *amicus curiae* briefs will have a positive impact on integrating human rights with investment protection.

Beginning with certain observations, non-disputing party interventions in international investment law were first seen in NAFTA investment disputes and, especially, in *Methanex* case where the tribunal concluded that it had the power to accept *amicus curiae* briefs.[70] In particular, the tribunal invoked the need for greater transparency and the dangers if seen as unduly secretive since the dispute was of public importance.[71] Additionally, both ICSID[72] and UNCITRAL[73] were recently amended to permit such submissions. As a result, there is an increasing number of *amicus curiae* briefs by concerned populations and Non-Governmental-Organizations (NGO). In a nutshell, *amicus curiae* briefs can be described as a practice, rather than a well-established right, whereby legal arguments or points of fact can be presented before the panel which would otherwise not be heard because they did not form part of the respective cases of the parties represented.[74]

CETA provides the possibility to non-disputing parties to participate in investment disputes. In particular, the tribunal may, after consultation with the disputing parties, invite submission from non-disputing parties regarding the interpretation of particular provisions.[75] In this way, the population of the host state may get involved in arbitral proceedings by virtue of *amicus curiae* briefs. As arbitral awards tend to have an impact on the host state's population, the participation of third parties is an important avenue through which human rights could be invoked and raised in the domain of an investment dispute. These kinds of interventions may inform the tribunal of anything related to the dispute, including the specific consequences of the legal issues under consideration.

---

[70] *Methanex Corporation v United States of America,* UNCITRAL Award 8/2005.

[71] *ibid*, para. 49.

[72] ICSID Convention, Rule 37.

[73] UNCITRAL Rules on Transparency in Treaty-based Investor-State Arbitration, Art. 4.

[74] Bellhouse and Lavers as cited in John (2016), pp. 82–83.

[75] CETA, Art. 8.38 (2). This provision is reflective of Article 1128 of NAFTA.

In this spirit, *amicus curiae* briefs in investment disputes, especially those concerned with human rights, environmental concerns or labour standards, might well enhance the legitimacy of arbitration proceedings by presenting the concerns of non-disputing parties. As Kube and Petersmann point out, human rights may play an important role in the acceptance of an *amicus* submission in cases where investment tribunals acknowledge that non-disputing parties and public interests are at stake.[76]

This kind of interventions are welcomed by tribunals if the petitioner is able to make a substantive point of law or fact and a procedural contribution to the proceedings, without encroaching on the parties due process and confidentiality rights.[77] The tribunal in the *Biwater* case held that the *amicus* submission by means of their interests and expertise in human rights, environmental and good governance issues, which had materially differed from those ones of the disputing parties, constituted a useful contribution to the arbitral proceedings.[78]

At the same time, it has been noted that *amicus curiae* would be welcomed as long as they don't politicise investment disputes and as long as this procedural innovation has a limited impact on substantive outcomes.[79] To achieve these goals, investment tribunals have emphasised that the role of *amicus curiae* briefs is to act as a volunteer, a friend of the court, not a party.[80] As will be shown, however, considering *amicus curiae* briefs merely as 'friends of the court' automatically limits their weight and, subsequently, their ability to integrate non-investment considerations.

While most commentators have viewed *amicus curiae* briefs as a positive development, there are also those who are not so optimistic about their impact.[81] This is because; the weight that has been given to *amicus curiae* briefs varies among different tribunals. Whilst some are more open to their involvement than others, all tribunals are limited by the institutional rules of the relevant arbitral venue. It is hardly surprising that *amicus curiae* briefs have been criticised as unable to influence outcomes due to the fact that several institutional rules do not give access to the documents of an investment dispute nor to the full evidence provided by the parties.[82] This limitation negatively affects a tribunal's ability to submit informed submissions.

These shortcomings leave no option to tribunals but to give little consideration to third-party interventions. For example, some tribunals in deeming it 'unnecessary' to

---

[76]*See generally* Kube and Petersmann (2018), pp. 87–91.

[77]Vinuales (2012), p. 118.

[78]*Biwater Gauff (Tanzania) Ltd. v. United Republic of Tanzania, ICSID Case No. ARB/05/22*, para. 187.

[79]Knahr (2011), p. 336.

[80]UN (2010), p. 11.

[81]Butler provides empirical evidence to argue that *amicus curiae* briefs have had a minimal impact on investment disputes. Butler further argues that the extent to which such briefs could affect the final outcome of a dispute is at the discretion of a tribunal. *See* Butler (2019). Also *See* Harrison (2009) and Wiik (2018).

[82]Harrison (2009), p. 412.

engage with non-disputing party submissions held that the petitioners were not fully aware of the mass evidence adduced in the proceedings.[83] Thus, it was inappropriate to take into serious consideration the submissions made by the non-disputing parties.[84]

Furthermore, there is no general legal principle regulating the extent to which a tribunal should, explicitly or implicitly, consider arguments made by third parties. In other words, tribunals are not obliged to take these submissions into consideration.[85] It appears to be the prerogative of tribunals to decide whether or not to engage with human rights concerns presented by third parties. For example, in the case of *Piero Foresti v South Africa*, Italian and Luxembourger investors commenced proceedings against South Africa in relation to the alleged expropriation of mining rights. A non-disputing party petitioned to the tribunal to submit *amicus curiae* brief justifying their involvement on the basis that the relevant state measure was intended to redress the racial inequalities resulting from the apartheid.[86] Having accepted this petition, the tribunal further allowed the non-disputing party to 'access those papers submitted to the tribunal by the Parties that are necessary to enable [them] to focus their submissions upon the issues arising in the case and to see what positions the parties have taken on those issues.'[87]

In contrast with the approach adopted by the tribunal in *Piero Foresti*, there were tribunals who favored a 'private law' approach to investment arbitration by focusing on the party-driven nature of arbitration. For example, in the case of *Biwater* the tribunal held that the non-disputing party could not attend the oral hearings because the rules of the ICSID Convention favor a party-driven interpretation that allows a party to refuse a non-disputing party to attend a hearing.[88] Hence, private law conceptions of investment arbitration result in restrictive approaches when it comes to accepting and assessing *amicus curiae* briefs by tribunals.

CETA provides the possibility to non-disputing parties to request from the tribunal pleadings, memorials and any other transcripts or evidence that have been tendered to the tribunals.[89] Furthermore, CETA stipulates that the tribunal shall accept, or after consultation with the disputing parties, may invite, oral or written submissions from the non-disputing party regarding the interpretation of the

[83]Cotula and Schroder (2017), p. 23; *United Parcel Service of America Inc. v. Government of Canada*, ICSID Case No. UNCT/02/1, para. 187.

[84]*ibid*, para. 187.

[85]The tribunal in *UPS* acknowledged that international tribunals have either ignored or given very low priority to third party interventions. *United Parcel Service of America Inc. v. Government of Canada*, ICSID Case No. UNCT/02/1 para. 40.

[86]*Piero Foresti, Laura de Carli & Others v. The Republic of South Africa*, ICSID Case No. ARB (AF)/07/01, Petition for Limited Participation as non-disputing parties in terms of articles 41(3), 27, 39, and 35 of the Additional Facility, p. 8.

[87]*ibid*, Letter Regarding Non-Disputing Parties.

[88]*Biwater Gauff (Tanzania) Ltd. v. United Republic of Tanzania,Procedural order No 5, ICSID Case No. ARB/05/22*, para. 71.

[89]CETA, Art. 8. 38 (1).

agreement.[90] Despite the provision that allows non-disputing parties to access case documents, CETA adopts a very limiting approach with regard to the issues a non-disputing party may raise.

As Schadendorf argues, a non-disputing party will be able to raise human rights only if there is an explicit provision on the applicability of non-investment considerations in an IIA or in a situation where a host state has previously raised such an issue.[91] The tribunal in *Pezold* confirmed this observation since it was held that the respondent state did not raise a human rights defense in the proceedings, therefore, the non-disputing party could not enlarge the choice of law by unilateral conduct.[92] In a similar fashion, the tribunal in *Pac Rim Cayman v El Salvador,* decided only to address those arguments of the non-disputing party which were related to the arguments raised by the responded.[93] These awards should be seen as a clear reminder that the ability of third parties to raise, independently from the disputing parties submissions, human rights principles are far from being guaranteed. Hence, it is regrettable to realise the absence of detailed provisions stipulating under what circumstances a non-disputing party may raise human rights.

In summation, *amicus curiae* briefs are meaningful to the extent that tribunals can demonstrate substantial engagement with the arguments raised by third parties. Non-disputing parties are not considered parties to the proceedings and, therefore, cannot introduce new arguments or evidence. The limited role of these interventions prevents the full introduction of human rights law in investment disputes. As such, *amicus curia*e briefs in CETA are intended to perform a supplementary role in further integrating human rights into international investment law. Regardless of the parties' intentions to give voice to non-disputing parties, this section argues that CETA is far from being a solution for those who don't have standing in investment disputes but are, nevertheless, affected by arbitral awards.

5.5 Appellate Mechanism

As pointed in the previous chapters, the impossibility of reviewing serious errors of law in investment awards undermines the trust in investment arbitration. Improving the quality of arbitral awards will inevitably enhance the legitimacy of investment arbitration since the present system so far has been unable to provide a mechanism

[90] *ibid.* Art. 8 38 (2).

[91] Schadendorf (2013), pp. 12–14. This is also reflected in Rule 37 of the ICSID Convention where it is stated that a non-disputing party could address a matter within the scope of the dispute.

[92] *Biwater Gauff (Tanzania) Ltd. v. United Republic of Tanzania,Procedural order No 2, ICSID Case No. ARB/05/22, para*, paras. 59–60.

[93] *Pac Rim Cayman LLC v. Republic of El Salvador*, Decision on the Respondent's Jurisdictional Objections, ICSID Case No. ARB/09/12, paras. 2.39–2.43.

that could correct a failure to apply the properly identified law correctly.[94] At this stage, it is necessary to differentiate between, on the one hand, a failure to apply the proper law, which may constitute a manifest excess of powers and, on the other hand, a failure to apply the properly identified law correctly, which would not constitute a ground of annulment under the ICSID convention.[95] Being able to challenge an award on the basis of a failure by a tribunal to apply the properly identified law correctly provides a more thorough analysis of legal issues.

The appellate body in CETA may uphold, modify or reverse an arbitral award based on errors in the application or interpretation of applicable law.[96] Under CETA, failing to apply the relevant legal rules correctly will invalidate the original award to its entirety. This option opens the possibility for greater integration of non-investment considerations within international investment law since the appellate body may reverse an award that fails to apply human rights law correctly.

Furthermore, it is generally understood that the appellate body of the WTO, which is authorised to accept appeals on issues of law,[97] is in a position to apply other international obligations in the context of trade disputes.[98] For example, in the *Hormones* case, the WTO appellate body had to decide whether the precautionary principle forms part of a general customary rule of international law.[99] To the extent this principle could have been considered as part of customary international law and utilised to interpret the SPS agreement, the European Communities could have avoided liability under WTO law. Despite that the appellate body held that the precautionary principle cannot override the SPS agreement, it was accepted that 'a standard not found in the text of the SPS Agreement itself cannot absolve a panel (or the Appellate Body) from the duty to apply the customary rules of interpretation of public international law.'[100] As argued by Hodu and Ajibo, an appeal heard by the WTO appellate body is more far-reaching in scope than annulment under the current ICSID framework since the former is able to look into the substantive correctness of the decision.[101]

The ability of an appellate body to review errors of law speaks to the fact that legal correctness is prioritised over finality. In addition to addressing inconsistent awards, therefore, an appellate mechanism could also assist in the de-fragmentation of international law and, subsequently, to the better integration of human rights with investment protection.[102] In the same spirit, an appellate mechanism could perform a

---

[94]*See* Kalnina and Di Pietro (2009), p. 240.

[95]Schreuer (2002), p. 193.

[96]CETA, Art. 8. 28 (2) (a).

[97]DSU, Art. 17 (6).

[98]*See generally* Ngangjoh Hodu and Qi (2016), ch. 3.

[99]DS26: European Communities—Measures Concerning Meat and Meat Products (Hormones).

[100]*ibid,* para. 118.

[101]Hodu and Ajibo (2015), p. 320.

[102]Butler and Musa (2018), p. 445. *See generally* H Qureshi (2008), pp. 1165–1168; Werner (2009); Kurtz (2016), ch.5.

constitutional role by guarding fundamental principles and norms in the development of the jurisprudence of CETA.[103] As Kurtz argues, the appellate body of the WTO has managed to sensitively adjudicate on trade-offs between different values following various accusations regarding a pro-trade bias of first-instance trade panels.[104]

All in all, it has been suggested that the most appropriate way of transforming investment arbitration is by marrying procedural and substantive reforms.[105] Accordingly, human rights will be taken into serious consideration by tribunals provided that IIAs include detailed and comprehensive provisions governing the relation between investment obligations and human rights. This realization also applies in the case of the appellate mechanism as it is unclear how applicable human rights norms should be taken into consideration in the context of investment disputes.

This difficulty has arisen in the context of a WTO dispute. In the *Sea Turtles* case, the WTO appellate body had to decide whether legislation prohibiting fishing technology harmful to sea turtles was in violation of the GATT.[106] One of the key questions the panel had to answer was whether the legislation could be saved by an environmental exception.[107] The panel held that the legislation was unjustifiable and aimed to produce a change in policy in exporting States rather than protecting sea turtles.[108] For this reason, it has been argued that the appellate body was more concerned with prioritising the free market values that underpin GATT.[109] It has been also noted that if it was so important to ensure responsiveness of the trading system to environmental objectives the Committee on Trade and Environment should have recommended changes to the WTO system.[110] As it seems from the report, a mere preambular reference to environmental protection was not sufficient to uphold that legislation.[111]

This realization leads again to the point where the lack of provisions in CETA regulating the relationship between competing obligations puts a serious obstacle to the greater integration of human rights within international investment law. Taking into account the problematic and limited provisions of CETA with respect to human rights protection, it is doubtful whether an appeal mechanism will achieve such an ambitious goal on its own. If harmonisation is impossible and normative hierarchy cannot be established, then human rights will remain in a conflictual relationship

[103]Qureshi (2008).

[104]Kurtz (2016), pp. 240–241.

[105]Miles (2013), p. 381.

[106]*United States-Import Prohibition of Certain Shrimps and Shrimp Products*, Appellate Body Report WT/DS58/R, 12 October 1998.

[107]*ibid*, para. 15.

[108]*ibid*, para. 187.

[109]Dine (2005), p. 197.

[110]*ibid*, paras. 154–155.

[111]*ibid*.

with international investment law. Without a solid effort to integrate human rights within international investment law, it is highly unlikely that a procedural innovation, such as an appellate mechanism, will increase coherence between the different branches of international law.[112]

Despite that the chapter is more about evaluating the text of CETA, it is proposed to the contracting parties to CETA to include specific provisions in order to clarify the normative content of the human rights they wish to protect. It is also imperative to include a method through which an appellate body could react to argumentation based on human rights law.[113] This can be achieved by means of a joint interpretative declaration. Ultimately, the implication of the above analysis is that more engagement with the substantive provisions of CETA is necessary in order to ease the tension between human rights law and investment obligations.

5.6 Conclusion

This chapter has attempted to examine whether CETA's provisions have the potential to better integrate human rights within investment obligations. As illustrated in previous chapters, the restricting jurisdiction and applicable clauses of most IIAs, the absence of a clear and watertight methodology as well as the silent text of IIAs put obstacles to the integration of human rights into this field of international law. For these reasons, investment tribunals have shown no particular enthusiasm for balancing human rights with investment protection. Despite this criticism, the drafters of CETA have missed an important opportunity to address this problematic aspect of investment arbitration.

As explained earlier, depending on the terms of both the jurisdictional and applicable law clause, the arbitrators may have some leeway to take into account human rights. Firstly, legality requirements at the jurisdictional stage may allow tribunals to deny protection to foreign investors who have breached human rights. Secondly, human rights may be considered as part of the applicable law. Over the years, this 'toolbox' has been instrumentalised to keep international investment law within certain boundaries. Yet, the effectiveness of these mechanisms tends to be rather limited. The analysis in this chapter indicates that the lack of hierarchy between different norms in international law as well as the vague formulation of a number of human rights norms makes their integration more difficult.

---

[112]An award-winning model treaty includes detailed provisions on human rights law as well as provisions giving the possibility to the appellate mechanism to request specialised international courts and tribunals, with core expertise on human rights, advisory opinions on legal questions arising within the scope of their activities. *See* Treaty on Sustainable Investment For Climate Change Mitigation and Adaptation, Art. 9. 11 (3) stockholmtreatylab.org/wp-content/uploads/2018/07/Treaty-on-Sustainable-Investment-for-Climate-Change-Mitigation-and-Adaptation-1.pdf.

[113]UN suggests that in order to provide guidance to tribunals the interaction between different branches of international law should be addressed. ILC Report (2005), p. 162.

Despite that certain other international instruments have made attempts to remedy this situation, the drafters of CETA have failed to take them into account. CETA does not clearly impose any binding obligations to foreign investors. Hence, human rights can become relevant in the context of investment disputes in very limited circumstances. Further, the observations made regarding the limitations of the general conflict rules to solve tensions between different branches of international law speak to the fact that there is a need for specific conflict rules. Such rules would introduce a clear methodology as to the way normative conflicts between investment and human rights could be resolved. In the same spirit, another option is to expressly condition the protection of IIAs to the extent a foreign investor respects human rights. Put differently, in order to successfully integrate different branches of international law, it is necessary to put forward a drastic change in the way IIAs are drafted.

Amicus curiae briefs have the potential to enhance the legitimacy of investment arbitration by further integrating human rights within investment protection. Although *amicus curiae* briefs are a step forward, particularly by raising other social concerns before tribunals, they are limited to a written submission. These submissions cannot provide direct relief for victims of violations of human rights or hold investors accountable. Non-disputing parties are not considered parties to the proceedings and, therefore, cannot provide new arguments or evidence to the dispute. For this reason, non-disputing parties are prevented from introducing human rights in arbitral disputes.

Last, but not least, the introduction of an appellate system in CETA with potential 'precedential' consequences is both promising and challenging for non-investment considerations. However, a path to reform will not be realised without a substantial shift in the way the provisions of IIAs address human rights law. In this regard, it is doubtful whether the novel mechanisms in CETA will make a substantial difference in better integrating human rights within international investment law. There are voices claiming that human rights could be better protected through counterclaims against investors. The same voices point out that human rights could be protected by rejecting enforcement of arbitral awards at the domestic level on the basis of overriding human rights norms. Yet, the 'public policy' defense at the enforcement stage has been rarely invoked and, most importantly, was never proved to be a successful method through which human rights could be protected. Therefore, the effectiveness of these methods remains at a theoretical level. The precise contours of whether, how and when these methods could be utilised are neither fully settled nor CETA provides a framework for this purpose.

In conclusion, although CETA is claimed to be a new ideal treaty when it comes to protecting human rights, this chapter argues that its provisions are more artificial than substantial. The text of CETA is merely a repetition of common provisions, which ultimately have failed to bring a balance between competing obligations. It is therefore unlikely that fundamental change will occur in investment arbitration until IIAs begin to include clear and detailed rules that attempt to draw a balance between competing obligations. The lack of hierarchy among different sources of international law dictates that States should put an effort in regulating the relationship between different branches of international law in order to ease the tension between human rights and investment obligations.

The absence of such mechanisms in CETA speaks to the fact that investment awards have a great risk to come into conflict with the Rule of Law. Morally empty awards run contrary to the fundamental purpose of the Rule of Law, which has been the protection of human rights. In this regard, the drafters of CETA have missed an important opportunity to better integrate human rights law into international investment law. Despite that some hoped that CETA would constitute a turn into a *constitutional moment* for international investment law that could address concerns of fragmentation,[114] this chapter argues otherwise.

In addition to the protection of human rights law, the Rule of Law requires procedural fairness during the arbitration proceedings. Taking into consideration the criticism made against investment arbitration regarding the level of fairness in proceedings, the following chapter asks whether CETA provides procedural fairness.

References

Acconci P (2014) The integration of non-investment concerns as an opportunity for the modernization of international investment law: is a multilateral approach desirable? In: Sacerdoti G et al (eds) General interests of host states in international investment law. Cambridge University Press, Cambridge

Adeleke F (2018) International investment law and policy in Africa: exploring a human rights based approach to investment regulation and dispute settlement. Routledge Publications, Abingdon, ch. 5

Amado J et al (2018) Arbitrating the conduct of international investors. Cambridge University Press, Cambridge, p 109

Anthony Van Duzer J et al (2012) Integrating sustainable development into international investment agreements: a guide for developing countries. Commonwealth Secretariat, London

Anthony VanDuzer J (2016) Sustainable development provisions in international trade treaties: what lesson for international investment agreements? In: Hindelang S, Krajewski M (eds) Shifting paradigms in international investment law: more balanced, less isolated, increasingly diversified. Oxford University Press, Oxford

Balcerzak F (2017) Investor-state arbitration and human rights. Brill Publications, Leiden, pp 134–146

Bartels L (2017) Human rights, labour standards and environmental standards in CETA. In: Griller S et al (eds) Mega-regional trade agreements CETA, TTIP and TiSA: new orientations for EU external economic relations. Oxford University Press, Oxford, p 210

Bellhouse and Lavers as cited in John G (2016) The 'de-fragmentation' of international investment law and international human rights law: a procedural basis for a host state human rights defence in ICSID arbitration. Brunel Univ Res Archive:82–83

Butler N (2019) Non-disputing party participation in ICSID disputes: Faux Amici? Netherlands Int Law Rev 66:1

---

[114] *See generally* Schill (2017).

Butler N, Musa S (2018) Systemizing human rights within investment arbitration. Am Rev Int Arbitr 28:4
Cali B et al (2017) The effects of international human rights law on other branches of public international law: an annotated compilation of case law. Center of Global Public Law. p 18
Cotula L (2012) Human rights, natural resource and investment law in a globalised world. Routledge Publications, Abingdon, p 78
Cotula L, Schroder M (2017) Community perspectives in investor-state arbitration. IIEL Land, Investment and Rights Series, p 23
Dine J (2005) Companies, international trade and human rights. Cambridge University Press, Cambridge, p 197
Dumberry P, Dumas-Aubin G (2012) When and how allegations of human rights violations can be raised in investor-state arbitration. J World Invest Trade 13:349–372
Dumberry P, Dumas-Aubin G (2014) A few pragmatic observations on how BITs should be modified to incorporate human rights obligations. Transnational Dispute Manag 11
Elisabeth Kjos H (2013) Applicable law in investor-state arbitration: the interplay between national and international law. Oxford University Press, Oxford, ch.3
Eric Peterson L (2009) Human rights and bilateral investment treaties: mapping the role of human rights law within the investor-state arbitration. International Center for Human Rights and Democratic Development, Montreal, p 22
European Commission (2010) Communication from the Commision to the Council, the European Parliament, the European Economic and Social Committee and the Committee of the Regions' COM(2010)343. Brussels, p 9
Fahner J, Happold M (2019) The human rights defence in international investment arbitration: exploring the limits of systemic integration. Int Comp Law Q 68:3
Fry J (2007) International human rights law in investment arbitration: evidence of international law's unity. Duke J Comp Int Law 18:1
Gehring M et al (2017) Sustainability impact assessments as inputs and as interpretative aids in international investment law. J World Invest Trade 18:163–199
Gonzalez Garcia L (2013) The role of human rights in international investment law. In: Calamita J et al (eds) The future of ICSID and the place of investment treaties in international law. BIICL, London, p 30
Harrison J (2009) Human rights arguments in Amicus Curiae submissions: promoting social justice? In: Marie Dupuy P et al (eds) Human rights in international investment law and arbitration. Oxford University Press, Oxford
Hirsch M (2008) Interactions between investment and non-investment obligations. In: Muchlinski P et al (eds) The Oxford handbook of international investment law. Oxford University Press, Oxford, pp 163–172
Hodu Y, Ajibo C (2015) ICSID annulment procedure and the WTO appellate system: the case for an appellate system for investment arbitration. J Int Dispute Settlement 6:320
Jacob M (2010) International investment agreements and human rights. INEF research paper series on human rights, corporate responsibility and sustainable development 03/2010, p. 11
Kalnina I, Di Pietro D (2009) The scope of ICSID review: remarks on selected problematic issues of ICSID decisions. In: Binder C et al (eds) International investment law for the 21st century: essays in Honour of Christoph Schreuer. Oxford University Press, Oxford, p 240
Knahr C (2011) The new rules on participation of non-disputing parties in ICSID arbitration: blessing or curse? In: Brown C, Miles K (eds) Evolution in investment treaty law and arbitration. Cambridge University Press, Cambridge, p 336
Kriebaum U (2007) Privatizing human rights: the interface between international investment protection and human rights. In: Reinisch A, Kriebaum U (eds) The law of international relations: Liber Amicorum Hanspeter Neuhold. Eleven International Publishing, The Hague, pp 172–177

Kube V, Petersmann EU (2018) Human rights in international investment arbitration. In: Gattini A et al (eds) General principles of law and international investment arbitration. Brill Publications, Leiden, pp 87–91
Kulick A (2012) Global public interest in international investment law. Cambridge University Press, Cambridge, ch. 2
Kurtz J (2016) The WTO and international investment law: converging systems. Cambridge University Press, Cambridge, ch.5
Lang A (2011) World trade after neoliberalism: reimagining the global economic order. Oxford University Press, Oxford, ch. 4
Marie Dupuy P, Vinuales J (2015) Human rights and investment disputes: integration in progress. In: Bungenberg M et al (eds) International investment law: a handbook. Nomos Publications, Baden-Baden
Mclachlan C (2005) The principle of systemic integration and Article 31(3) of the Vienna Convention. Int Comp Law Q 54:279
Miles K (2013) The origins of international investment law: empire, environment and the safeguarding of capital. Cambridge University Press, Cambridge
Mota A (2018) #Defend the sacred: harnessing hard and soft law mechanisms to integrate international investment and cultural rights. King's College Repository, p 221
Newcombe A (2011) Investor misconduct: jurisdiction, admissibility or merits? In: Brown C, Miles K (eds) Evolution in investment treaty law and arbitration. Cambridge University Press, Cambridge, p 199
Ngangjoh Hodu Y, Qi Z (2016) The political economy of WTO implementation and China's approach to litigation in the WTO. Elgar Publications, Camberley, ch. 3
Qureshi AH (2008) An appellate system in international investment arbitration? In: Muchlinski P et al (eds) The Oxford handbook of international investment law. Oxford University Press, Oxford, pp 1165–1168
Radi Y (2011) Realizing human rights in investment treaty arbitration: a perspective from within the international investment law toolbox. North Carolina J Int Law Commer Regul 37:4
Report of the ILC (2005) 57th session, UN Doc A/60/10, para. 236
Schadendorf S (2013) Human rights in Amicus Curiae submissions: analysis of ICSID and NAFTA investor-state arbitration. Transnational Disp Settlement 10(1):12–14
Schill S (2017) Authority, legitimacy, and fragmentation in the (envisaged) dispute settlement disciplines in mega-regionals. In: Griller S et al (eds) Mega regionals trade agreements: CETA, TTIP and TiSA: new orientations for EU external economic relations. Oxford University Press, Oxford
Schreuer C (2002) Failure to apply the governing law in international investment arbitration. Aust Rev Int Eur Law 7:193
Simma B, Kill T (2009) Harmonizing investment protecting and international human rights: first step towards a methodology. In: Binder C et al (eds) International investment law for the 21st century: essays in Honour of Christoph Schreuer. Oxford University Press, Oxford, p 694
Thielborger P (2009) The human right to water versus investors rights: double-dilemma or pseudo-conflict? In: Dupuy PM (eds) Human rights in international investment law and arbitration. Oxford University Press, Oxford, p 488
United Nations Commision on International Trade Law (2010) Report of Working Group II (Arbitration and Conciliation) A/CN.9/712
Vadi V (2012) Public health in international investment law and arbitration. Routledge Publications, Abingdon, pp 187–188
Vinuales JE (2012) Foreign investment and the environment in international law. Cambridge University Press, Cambridge, pp 34–38
Wandahl Mouyal L (2016) International investment law and the right to regulate: a human rights perspective. Routledge Publications, Abingdon, pp 59–65

Werner J (2009) Limits of commercial investor-state arbitration: the need for appellate review. In: Marie Dupuy P et al (eds) Human rights in international investment law and arbitration. Oxford University Press, Oxford

Wiik A (2018) Amicus Curiae before international courts and tribunals. Nomos Publications, Baden-Baden

Yotova R (2017) Systemic integration: an instrument for reasserting the state's control. In: investment arbitration? In: Kulick A (ed) Reassertion of control over the investment treaty regime. Cambridge University Press, Cambridge

Zia-Zarifi S (2007) Protection without protectionism. Linking a multilateral investment treaty and human rights. In: Nieuwenhuys EC, Brus M (eds) Multilateral regulation of investment. Kluwer Law International, Alphen aan den Rijn

Chapter 6
Procedural Fairness and CETA: Ghosts of Decades Past

6.1 Introduction

To ensure the application of the law and avoid potential abuses, the Rule of Law sets out certain procedural conditions that should be met by tribunals. The observance of procedural constraints by investment tribunals enables the law to be correctly ascertained and applied, revent arbitrators from taking extra-legal considerations into account and ensure that arbitral awards are issued without bias. For this purpose, the drafters of the CETA have introduced a permanent investment tribunal with a roster of adjudicators, a code of conduct and ethics provisions for the members of a tribunal, a mechanism for the appointment and compensation of adjudicators, and a series of other provisions to ensure procedural fairness. These provisions are supposed to deal with concerns about the arbitrators' impartiality at an individual level and a pro-investor institutional bias that is associated with the system's *ad hoc* nature. This chapter seeks to evaluate whether the institutional safeguards in CETA have the potential to ensure procedural fairness during the arbitration proceedings. Although that the contracting parties to CETA have put in place concrete provisions to ensure procedural fairness, the chapter argues that investors run the risk of being subjected to bias in favor of States in the context of investment disputes. The view of this chapter is that the method of appointment and compensation in CETA could jeopardise procedural fairness since it creates incentives for arbitrators to lean towards the state parties. Lastly, the lack of detailed criteria requiring greater diversity in the CETA tribunal is regrettable.

K. Dionysiou, *CETA's Investment Chapter*, European Yearbook of International Economic Law 13, https://doi.org/10.1007/978-3-030-66992-8_6

6.2 Code of Conduct and Enforcement Mechanism

6.2.1 IBA Guidelines and Ethics Provisions

Fair proceedings are guaranteed as long as adjudicators are *independent* of any kind of financial or personal relationship with a party to the dispute, while *impartiality* is maintained only where adjudicators do not appear to have pre-judged some issues. According to the European Commission, the independence of the CETA Investment Court should be ensured through strict requirements on ethics and impartiality, full-time employment of the members of the panel, non-renewable appointments and an independent mechanisms for appointment of the members of the panel.[1]

Starting with impartiality, arbitrators commonly engage in other professional activities, which might give rise to connections with a particular dispute and may have a bearing on their impartiality. In an effort to respond to several of the legitimacy concerns advanced against investment arbitration, CETA includes ethics provisions for the members of the tribunal and the appellate mechanism.[2] In contrast with previous practices, CETA provisions build on past and recent attempts to effectively precisely regulate adjudicators' ethics and conduct. In particular, CETA includes the IBA Guidelines on Conflicts of Interest (IBA Guidelines) and separate ethics provisions in its text.[3] This part aims to examine whether these provisions constitute a decisive response to the criticism made about the lack of impartiality of arbitrators.

Turning to the separate ethics provision in CETA, the principal phenomenon that gives rise to concerns about the impartiality of arbitrators is the 'double-hatting' by certain individuals. As argued in previous chapters, the 'double-hatting' phenomenon, also called 'role-confusion', raises concerns regarding arbitrators' impartiality to investment disputes.[4] These concerns are based on a presumption that adjudicators will not be able to exercise impartial reasoning due to the fact that their previous interactions with an issue, which is relevant to the particular dispute, will prevent them from exercising judgment without bias.[5] In the same vein, in the domain of investment arbitration, arbitrators are *de facto* generating law by elaborating on the scope and content of certain key investment obligations in IIAs, as well as the meaning of customary international law.[6] Nevertheless, this law that arbitrators are creating when deciding disputes is the same law in which the same arbitrators, when acting as counsel or expert, argue should be given a particular interpretation. On this basis, individuals who concurrently act as counsel on such occasions become judges of their own arguments.

---

[1] *See generally* European Commission (2017).

[2] CETA, Art. 8. 30.

[3] *ibid.*

[4] Van Harten (2016).

[5] *See generally* Sand (2011).

[6] Van Harten (2007), pp. 122–124.

CETA's approach to the 'double-hatting' phenomenon leaves no grey areas by clearly prohibiting adjudicators to simultaneously act as counsels, experts or arbitrators.[7] According to article 8 of CETA's Investment Chapter, adjudicators are prevented from acting as counsels or party-appointed experts or witnesses in any other dispute during their 5-year appointment to the CETA tribunal.[8] Furthermore, adjudicators must be independent of the state parties to CETA since they should not be affiliated with any government.[9] This provision then specifies that members of the tribunal 'shall not take instructions from any organization, or government with regard to matters related to the dispute' and 'they shall not participate in the consideration of any disputes that would create a direct or indirect conflict of interest.[10]

The rationale behind this complete restriction of a 'dual role' by adjudicators in different disputes is not surprising as it is one of the main points of criticism against investment arbitration. Furthermore, the clear prohibition of 'double-hatting' in CETA text is recognition of the fact that the IBA Guidelines are missing specific provisions dealing with this phenomenon. In this way, the parties to CETA recognised the particularism of investment disputes through additional provisions prohibiting this practice.[11]

In addition to the complete prohibition of 'double-hatting for arbitrators', CETA includes a reference to the IBA Guidelines in an effort to tackle other situations where the impartiality of arbitrators might be at risk. The IBA Guidelines address among other things: arbitrators' obligations of impartiality, disclosure duties, obligations to withdraw, and the 'justifiable doubts' test which represents a baseline of independence and impartiality for all those involved in investment disputes.[12] The remaining of this section will closely examine these obligations.

Starting with the latter, the IBA Guidelines invoke the much lower test of 'justifiable doubts' in order to assess whether an individual may be influenced by

[7]Simoes (2018), p. 109. The clear prohibition is of paramount importance due to that certain tribunals went to dismiss the claim that 'double-hatting' is problematic for fair proceedings. 'It is at the core of the job description of legal counsel—whether acting in private practice, in-house for a company, or in government—that they present the views which are favorable to their instructor and highlight the advantageous facts of their instructor's case. The fact that a lawyer has taken a certain stance in the past does not necessarily mean that he will take the same stance in a future case.' *See Saint-Gobain Performance Plastics Europe v. Bolivarian Republic of Venezuela*, ICSID Case No. ARB/12/13, Decision on Claimant's Proposal to Disqualify Mr. Bottini from the Tribunal under Article 57 of the ICSID Convention, para.80.

[8]CETA, Art. 8. 30 (1).

[9]*ibid.*

[10]*ibid.*

[11]Horodyski (2010), p. 15.

[12]General standard 2 (d) of the rules state further that 'doubts are justifiable if a reasonable and informed third party would reach the conclusion that there was a likelihood that the arbitrator may be influenced by factors other than the merits of the case as presented by the parties in reaching his or her decision.'

factors other than the merits of the case.[13] However, before examining the merits of the 'justifiable doubts' test it should be contrasted with the much higher ICSID threshold of 'manifest lack'. In the *RFCC* case, the tribunal had to decide whether an individual should be disqualified on the basis of the ICSID threshold. In this case, an arbitrator was challenged because he was acting as counsel in another dispute with common features. Ultimately, it was held that only in *exceptional circumstances* there is a reason to assume that an arbitrator would be biased in situations he had to decide on a similar question pertaining to which he has previously, in another dispute, defended a point of view.[14]

Another example of an unsuccessful challenge occurred in *Urbaser v Argentina*, where the tribunal held that "the mere showing of an opinion, even if relevant in a particular arbitration, is not sufficient to sustain a challenge for lack of independence or impartiality of an arbitrator.'[15] The negative outcome of these challenges correlates with the high disqualification threshold of the ICSID Convention.[16] In the words of Sobota, the determination of actual bias of the challenged arbitrator entails an elusive inquiry into his mind.[17]

In contrast with the previous awards, the tribunal in *Perenco,* applying the 'justifiable doubts' test, held that the claimant-appointed arbitrator, who made comments about the pending proceedings, showed a clear appearance of bias against the respondent state.[18] In particular, the tribunal examined whether 'a *reasonable* person and *informed* third party would reach the conclusion that there was a likelihood that the arbitrator may be influenced by factors other than the merits of the case.'[19] The fact that the particular arbitrator expressed his opinion on a matter that he considered a pressing issue in international arbitration, which was relevant for the purpose of the pending dispute, raised doubts regarding his open-mindedness.[20]

---

[13]IBA Guidelines, General Standards 2 (c). The IBA threshold stands in contrast with the much higher threshold in the ICSID convention that imposes an excessive burden of proof on the challenging party. The ICSID Convention states that a party seeking to challenge an arbitrator may request its disqualification on the basis of any fact indicating a manifest lack of independence and/or impartiality.

[14]*Consortium RFCC v. Royaume du Maroc*, ICSID Case No. ARB/00/6, Decision on Annulment.

[15]*Urbaser S.A. and Consorcio de Aguas Bilbao Bizkaia, Bilbao Biskaia Ur Partzuergoa v. The Argentine Republic*, ICSID Case No. ARB/07/26, Decision on Claimant's Proposal to Disqualify Professor Campbell McLachlan, Arbitrator, para. 45.

[16]Further on this point *See* Giorgetti (2013a, b).

[17]Sobota (2015), p. 316.

[18]*Perenco Ecuador Ltd. v. The Republic of Ecuador and Empresa Estatal Petróleos del Ecuador (Petroecuador)*, ICSID Case No. ARB/08/6, Decision on Challenge to Arbitrator.

[19]*ibid*, para.41.

[20]*ibid*. Relevant to this test, practical standard 2 (d) in the IBA Guidelines states that if an arbitrator had a strong opinion or interest in an issue relevant to the particular dispute will trigger the 'justifiable doubt' test.

Along the same lines, in *Vito Gallo* the tribunal had to elaborate on the 'justifiable doubts' test enshrined in the UNCITRAL rules. In the tribunal's view there would be justifiable doubts about Mr. Thomas' impartiality and independence as an arbitrator if he were not to discontinue his advisory services to Mexico for the remainder of the arbitral proceedings.[21] The tribunal subsequently called Mr. Thomas to choose whether he will continue to advise Mexico, or continue to serve as an arbitrator in this case. A week after the ruling, the challenged arbitrator resigned from his duties.[22] As Clein points out, the 'justifiable doubts' threshold signals a stricter standard of independence and impartiality to arbitrators, thereby increasing the chances of ethical behavior.[23] The above approaches illustrate that the 'justifiable doubts' test in the IBA Guidelines could untie the hands of concerned disputing parties seeking to challenge an arbitrator's impartiality.

Moreover, the IBA Guidelines contain two parts that aim to provide concrete examples of situations in which arbitrators could be considered as being biased. The first part lays down the general standards of conduct to be kept in mind by arbitrators and parties when deciding on issues of bias. An explanatory note accompanies this section. The general standards are then followed by another part that includes a non-exhaustive list of specific conflict situations. In particular, the 'non-waivable red list' includes situations, which arbitrators are considered biased, and should decline appointment or withdraw. In other words, this list describes circumstances that raise justifiable doubts and cannot be cured.[24] These circumstances include situations when an arbitrator has a significant interest in the outcome of the award or has a controlling influence on a party or entity that has a direct economic interest in the award.[25] The 'waivable red list' covers situations that are serious but not as severe. For example, this list includes situations where an arbitrator has given legal advice or expert opinion on the dispute to a party or an affiliate of one of the parties or had prior involvement with the particular dispute.[26]

The IBA Guidelines further contain the so-called 'orange list' that contains several situations that may give rise to justifiable doubts as to the arbitrator's impartiality and/or independence.[27] The situations contained in the 'orange list' should be considered waivable, but only if and when the parties, being aware of the conflict of interest, state their willingness to proceed with the particular

[21] *Vito G. Gallo v. The Government of Canada*, UNCITRAL, PCA Case No. 55798, Decision on the Challenge to Mr. J. Christopher Thomas, QC, para. 36.

[22] *ibid*, Resignation letter of Arbitrator J. Christopher Thomas.

[23] Nicole Cleis (2017), p. 212. In the same vein, despite that ICSID tribunals have begun to equate 'manifest' with 'easily recognizable' authors still support that a general lowering of the standard required for ICSID arbitrator challenges is necessary. *See* Vasani and Palmer (2015) and Sheppard (2009).

[24] IBA Guidelines, Explanation of General Standard 2 (d).

[25] *ibid*. 1.2.

[26] *ibid*. 2.1.

[27] *ibid*, Practical Application 2.

individual.[28] In particular, the 'orange list' targets situations in which 'the arbitrator has within the past 3 years been appointed as arbitrator on two or more occasions by one of the parties or an affiliate of one of the parties.'[29] In regards to the 'orange list', some uncertainty with regard to the grounds an arbitrator could be challenged is inevitable. In other words, CETA text does not address all the potentially problematic situations that might arise with regard to issues of conflict.[30] The uncertainty, however, may have positive effects since the flexibility of these grounds might have a deterrent effect.[31] At the same time, taking into consideration that any qualitative standard for the challenges of arbitrators is inherently vague, it could be argued that this set of lists puts the justifiable doubts thresholds into more concrete terms. As Cleis argues, the IBA Guidelines may effectively reduce the incidence of quantifiable conflicts of interest, including those caused by repeat appointments.[32]

Turning to the disclosure obligations in the IBA Guidelines, it is of paramount importance that more information is made available to the disputing parties to promote a level playing field among parties and counsel. The arbitrator's duty of disclosure, therefore, rests on the idea that disputing parties have an interest in being fully informed of any facts that may be relevant for the purpose of their dispute. The duty of disclosure is an essential instrument for the prevention of conflicts of interest and the promotion of procedural fairness, which is clearly connected with the Rule of Law benchmark.[33] As it was held in the *Vivendi* case, all the circumstances need to be considered in order to determine whether the relationship between a party and an arbitrator is significant enough to raise reasonable doubts as to the capacity of the arbitrator to render a decision independently.[34]

For this reason, the IBA Guidelines stipulate that the arbitrators shall disclose such facts or circumstances to the parties or other appointing authority that may, in the eyes of the parties, give rise to doubts as to their independence and/or impartiality.[35] Yet, such a general obligation exists in the ICSID convention as well.[36] What is unique with CETA is that a non-exhaustive list is provided that stipulates what

[28]*ibid.*

[29]IBA Guidelines on Conflicts of Interest in International Arbitration, Part II: Practical Application of the General Standards, para. 3.

[30]In *UPS* case, the applicants challenged the appointment of an arbitrator because the arbitrator was a partner and chairman of a law firm with a longstanding and significant ongoing relationship with a company that was not a disputing party but, nevertheless, had a significant interest in the outcome of the particular dispute. Relying on the ICSID standard, the tribunal rejected the challenge. *See United Parcel Service of America Inc. v. Government of Canada, ICSID Case No. UNCT/02/1.*

[31]Nicole Cleis (2017), p. 238.

[32]*ibid*, p. 175.

[33]Fach Gomez (2018), p. 26.

[34]*Suez, Sociedad General de Aguas de Barcelona, S.A.and Vivendi Universal, S.A. v. Argentine Republic*, ICSID Case No. ARB/03/19, Decision on the Challenge to the President of the Committee, para. 28.

[35]IBA Guidelines, General Standards 3 (a).

[36]ICSID Convention, Chapter 1, Rule 6 (2).

kind of personal or professional contacts an arbitrator will have to disclose. The text of CETA stipulates that candidate arbitrators shall disclose, among others, any financial interest in the proceedings or in their outcome, and any financial interest their employer, partner or family member might have in the proceedings or in their outcome.[37]

As a general rule, all the facts or circumstances that may, in the eyes of the parties, give rise to doubts as to the arbitrator's impartiality should be disclosed.[38] As it is made clear from the IBA Guidelines, a reasonable third-party standard is prioritised. This standard shifts away from an arbitrator-centered approach towards a more party-centered approach. This means that in a situation where an arbitrator's challenge takes place under CETA, the question will be whether a reasonable third-party would have assumed that there is a reasonable suspicion of bias. This is different from a party-centered approach, according to which an arbitrator's impartiality would be examined from the parties' perspectives. Although the former approach has been criticised for bearing the risk to generate frivolous challenges,[39] the subjective standard is the most promising to enhance the legitimacy of investment arbitrator in the public eye.

In the *Vivendi* case, the state requested the disqualification of an arbitrator on the basis that he had not disclosed important information, thus, violated an important procedural requirement.[40] Adopting the parties perspective test, the committee concluded that 'it is, in any event, difficult to understand why the bank was notified by [the arbitrator] of her existing arbitrations but not the arbitrating parties of her (impending) directorship of the bank at the same time.'[41] In light of the above, the body deciding in disqualification proceedings should be encouraged to refer to the parties point of view in making a decision.

Most importantly, the duty of disclosure in the IBA Guidelines is ongoing, meaning that arbitrators should disclose relevant information that may give rise to doubts as to their impartiality and/or independence, as soon as they are discovered.[42] Disclosure does not end with an individual's appointment to the tribunal. Imposing a continuing duty to disclosure has been a proposal for a long time, which is expected to enhance the fairness of the arbitral proceedings.[43] Any doubt as to whether an arbitrator should disclose certain information should be resolved in favor of

[37]CETA, Annex 29-B, Code of Conduct for Arbitrators and Mediators, Art. 3.

[38]IBA Guidelines, General Standards 3 (b) (a).

[39]Fach Gomez (2018), p. 39.

[40]*Suez, Sociedad General de Aguas de Barcelona, S.A.and Vivendi Universal, S.A. v. Argentine Republic,* ICSID Case No. ARB/03/19, Decision on the Challenge to the President of the Committee.

[41]*ibid,* para. 229.

[42]*ibid,* para. 229. General Standards 3 (b). This obligation is critical given that the duty to disclose is complicated by a presumed static character. *See* Fernandez Perez (2018), p. 113.

[43]Malintoppi (2008), p. 825.

disclosure.[44] Even if the latter leads to over-disclosure it's preferable to opacity. At the same time, the duty to disclose is double-sided. This is because; the IBA Guidelines further oblige the disputing parties to inform both the arbitrators and the other parties of any relationship, direct or indirect, between the arbitrator and the party.[45]

As a final remark, the explicit inclusion of the IBA Guidelines in the investment chapter of CETA is a significant departure from the usual practices since these standards of conduct were usually binding in a dispute only if the disputing parties agreed so. Along the same lines, the IBA Guidelines were considered as 'soft law instruments that can only induce voluntary adherence, unless a forum binds its arbitrators to the guidelines or if the procedural rules of an arbitration incorporate them by reference.'[46] For example, the remaining members in *Tidewater v Venezuela* held that the ICSID Convention mandates a general standard for disqualification that differs from the 'justifiable doubts' test formulated in the IBA Guidelines.[47]

In parallel, the 'soft law' nature of the IBA Guidelines was also confirmed in disputes where it was held that these rules evidence authoritative practices and guidelines for the conduct of investment disputes.[48] The adoption of these rules by CETA gives them the long-awaited teeth and regulatory prowess to raise the level of ethics in investment disputes.[49] The clear reference to the IBA Guidelines speaks to the fact that the duties enshrined therein should not be considered as voluntary in nature but should be positively valued as they provide the disputing parties with certainty.

6.2.2 Enforcement Mechanism

Menon pointed out that as stakeholders contemplate moral hazards in international arbitration, it seems surprising that there are no effective control mechanisms to maintain the quality and legitimacy of international arbitration as a method of international dispute settlement.[50] As will be explained, this is mostly attributed to the unsuitability of the current methods to disqualify an arbitrator. Considering this, another principal mechanism to ensure impartiality on the part of members of the

[44] *ibid* p. 825. General Standards 3 (d). This provision is also critical given that arbitrators might underestimate their connection with a party.

[45] *ibid.* General Standards 7 (a).

[46] Anderson (2018), p. 1162.

[47] *Tidewater Inc., Tidewater Investment SRL, Tidewater Caribe, C.A., et al. v. The Bolivarian Republic of Venezuela*, ICSID Case No. ARB/10/5, Decision on Claimants' Proposal to Disqualify Professor Brigitte Stern, Arbitrator, para. 43.

[48] *Alpha Projektholding GmbH v. Ukraine*, ICSID Case No. ARB/07/16, Decision on Respondent's Proposal to Disqualify Arbitrator Dr. Yoram Turbowicz, paras. 62–66.

[49] Niedermeyer (2014), p. 5.

[50] Menon (2010), para. 43.

tribunal is the procedures to challenge adjudicators on the basis of lack of impartiality. Enforcement of ethical standards could take the form of holding an individual in contempt, professional discipline or permanent disqualification.[51] In any case, as a UN report indicates, an effective challenge mechanism must fulfill two main functions: the first function is to provide the teeth of the requirements for fair proceedings and, secondly, it must be sufficiently robust to allow for disputes to proceed.[52]

When it comes to enforcing the above provisions, CETA distances itself from other treaties for the challenge and disqualification of adjudicators. Under the ICSID Convention, the decision on any proposal to disqualify an adjudicator shall be taken by the other members of a tribunal. The ICSID Administrative Council will get involved only if the two co-adjudicators do not agree on the challenge or if a sole adjudicator or more than one adjudicators of a three-member tribunal is or are being challenged.[53] The decision of arbitrator challenges by the remaining arbitrators has frequently been criticised. As Cleis explains, it is generally accepted that arbitrators of such high caliber are sympathetic towards each other and that they might have a tendency to protect each other against challenges.[54] By the same token, the distance thought that they might one day find themselves in the same situation raise doubts as to their willingness to stand on principle when it comes to arbitrators' challenges.[55] Apart from this problematic situation, the co-arbitrators' evaluations of a challenge, after proceedings have begun, might be influenced by the challenged arbitrator views on the merits of a particular dispute.[56]

Against this background, it seems desirable to delegate decisions on arbitrator challenges to another independent body. According to CETA, 'if a disputing party considers that a Member of the Tribunal has a conflict of interest, it may invite the President of the International Court of Justice to issue a decision on the challenge to the appointment of such Member.'[57] 'If, within 15 days from the date of the notice of challenge, the challenged Member of the Tribunal has elected not to resign from the division, the President of the ICJ may, after receiving submissions from the disputing parties and after providing the Member of the Tribunal an opportunity to submit any observations, issue a decision on the challenge.'[58] Another avenue through which a member of the tribunal can be removed is by a joint initiative of the

---

[51]For a brief overview of the various enforcement mechanisms that guide and control the behavior of adjudicators in both public and private international law *See* Fisher (1996).

[52]UN General Assembly (2018, p. 12. Furthermore, out of 75 disqualifications proposals brought at ICSID by 2019, only 5 were upheld. *See* ICSID Database, Decisions on Disqualifications. icsid.worldbank.org/en/Pages/Process/Decisions-on-Disqualification.aspx.

[53]ICSID Convention, Art. 58.

[54]Clein (2017), p. 231.

[55]*ibid.*

[56]*ibid.*

[57]CETA, Art. 8. 30 (2).

[58]*ibid.* Art, 8. 30 (3).

disputing parties through a decision of the Joint Committee.[59] Finally, in the event of a disqualification or resignation of a member of the tribunal, the vacancy 'shall be filled promptly' from the roster.[60]

This mechanism attempts to address the critiques on investment arbitration by establishing the circumstances under which members of a tribunal can be removed when one or more of its members failed to meet the IBA Guidelines and ethics provisions. This concrete approach attempts to give more enforcement capabilities to the IBA Guidelines, which have been criticised for lacking teeth.[61] In the same manner, the transfer of the authority to the ICJ would improve the consistency of future challenges and permit for an in-depth consideration of the challenging party's claims. Furthermore, the enforcement mechanism in CETA is in line with the Kyiv Recommendations on Judicial Independence that stipulate that disciplinary proceedings should be undertaken by an independent body of judicial discipline to ensure effectiveness and fairness.[62]

In summation, the above analysis suggests that the parties have made a bold attempt to address the critiques on the lack of impartiality of arbitrators. The clear prohibition of 'double-hatting', the inclusion of the 'justifiable doubts' tests in combination with a detailed outline of the situations that might raise doubts as to the arbitrator's impartiality could effectively reduce the number of conflicts of interest. Furthermore, emphasising the duty of disclosure's continuous nature and its wide scope will prove useful in the struggle against biased proceedings by leading to resignations or challenges of members of the tribunal. A comprehensive duty of disclosure may also assist in the fight against the harmful phenomenon of 'double-hatting'. Lastly, the introduction of a robust enforcement mechanism constitutes a bold attempt towards procedural fairness and comprises a direct response against the belief that the self-regulatory nature of the arbitrator's community will eventually remove any suspicion of conflicts of interest.[63]

6.3 Investment Court System

6.3.1 Appointing Mechanism

The lowering of the disqualification standard of arbitrators, the accompanying guidelines in the IBA Guidelines and the strong enforcement mechanism attempt

[59]*ibid*, Art. 8. 30 (4).

[60]*ibid*, Art. 8. 30 (3).

[61]Niedermeyer (2014), p. 8.

[62]Kyiv Recommendations on Judicial Independence in Eastern Europe, para. 26.

[63]Empirical studies indicate that voluntary restraints have been insufficient to deal with the concerns arising from 'double-hatting' and other concerns relating to conflicts of interest. Nicole Cleis (2017).

to reduce bias. Yet, these provisions inevitably contain a few loopholes. Several authors claim that creating standards that 'explicitly disallow arbitrators from simultaneously making investor-state arbitration their main economic activity as counsel' would be a modest reform when compared to proposals that aim to completely transform the way the ISDS functions.[64] To this point, it has been argued that there is 'tentative support for expectations of systemic bias arising from the interests of arbitrators in light of the system's asymmetrical claims structure and the absence of conventional markers of judicial independence.'[65] Markers of judicial independence include an autonomous budget and a fixed salary for adjudicators, transparent appointing method, objective case assignment and security of tenure. This section will examine the appointing mechanism and the qualification requirements for arbitrators as well as the method of financing of the tribunal to evaluate whether CETA introduces suitable safeguards to ensure institutional independence.

Turning to the appointing mechanism, CETA does not only introduce standards of behavior for members of the tribunal but also alters the way in which arbitrators are appointed.[66] In particular, the members of the tribunal will not be appointed by the disputing parties but must be appointed from a roster created by the parties to CETA instead. From that roster, the President of the tribunal will select three members to adjudicate a dispute.[67] The President should give equal opportunity to all members to serve, while neither States nor investors can directly appoint any member to hear their dispute.[68] The same prohibition applies to the members of the appellate body, where the involvement of the disputing parties in appointing its members is restricted.[69] Like the first-instance tribunal, the members of the appellate mechanism will be appointed randomly, thereby ensuring that the composition of each panel is unpredictable.[70]

The standing roster of adjudicators and the selection process in CETA for particular disputes shifts away from the traditional party-appointed system.[71]

---

[64]Bernasconi-Osterwalder and Robert (2014), p. 13. This view is also supported by another study suggesting structural and procedural safeguards to decrease the risk of errors and systemic bias. *See* Franck et al. (2017).

[65]Van Harten (2012), p. 252.

[66]For a general overview *See* Gaukrodger (2018).

[67]CETA, Art. 8. 27 (6).

[68]*ibid*, Art. 8. 27 (7).

[69]*ibid*, Art. 8.28 (3).

[70]*ibid*, Art. 8.28 (3). Randomization in case assignment is expected to better guarantee institutional independence because it eliminates risks of outside and internal interference. By contrast, placing case assignment powers within the discretionary powers of the President of the tribunal or another body poses various risks, such as pressures and/or interferences from outsiders. *See* Kaufmann-Kohler and Potesta (2017), pp. 104–105.

[71]CETA, Art. 8. 27. Puig suggests that the party appointed method characterises the dynamics of the field of investment arbitration. Since the appointment of an arbitrator may be translated into direct and indirect economic gains, it is suggested that the current method should be investigated further to limit the negative consequences. *See* Puig (2014).

While the state parties to CETA have a say over the initial constitution of the roster of arbitrators, the agreement attempts to move away from a situation where the disputing parties have direct involvement in selecting who will determine their investment dispute. The aim was to take away a substantial amount of party autonomy, both from investors and States, in appointing arbitrators. As argued in previous chapters, in situations where the disputing parties make the appointments arbitrators will lean towards the party that appointed them. By the same token, what is important for disputing parties is whether a particular arbitrator will enhance their chances of winning a case.[72]

The ultimate objective of this system, therefore, is to address key residual pre-conceptions and institutional biases for which the ISDS has been criticised. Most importantly, this appointing mechanism attempts to halt any kind of incentives that might cause arbitrators to favor foreign investors. The symbolic removal of the term 'arbitrator' and its replacement with the neutral term 'members of the tribunal' is part of a wider attempt to address the critiques expressed about institutional bias in investment arbitration.[73]

Considering the above, it has been suggested that the ISDS mechanism in CETA more closely resembles an Investment Court System (ICS) rather than *ad hoc* arbitration.[74] It remains to be seen, however, whether the ICS in CETA is substantially different from the traditional ISDS or if it is more of a system that aims to reassure an unsuspicious audience.[75] In other words, the transition from an *ad hoc* tribunal to the ICS in CETA poses several theoretical and policy questions that need to be further explored.

While the abandonment of the party appointing system is one way through which the pendulum is likely to swing towards an accrued role for States, the ICS could be skewed in favor of respondents.[76] The potential for renewal by States could create a perceived incentive for members of the tribunal to render pro-state awards, or awards in favor of the appointing state party.[77] As Sardinha asks: will the state parties not take into consideration an arbitrator's predispositions to allocate their portions of members to CETA tribunal?[78] Even the perception of a biased system could undermine the authority of the ICS and affect the behavior of foreign investors.[79] In the words of Horodyski, the roster system in CETA is more of a superficial

[72]*ibid.*

[73]Sardinha (2017), p. 633.

[74]*ibid.*. *See generally* Kaufmann and Potesta (2016), pp. 34–41.

[75]Koskenniemi (2017), p. 352.

[76]Waibel (2016), p. 355.

[77]Sardinha (2018), p. 129. Along the same lines, Schwebel asks if it is to be presumed that a member of the panel appointed by a foreign investor is biased in favour of him, is there a reason to presume that adudicators appointed only by States will not be biased in favour of them ? *See* Stephen Schwebel as cited in Lowenfeld (2009), p. 24. According to Article 8.27 (5), fifteen members of the CETA tribunal shall be appointed for a 5-year term, renewable once.

[78]*ibid*, p. 126.

[79]Fontanelli et al. (2016), p. 205.

decoration that is designed to truly solve a problem with impartiality and pressure made by appointing parties on arbitrators.[80] A task force paper regarding the ICS in CETA issued by the European Federation of Investment Law and Arbitration (EFILA) argues that it is expected that the State parties will have regard to the fact that they will be potentially respondents when appointing arbitrators and appoint those who may be considered more likely to be sympathetic to the State's position. It is therefore arguable that the ICS could be weighted in favor of the Respondent.[81]

In a wider context, Rogers explains that the state-controlled appointment mechanisms of a number of international courts and tribunals, including the ICJ, are regarded as essential to keep States continuing to use these venues for their dispute.[82] These control mechanisms allow States to acquire greater influence and, ultimately, to control the composition of the panels. Therefore, bringing the power to appoint arbitrators back to the States is not synonymous with greater procedural fairness.

Supposedly, the IBA Guidelines mentioned in CETA could also be applied in situations where a member of the tribunal is perceived to be biased in favor of a respondent state. Yet, CETA stipulates that 'for greater certainty, the fact that a person receives remuneration from a government does not in itself make that person ineligible.'[83] This provision stands in sharp contrast with the requirement for the members of the CETA tribunal to exercise their judgment in an independent manner. This provision ultimately opens up the door for appointments of adjudicators who might be perceived as biased in favor of States due to their independence by States. It is doubtful whether the contracting parties to CETA aimed to ensure fairness during the arbitral proceedings. With regards to the composition of the tribunal, it appears that rather than establishing a robust and fair mechanism for the appointment of arbitrators the ultimate objective was to reassert state control regardless of the negative consequences that might have.[84]

In contrast with the method of appointment in CETA, scholars have suggested that arbitrators should be appointed by an independent committee of jurists, whose compositions reflect multiple stakeholders (not only States but the private sector, NGOs and academia), in the nomination process.[85] Other scholars further argue that to deal with concerns about institutional bias a pool of potential candidates should be established, who can function as presidents, drawn from those who have not systematically over-represented investors or respondent States in previous

---

[80]Horodyski (2010), p. 16.

[81]EFILA Paper (2015), p. 15; Also *See* Schacherer (2016).

[82]Rogers (2013), p. 245.

[83]CETA, Annexes to CETA note 12.

[84]This section's argument stands in sharp contrast with the assurances given by the EU regarding the remote event that the parties to CETA will 'pack' the roster of arbitrators with pro-state individuals. Sardinha (2018), p. 25.

[85]Howse (2017), p. 225; For a similar proposal *See* Devaney (2019).

disputes.[86] This proposal is based on the hypothesis that the president's crucial functions and influence in a three-member tribunal would substantially alleviate bias.[87]

Ultimately, every method that aspires to bring greater procedural fairness brings forward the famous Latin phrase: *Quis custodiet ipsos custodes?* (Who will guard the guardians themselves?). In other words, even if an independent appointing authority is established to ensure the independence of the members of the tribunal there would always be the question of whether those with the authority to appoint arbitrators are independent and impartial themselves.

From a Rule of Law perspective, it is suggested that a pragmatic way of ensuring greater procedural fairness is by severing the direct link between potential disputing parties and the nominee members of the tribunal. This could be achieved by broadening the scope of participation during the appointment procedure in the roster of the members of the tribunal. Engaging NGOs, academics, and jurists, which have a more neutral position to the dispute, in the appointing procedure, may serve as a correcting mechanism to institutional bias as arbitrators will not be directly dependent on the state parties to receive re-appointment. Granting individual arbitrators tenure of appointment or making arbitrators eligible for appointment only for a single term could combine this method.[88] In this way, arbitrators will not have at the back of their mind the fact that a particular state party will have to sponsor their candidacy for re-appointment in the roster.

The above point out to the existence of a variety of well-thought-out methods to achieve procedural fairness that the parties to CETA have unfortunately ignored. Despite the structural deficiencies of CETA, which could be addressed in their entirety only by means of an amendment, States could choose to appoint adjudicators from a variety of professional backgrounds. Most importantly the parties could appoint individuals with a reputation for neutrality in order to ensure procedural fairness. This could be achieved by wide consultations with all stakeholders.[89] Furthermore, States could appoint the members of a tribunal in a transparent manner, especially during the preparation of the disclosure lists of proposed arbitrators and the process of selection for a particular dispute.[90] This consultative process could potentially reduce time-consuming arbitrators' challenges during the arbitral proceedings.[91] Along the same lines, it was also suggested that the selection criteria of

---

[86]Donaubauer et al. (2018), p. 20.

[87]*ibid.*

[88]Investment Treaty Working Group: Task Force Report on the Investment Court System Proposal (2016), p. 14.

[89]*ibid.* There is no suggestion in the investment chapter of CETA that the appointment of members to the tribunal will be conducted in a transparent manner or whether other stakeholders will be asked to provide their opinion on the suitability of candidates.

[90]This is very similar to the method of appointment adopted by the Court of Justice of the European Union. *See generally* Kuiper (2017).

[91]A recent proposal by the EU Commision about the independence of arbitrators does not permit any optimistic expectations. No reference is made to transparent proceedings or consultations with

the members of the tribunal could be published to enhance the legitimacy of the tribunal in the public eye.[92]

6.3.2 Compensation Scheme

In addition to the appointment of arbitrators' method, the system on the basis of which adjudicators are compensated for their services is also considered a core issue for judicial independence in the institutional design of a dispute settlement mechanism.[93] As a matter of institutional design, tenure of appointment and fixed compensation are seen as important requirements for the purpose of ensuring the Rule of Law. In this context, according to various institutions, such as the Permanent Court of Arbitration (PCA) and UNCTAD, legal fees in investment arbitration disputes have been estimated to amount to 60 and sometimes even 90% of the overall cost.[94] These figures, coupled with the lack of fixed compensation, raise credible concerns regarding the independence of arbitrators from external economic pressures.

Considering this, CETA stipulates that in order to ensure availability, the Members of the Tribunal shall be paid a monthly retainer fee to be determined by the CETA Joint Committee.[95] This retainer fee is later to be converted into a regular salary.[96] Furthermore, members of the tribunal hearing a case will receive fees and expenses reimbursements from the disputing parties in accordance with the Administrative and Financial Regulations of the ICSID Convention, unless the Joint Committee decides otherwise.[97] The Joint Committee will also decide on the compensation regime for the appellate body.[98] This means that CETA leaves key aspects of the compensation arrangements for members of the tribunal for future decisions or adjustments.[99]

In addition to the problems that may result by the open issues highlighted above, the institutional structure of the ICS also raises Rule of Law-related concerns. ICS has a mix system of compensation for the members of the tribunal. Part of the arbitrator's income will come from the state parties through a retainer fee and

other stakeholders. *See* 'Proposal for a Council Decision as regards the adoption of a code of conduct for Members of the Tribunal, the Appellate Tribunal and mediators (2019).

[92]UNCTAD (2018a), p. 9.

[93]Gaukrodger (2017).

[94]UNCTAD (2018b), p. 5.

[95]CETA, Art. 8. 27 (12).

[96]*ibid.*

[97]*ibid.*

[98]*ibid.*

[99]The EU Commision recently proposed security of tenure and a monthly retainer fee for the members of the appellate tribunal. Approval by Council, Member States and Canada is pending. *See* 'Proposal for a Council Decision on matters regarding the functioning of the Appellate Tribunal (2019).

another part of their income comprise of per day fees payable by the disputing parties. This system has the potential to generate multiple problems.

First and foremost, the per day fees by the disputing parties may create incentives for arbitrators to prolong the proceedings and encourage complexity in an effort to increase their income.[100] For example, scholars claim that arbitrators tend to interpret jurisdictional clauses widely and favor the admissibility of claims to sit longer and receive greater remuneration. This is why Article 6 of the European Charter on the Statute for Judges stipulates that the remuneration of judges must be fixed 'so as to shield them from pressures aimed at influencing their decisions' and prevents the impairment of their independence and impartiality.[101] The potential financial leverage over adjudicators by a fee-based compensation scheme is a critical Rule of Law concern. This situation will eventually advantage financially strong disputing parties and disadvantage financially weak parties.

Additionally, the mix compensation structure, in combination with the authority of the state parties to appoint the members of the roster, creates a situation where arbitrators are directly appointed and paid by States. As a consequence, members of the tribunals have an incentive to act in a pro-state manner. This feature should be considered as a gravitational force that pulls away procedural fairness. Most importantly, the analysis in the previous two sections stands in sharp contrast with the opinion of the CJEU regarding CETA's Investment Chapter. According to the CJEU, fixed appointments and the guaranteed remuneration assure the ICS's institutional independence for members of the tribunal.[102] However, the framework adopted by the CJEU to examine whether CETA's ICS is susceptible to external pressures fails to grasp the challenges that may arise as a result of exclusive power of the contracting parties to decide who is going to be appointed in the roster of arbitrators.[103] The question whether this limited understanding of institutional independence was adopted as a result of a conscious choice or by mistake is interesting but, nevertheless, falls outside the scope of this study. Ultimately, CETA's tribunal is not compatible with the requirement of independence, as it is not protected from 'external interventions or pressure liable' that could influence a tribunal's decision.[104]

[100]In domestic legal systems, disputing parties do not pay adjudicators directly. Furthermore, remuneration of adjudicators does not depend on the amount of the fees collected from the disputing parties.

[101]European Statute on the Statute of Judges, Art. 6.

[102]Opinion 1/17 of the CJEU, ECLI:EU:C:2019:341, para. 202.

[103]*ibid*, para. 202.

[104]*ibid*, para. 61.

6.3.3 *Qualification Requirements*

What are also relevant for addressing the concerns regarding an inherent pro-investor bias in investment arbitration are the qualification requirements for the members of the CETA tribunal. Drafting the qualification requirements for CETA tribunal in a way that attracts individuals from all walks of life will arguably make the group better 'cognitively' as it were.[105] Moreover, sociological studies in investment arbitration indicate that diverse tribunals are more likely to avoid collective biases in the context of an investment dispute.[106] Put differently, diversity ensures that a single perspective does not dominate judicial reasoning. Consequently, the selection of the members of the tribunal is of great importance not only for the quality of the awards but also, for what the disputing parties may expect with regard to the substantive outcome of the award. As Gomez argues, 'a homogenous court is not sustainable from the Rule of Law perspective.'[107] Waibel and Wu have opined that it is a possibility that the arbitrators' background, life experience, and ideology may inâuence how they decide cases.[108]

Turning to the text of CETA, a member of the tribunal must 'possess the qualifications required in their respective countries for appointment to judicial office, or be jurists of recognised competence. They shall have demonstrated expertise in public international law.'[109] It is also desirable to have expertise in international investment law and the resolution of disputes arising under international investment.[110] This provision is of significant value taking into consideration that the commercial law background of many arbitrators has led many to argue that it's one of the reasons behind the pro-investor bias of arbitrators.[111] A pluralistic dispute settlement mechanism that is designed in accordance with the Rule of Law favors this variety of types of adjudicators since it helps to counteract a pro-investor bias of commercial arbitrators.[112]

Despite this provision, the state-controlled appointment mechanism in CETA could lead to the opposite results since the State parties could exclusively appoint adjudicators who are specialised in a particular field of law.[113] Furthermore, the text of CETA does not elaborate on what diversity is and, in particular, which different

[105] *See generally* Schultz (2019).

[106] Kidane (2017), p. 145.

[107] Gomez (2018), p. 81. In the same paper it is highlighted that since different arbitrators are from different countries the bias of other judges can mitigate one arbitrator. It is also suggested that arbitrators with homogenous profiles tend to share the same attitudes. On this basis, diversity could serve as a de-biasing agent.

[108] Waibel and Wu (2012), p. 4.

[109] CETA, Art. 8. 27 (4).

[110] *ibid.*

[111] For the relevant statistics *See* Giorgetti (2013a, b), pp. 459–460.

[112] Dimitropoulos (2018), p. 32.

[113] Kaufmann-Kohler and Potesta (2017), pp. 64–65.

aspects of diversity (such as gender, and social and educational background) should be considered.[114] The absence of clear criteria in CETA, on the basis of which competent arbitrators can be chosen, does not help to facilitate the establishment of a broader and more representative roster of arbitrators.[115] In a nutshell, there are very few elements in the design of CETA that require greater diversity.[116]

In summary, despite the bold statements regarding procedural fairness, it is impossible to ignore that the transition from *ad hoc* arbitration to an institutionalised court, and from party-appointed arbitrators to members of a tribunal with quasi-judicial status is not trouble-free. A problematic aspect with regard to the ICS is the fact that investors are deprived of any role in the appointment of the members of the tribunal, while States are granted the exclusive authority to do so. Furthermore, the lack of comprehensive criteria in the design of the CETA tribunal requiring greater diversity is regrettable since a prominent Rule of Law critique is the monothematic commercial background of arbitrators. Last, but not least, the method of financing of the tribunal could raise criticism about a pro-state bias and, subsequently, raise concerns about a lack of institutional independence.

6.4 Conclusion

This chapter attempted to examine whether CETA's Investment Chapter provides a framework that ensures procedural fairness in the context of investment disputes. As explained, the attempt to reform the ISDS mechanism in CETA is an attempt to ensure independence and impartiality of the arbitrators, which are key elements of any system of justice, meant to ensure a fair trial and the Rule of Law. Answering this question, therefore, is of major importance since ensuring independence and impartiality of arbitrators is not only important for the purpose of creating a more level playing field in investment disputes, but also for maintaining the Rule of Law.

---

[114]Article 8. 27 of CETA states that the members of a tribunal will be selected on the basis of their national and, in particular, one from the EU, one from Canada and the presiding member from a neutral state. However, a prominent study by Franck maps the contours of diversity to six factors: (1) gender (2) nationality (3) age (4) linguistic capacity (5) legal training and (6) professional experiences related to arbitration. *See* Franck et al. (2015), p. 440. *See generally* Polonskaya (2018). For example, others have taken a pledge for equal representation in arbitration. *See* Equal Representation in Arbitration. Another example of strong assurances to diversity by an international tribunal is the International Criminal Court. Article 36 (8) of the Rome Statute provides that the State parties shall, in the selection of judges, take into account the need, within the membership of the Court, for the representation of the principal legal systems of the world, equitable geographical representation and a fair representation of female and male judges.

[115]CETA merely stipulates that five of the members of the tribunal must be EU nationals (appointed by the EU), five shall be Canadian nationals (appointed by Canada) and the remaining five must be third-country nationals (appointed by the CETA Joint Committee).

[116]The absence of guidance on diversity in CETA was further noted by Sornarajah. *See* Sornarajah (2016).

In other words, the ultimate goal was to put in place a dispute settlement mechanism that functions in accordance with the concept of the Rule of Law and more closely resembles an institutionalised arbitration court rather than a private law dispute settlement mechanism.

Starting with issues of impartiality, the clear reference to the IBA Guidelines in CETA should be welcomed as a clear contrast to other IIAs that include scattered references to various arbitrators' duties. The fact that the IBA Guidelines have been incorporated into the CETA text means they have the force of regulation rather than serving as 'soft law'. These relatively loose obligations have been creating concerns, including information gaps that permit obvious conflicts to go undetected. Likewise, making arbitrators' duties more visible in combination with a lower threshold for arbitrators' challenges illustrate the willingness of the signatory parties to establish this code of conduct as an essential procedural requirement for fair proceedings. In addition to the above, the lists in the IBA Guidelines that contain several situations that may give rise to justifiable doubts as to the arbitrator's impartiality and/or independence may reduce the incidence of several quantifiable conflicts of interest.

In parallel, the text of CETA constitutes a weapon of combating several systemic deficiencies, such as the well-known 'double-hatting' phenomenon. Despite concerns that the prohibition to engage in any outside occupation will make the appointment to CETA tribunal unattractive for experienced lawyers, this requirement was put in place to ensure arbitrator's actual impartiality. Therefore, from a Rule of Law perspective, this feature opens the way for fairer arbitration proceedings.

However, a dispute settlement system that is based on a strong Rule of Law should not be solely concerned with ensuring impartiality. Rather socio-cultural factors are involved in shaping the Rule of Law, including transforming the cultural norms that underpin investment arbitration. Namely, creating a culture among adjudicators that emphasises institutional independence rather than focusing on keeping investors satisfied to gain repeat business or taking the side of the state parties to receive re-appointment in the roster of arbitrators. Beyond issues of impartiality, therefore, other kinds of adjudicators' incentives are an important consideration for institutional design, desired outcomes, and, ultimately, for the Rule of Law.

As argued in the second part, the roster of members of the tribunal, selected solely by the treaty parties, might raise criticism about a pro-state bias. With regard to greater diversity, the wide discretion of the state parties could threaten the Rule of Law since States could appoint individuals from a particular group. Moreover, the absence of clear criteria for greater diversity in the CETA tribunal does not help towards realising pluralist participation. Lastly, the financial incentives created by litigant fees, as opposed to fixed salaries for the members of the tribunal, raise reasonable doubts as to the independence of the body of arbitrators. As the chapter argues, the ISDS mechanism in CETA is far from being perfect with regard to ensuring institutional independence. Quite paradoxically, such features bring us again to a situation where investment dispute settlement can be perceived as operating in the interest of States and at the detriment of investors. From a historical point of view, therefore, it appears that ghosts of decades past could come back. Those are the ghosts of States' governments having excessive control over tribunals's decisions and key functions.

From a Rule of Law perspective, the parties to CETA would have been better advised to delegate the appointment of the members of the tribunal to an independent body that could deal with the appointment of arbitrators. Another way of ensuring greater procedural fairness is by severing the direct link between potential disputing parties and the nominee members of the tribunal. This can be achieved by broadening the scope of participation during the appointment procedure in the roster of the members of the tribunal. Engaging NGOs, academics, and jurists, which have a more neutral position, to the disputes in the appointing procedure, may serve as a correcting mechanism to institutional bias as arbitrators will not be directly dependent on state parties to receive re-appointment. Another method to be considered is by granting individual arbitrators tenure of appointment. In this way, arbitrators will not be motivated by the need to obtain re-appointment in the roster by States.

In parallel, it would have been preferable to introduce comprehensive criteria to ensure pluralist participation in the roster of the members of the tribunal as well as a fixed salary to ensure institutional independence. Such mechanisms would have significantly contributed to the better functioning of investment arbitration. The absence of mechanisms of this kind raises credible concerns. Ultimately, while, CETA abolishes the party-appointment of adjudicators, completely prohibits 'double-hatting', and lowers the threshold for arbitrators' challenges, the institutional safeguards to ensure institutional independence are not that promising.

In addition to procedural fairness, the last elements of the Rule of Law are transparency and access to justice. The final chapter of the monograph, therefore, will examine the extent to which the parties have achieved greater transparency and access to justice to both disputing and non-disputing parties for the purpose of the arbitral proceedings under CETA's Investment Chapter.

References

Anderson A (2018) Saving private ISDS: the case for hardening ethical guidelines and systematizing conflict checks. Georgetown J Int Law 49(3):1162

Bernasconi-Osterwalder N, Robert D (2014) Investment treaty arbitration: opportunities to reform arbitral rules and processes. The International Institute for Sustainable Development, Winnipeg, p 13

Devaney J (2019) Selecting investment arbitrators: reconciling party autonomy and the international rule of law. KFG Working Papers Series No. 33

Dimitropoulos G (2018) Investor-state dispute settlement: reform and theory of institutional design. J Int Dispute Settlement 9(4):32

Donaubauer J et al (2018) Winning or losing in investor-state dispute resolution: the role of arbitrator bias and experience. Rev Int Econ 26(4):892–916, p. 20

EFILA Paper (2015) Task force paper regarding the proposed International Court System (ICS), p 15

European Commission (2017) Recommendation for a Council Decision authorising the opening of negotiations for a Convention establishing a multilateral court for the settlement of investment disputes
Fach Gomez K (2018) Key duties of international investment arbitrators: a translational study of legal and ethical dilemmas. Springer Publications, New York, p 26
Fernandez Perez A (2018) Conflicts of interests of arbitrators in international law firms. Arbitr Int 34(1):113
Fisher L (1996) The international legal profession: a need for more governance. Am J Int Law 90:250
Fontanelli F et al (2016) Lights and shadows of the WTO-inspired international court system of investor-state dispute settlement. In: European investment law and arbitration review. Brill Publications, Leiden, p 205
Franck S et al (2015) The diversity challenge: exploring the 'invisible college' of international arbitration. Columb J Translational Law 53(429):440
Franck S et al (2017) Inside the arbitrator's mind. Emory Law J 66:5
Gaukrodger D (2017) Adjudicator compensation systems and investor-state dispute settlement. OECD Working Papers, p 11
Gaukrodger D (2018) Appointing authorities and the selection of arbitrators in investor-state dispute settlement: an overview (consultation paper). OECD, Paris
Giorgetti C (2013a) Challenges of international investment arbitrators: how does it work, and does it work? World Arbitr Mediat Rev 7:2
Giorgetti C (2013b) Who decides who decides in international investment arbitration? Univ Pa J Int Law 35(431):459–460
Gomez K (2018) Diversity and the principle of independence and impartiality in the future multilateral investment court. Law Pract Int Courts Tribunals 17:81
Horodyski D (2010) Code of conduct of arbitrators in CETA - a step forward in investment arbitration. Jagiellonian Univ Kraków Rev 2(11):15
Howse R (2017) Designing a multilateral investment court: issues and options. Yearb Eur Law 36 (1):225
Investment Treaty Working Group: Task Force Report on the Investment Court System Proposal (2016) American Bar Association Section on International Law, p 14
Kaufmann G, Potesta M (2016) Can the Mauritius Convention serve as a model for the reform of investor-State arbitration in connection with the introduction of a permanent investment tribunal or an appeal mechanism?Analysis and roadmap. Geneva Center for International Dispute Settlement, pp 34–41
Kaufmann-Kohler G, Potesta M (2017) The composition of a multilateral investment court and of an appeal mechanism for investment awards. CIDS Supplementary Report, pp. 104–105
Kidane W (2017) The culture of international arbitration. Oxford University Press, Oxford, p 145
Koskenniemi M (2017) It's not the cases, it's the system. J World Invest Trade 18(343):352
Kuiper PJ (2017) The court of justice of the European Union. In: Howse R et al (eds) The legitimacy of international trade courts and tribunals. Cambridge University Press, Cambridge
Lowenfeld A (2009) The ICSID convention: origins and transformations. Georgia J Int Comp Law 38:47
Malintoppi L (2008) Independence, impartiality and duty of disclosure of arbitrators. In: Muchlinski P et al (eds) The Oxford handbook of international investment law. Oxford University Press, Oxford
Menon S (2010) International arbitration: the coming of a new age for Asia (and elsewhere). (ICCA Congress. Opening Plenary Session), para. 43. www.arbitration-icca.org/media/0/13398435632250/ags_opening_speech_icca_congress_2012.pdf
Nicole Cleis M (2017) The Independence and impartiality of ICSID arbitrators. Brill Publications, Leiden, p 212
Niedermeyer M (2014) Ethics for arbitrators at the international level: who writes the rules of the game? Am Rev Int Arbitr 25(480):5

Polonskaya K (2018) Diversity in the investor-state arbitration: intersectionality must be a part of the conversation. Melb J Int Law 19:1

Proposal for a Council Decision as regards the adoption of a code of conduct for Members of the Tribunal, the Appellate Tribunal and mediators (2019) Brussels, 11.10.2019 COM

Proposal for a Council Decision on matters regarding the functioning of the Appellate Tribunal (2019) Brussels, 11.10.2019 COM

Puig S (2014) Social capital in the arbitration market. Eur J Int Law 25:2

Rogers C (2013) The politics of international investment arbitrators. Santa Clara J Int Law 12:245

Sand P (2011) Conflicts and conflicts in investment treaty arbitration: ethical Standards for counsel. In: Brown C, Miles K (eds) Evolution in investment treaty law and arbitration. Cambridge University Press, Cambridge

Sardinha E (2017) The new EU-led approach to investor-state arbitration: the investment tribunal system in the Comprehensive Economic Trade Agreement (CETA) and the EU-Vietnam Free Trade Agreement. ICSID Rev 32(3):633

Sardinha E (2018) Party-appointed arbitrators no more: the EU-led investment tribunal system as an (Imperfect) response to certain legitimacy concerns in investor-state arbitration. The Law and Practice of International Courts and Tribunals, p 129

Schacherer S (2016) TPP, CETA and TTIP between innovation and consolidation- resolving investor-state disputes under mega-regionals. J Int Disp Settlement 7:3

Schultz T (2019) The Ethos of arbitration. In: Schultz T, Ortino F (eds) The Oxford handbook of international arbitration. Oxford University Press, Oxford

Sheppard A (2009) Arbitrator independence in ICSID arbitration. In: Binder C et al (eds) International investment law for the 21st century: essays in Honour of Christoph Schreuer. Oxford University Press, Oxford

Simoes D (2018) Hold on to your hat! Issue conflicts in the investment court system. Law Pract Int Courts Tribunals 17:109

Sobota L (2015) Repeat arbitrator appointment in international investment disputes. In: Giorgetti C (ed) Challenges and recusals of judges and arbitrators in international courts and tribunals. Brill Publications, Leiden, p 316

Sornarajah M (2016) An international investment court: panacea or purgatory?. Columbia FDI perspectives: perspectives on topical foreign direct investment issues, No. 180

UNCTAD (2018a) Possible reform of investor-State dispute settlement (ISDS) Arbitrators and decision makers: appointment mechanisms and related issues' A/CN.9/WG.III/WP.152, p 9

UNCTAD (2018b) Possible reform of investor-State dispute settlement (ISDS) — cost and duration', A/CN.9/WG.III/WP.153 (31th August 2018), p 5

Van Harten G (2007) Investment treaty arbitration and public law. Oxford University Press, Oxford

Van Harten G (2012) Arbitrator behaviour in asymmetrical adjudication: an empirical study of investment treaty arbitration. Osgoode Hall Law School 50(1):252

Van Harten G (2016) The European Commission and UNCTAD reform agendas: do they ensure independence, openness, and fairness in investor-state arbitration? In: Hindeland S, Krajewski M (eds) Shifting paradigms in international investment law: more balanced, less isolated, increasingly diversified. Oxford University Press, Oxford

Vasani B, Palmer S (2015) Challenge and disqualification of arbitrators at ICSID: a new dawn? ICSID Rev 30:1

Waibel M (2016) Arbitrator selection-towards greater state control. In: Kulick A (ed) Reassertion of control over the investment treaty regime. Cambridge University Press, Cambridge, p 355

Waibel M, Wu Y (2012) Are arbitrators political? Evidence from international investment arbitration, p 4. www.bcf.usc.edu/~yanhuiwu/arbitrator.pdf

Chapter 7
Transparency and Access to Justice in CETA: Issues and Shortcomings

7.1 Introduction

Both the principle of transparency and access to justice are essential prerequisites for upholding the Rule of Law and ensuring that anyone who is affected by the outcome of a dispute has access to the proceedings. The chapter aims to examine the extent to which the contracting parties have achieved greater transparency and access to justice. In particular, this chapter examines whether the UNCITRAL Transparency Rules and other related provisions constitute a decisive step towards greater transparency as well as elaborating whether the transparency requirements interfere with other considerations, such as confidentiality and procedural fairness. This chapter will further assess whether the parties have confronted the challenges pertaining to the access to justice resulting from the high costs of investment disputes. The chapter finally argues that CETA's provisions on transparency have the potential to ease the tension between the public law nature of investment disputes and the lack of transparency in investment arbitration. The same cannot be argued, however, with respect to access to justice concerns as the parties have missed an important opportunity to confront these pressing issues in investment arbitration. Despite the fact that the high costs of a dispute can be covered by third-party funding, it is argued that this method is not a panacea and, most importantly, it could jeopardise the integrity of the arbitral proceedings.

7.2 Transparency

7.2.1 Preliminary Observations

There is a consensus among scholars and various stakeholders that greater transparency would be achieved by publishing the initiation of arbitral proceedings; a list of

K. Dionysiou, *CETA's Investment Chapter*, European Yearbook of International Economic Law 13, https://doi.org/10.1007/978-3-030-66992-8_7

dispute-related documents (i.e. pleadings, procedural orders, evidence etc.), the submissions by third parties, and the arbitral award.[1] Furthermore, the transparency requirement dictates for open hearings.[2] Accordingly, this section will examine whether information about the arbitral proceedings and dispute-related documents, including the arbitral award, will be made available to the public. This section will also briefly examine whether non-disputing parties have access to the arbitral proceedings. Nonetheless, before proceeding to analyse CETA provisions on transparency, some general remarks will be outlined.

Regardless of an emerging consensus on the scope and content of transparency, there is no general principle in international law to impose transparency in investment treaty arbitration.[3] At the same time, tribunals have been reluctant to publish any dispute-related documents without the previous express consent of the disputing parties.[4] This means that one has to look at the institutional rules of an arbitral venue to examine the way through which greater transparency can be achieved in investment arbitration.

ICSID is arguably the most transparent arbitral venue among those used for investment disputes.[5] In particular, the ICSID Secretariat is under an obligation to publicly register all requests for conciliation and arbitration as well as the names of the disputing parties and the date of registration of the dispute.[6] ICSID secretariat also posts the most recent developments in each investment dispute. At the same time, a several awards rendered under ICSID have been made available to the public. Unless both parties have agreed to keep the decision confidential or unless there is a confidentiality order issued by a tribunal, the ICSID regulations do not prohibit any of the parties from publicising the award.

Despite that ICSID recognises the need for greater transparency, the principles of confidentiality and privacy applied in commercial arbitration are also recognised. For example, the ICSID Convention provides that awards will not be published by the Secretariat without the parties' consent.[7] Additionally, the convention states that a disputing party may object to the tribunal to prevent other persons to attend the

[1]United Nations Commission on International Trade Law (2010), p. 9. The way transparency is understood across different legal systems is not the same. However, a comparative study suggests that open hearings and access to dispute-related documents are key aspects of this notion. *See* Asteriti and Tams (2010) and UNCTAD (2012).

[2]*See generally* Szilagyi (2017).

[3]*See generally* Maupin (2013).

[4]Brabandere (2014), pp. 155–159.

[5]For a comparative study *See* Delaney and Magraw (2008).

[6]ICSID Administrative and Financial Regulations, Regulation 22 and 23. It is interesting to note that this regulation was adopted because of the 'public nature of the institution'. *See* Parra (2012), p. 104.

[7]ICSID Convention, Art. 48 (5). An OECD finds that approximately 50% of the cases obtain consent from the disputing parties in order to be published. Furthermore, the disputing parties take several months to send their consent to ICSID to publish the award. *See generally* OECD (2005).

hearings of a dispute.[8] Although tribunals have certain inherent powers with respect to the way arbitral proceedings are conducted, they are not authorised to exercise such powers in opposition to a clear directive in the rules governing the arbitration proceedings.[9] This means that regardless of the growing consent that investment disputes are of public interest, the final say over what is published remains with the disputing parties.

Even NAFTA, which is considered a progressive treaty with regard to transparency, allows investors to bring their claims under various institutional rules that provide diverging, if any, rules on transparency.[10] Even though the NAFTA Trade Commission issued a number of recommendations and guidelines regarding open hearings and third-party submissions, it ultimately falls within the discretion of a tribunal whether to accept these recommendations.[11] As Shirlow argues, treaties and institutional rules prior to the UNCITRAL Convention failed to provide strong assurances about transparency, leaving the disputing parties the discretion to decide on issues of transparency.[12] It is this realisation that forced the parties to CETA to include an explicit reference to the UNCITRAL Convention on Transparency.[13] Consequently, the following section will assess whether CETA's provisions are robust enough to ensure greater transparency.

7.2.2 UNCITRAL Transparency Rules and Other Related Provisions

As illustrated in the second chapter, the old generation of IIAs do not address transparency in investment arbitration, let alone make it compulsory. As a response to this situation, article 8.36 of the investment chapter in CETA stipulates that UNCITRAL Transparency Rules ('rules') shall apply in investment disputes. These rules form the basis on which the contracting parties have attempted to secure transparency in investment arbitration. In general, the rules ensure the public release of information and dispute-related documents as well as the ability of third parties to intervene in the arbitral proceedings. As will be argued, strong transparency provisions in CETA constitute a meaningful opportunity to promote the Rule of Law in investment arbitration.

---

[8]ICSID Convention, Rule 32 (2).

[9]*Suez, Sociedad General de Aguas de Barcelona, S.A.and Vivendi Universal, S.A. v. Argentine Republic, ICSID Case No. ARB/03/19*, Order in Response to a Petition for Transparency and Participation as Amicus Curiae, para.7.

[10]NAFTA, Chapter 5.

[11]Maupin (2013), pp. 21–26.

[12]Shirlow (2016), p. 626.

[13]For an overview of the debates in the EU regarding transparency *See* Calamita (2014); Jemielniak and Unuvar (2016), No. 75.

First and foremost, the express reference to the rules in CETA means that they cannot be waived by the tribunal or by the disputing parties. It could be argued, therefore, that the rules shift the decision-making power on matters of transparency away from the disputing parties and, thus, inject a Rule of Law principle into arbitral decision-making.[14] The simplest and most fundamental form of transparency requires that basic information about a dispute should be made available at the commencement of the arbitral proceedings.[15] Turning to the substantive provisions of the rules, it is stated that once the respondent has received the notice of arbitration, the repository shall make available to the public, information regarding the name of the disputing parties and the economic sector involved.[16] This information is of paramount importance as it allows third parties to become aware of the existence of a dispute.[17]

Furthermore, the rules state that a list of case documents shall be made public, including the statement of claim and defense, the written submissions by the disputing parties, any written submission by the non-disputing party, and any orders, decisions, and awards of the arbitral tribunal.[18] CETA text also states that the request for consultation, the notice requesting a determination of the respondent and the notice of determination, and the notice of intent to challenge a member of the tribunal and the decision on the challenge shall be made available to the public.[19] Exhibits shall be included in the list of documents to be made available to the public.[20] In essence, this provision provides that a number of documents should always be published. Taking into consideration that a few arbitration rules are silent on this, the rules constitute a bold step towards greater transparency and signify a departure from what existed so far with regard to publicly available dispute-related documents.[21]

Moreover, hearings for the presentation of evidence or for oral arguments shall be public.[22] The tribunal shall make logistical arrangements to facilitate the public access to hearings, including organising attendance through video link.[23] CETA

---

[14]In a seminal paper it is argued that despite various attempts to promote greater transparency, there are a few loopholes in place permitting secrecy in investment disputes. The paper concludes with a suggestion that greater transparency will be achieved with explicit provisions requiring the mandatory disclosure of arbitral awards and documents and/or information. *See* Hafner-Burton and Victor (2016).

[15]NGOs advocate in favor of the publication of information related to disputes. *See generally* Bernasconi and Johnson (2011).

[16]UNCITRAL Rules, Art. 2.

[17]Bianco (2015), p. 89.

[18]UNCITRAL Rules. Art. 3 (1).

[19]CETA, Art. 8.36 (2).

[20]*ibid*, Art. 8. 36 (3).

[21]Kee (2015), p. 92.

[22]UNCITRAL, Art. 6 (1). Under various sets of procedural rules, arbitral proceedings are confidential unless the parties agree to waive confidentiality (AAA, ICC, LCIA, SCC, etc.).

[23]*ibid*. Art. 6 (2).

text reaffirms that a hearing shall be open to the public. Thus, a disputing party may not object to open hearings.[24] Together with the publication of documents, open hearings represent a bold step towards greater transparency in investment arbitration.[25]

In addition to the benefits of transparency, bringing greater transparency in investment arbitration is not without its critics due to concerns that confidential and/or private information might be disclosed.[26] As argued by Feldman, confidentiality is an essential element not only of commercial arbitration, but also investment arbitration. The inclusion of provisions on public access to documents and hearings in international investment treaties consistently has been accompanied by safeguards to protect confidential business information.[27] In view of these concerns, in the context of the UN discussions on transparency and investment arbitration, it was pointed out that not all documents need to be published.[28] In other words, the public's right to know and the disputing parties' expectations of privacy calls for a middle ground between transparency and confidentiality.

Without a balance between these two competing considerations, investment arbitration can no longer be considered as a viable dispute settlement method and subsequently the parties will be deterred from using it. Consequently, the inclusion of certain limitations to transparency seems not only desirable but a necessity to strike a balance between the interests of the disputing parties to keep certain information away from the public eye and the need for greater openness. As Feliciano argues, confidentiality and transparency are sometimes competing values which need to be accommodated and adjusted to the other in each specific case.[29]

The tribunal reasoning in *Biwater* with respect to the right balance between confidentiality and transparency provides us with an authoritative foundational benchmark that can be utilized to examine CETA's transparency provisions.[30] In this case, the tribunal emphasised the significance of the public interest in the dispute and therefore determined that any restriction on greater transparency should be narrowly delimited.[31] For this purpose, the tribunal differentiated certain types of documents and information to assess the permissibility of their publication.[32] In addition to confidential information, it was held that correspondence between the disputing parties' counsels and any other document that may undermine these information should be exempted from public disclosure.[33] Finally, the tribunal called

[24]CETA, Art. 8.36 (5).

[25]Alexander (2015), p. 247.

[26]Mollestad (2014), p. 14.

[27]Feldman (2016), p. 16.

[28]UN (2010), pp. 11–12.

[29]Feliciano as cited in Lam and Unuvar (2019), p. 10.

[30]Knahr and Reinisch (2007), p. 103.

[31]*ibid*, p. 107.

[32]*ibid.*

[33]*ibid.*

the parties to refrain from any actions that might undermine the integrity of the arbitral proceedings.[34]

Consistent with *Biwater*, the rules provide that hearings are open to the public unless there is a need to protect the integrity of the process or to safeguard confidential information.[35] Protected information consist of confidential business information and any other information that is protected against being made available to the public.[36] To counter the disputing parties' concerns, therefore, both the disclosure of documents and open hearings are subject to limitations when it comes to keeping confidential information protected.[37]

Furthermore, the rules and CETA's text states that if the tribunal determines that there is a need to protect confidential or protected information, the tribunal shall make the appropriate arrangements to hold in private that part of the hearing requiring such protection.[38] CETA further states that a respondent state may communicate to the public, information it is required to disclose by its laws (i.e. expenses, outcome etc.), but that it must do 'in a manner sensitive to protecting from disclosure that has been designated as confidential or protected information.'[39] With regard to documents and/or information, the rules state that the tribunal, 'after consultation with the disputing parties, shall make arrangements from any confidential or protected information from being made available to the public.'[40] These arrangements include, among others, time limits, and prompt designation and redaction of the confidential documents.[41] This provision introduces a relatively new obligation that ultimately protects sensitive information in situations where a disputing party is obliged to share such information with another entity.[42]

Despite its merits, it has been argued that the confidentiality exception could 'allow a state to substantially backtrack from transparency through the device of domestic law'.[43] In the context of the UN discussion on transparency and investment arbitration, it was argued that such exception could ultimately weaken the rules on transparency.[44] However, the rules include robust safeguards for this contingency. In particular, the rules provide to tribunals the exclusive power to decide which information should be excluded from disclosure on the basis of its confidential nature. This provision will ultimately protect the *Biwater* compromise by preventing

[34] *ibid*, p. 104.
[35] UNCITRAL Rules, Art. 6 (2).
[36] *ibid*, Art. 7 (2).
[37] CETA. Art. 8.36 (4-5).
[38] *ibid*, Art. 8.36 (4-5).
[39] CETA, Art. 8. 36 (6).
[40] UNCITRAL Rules, Art. 7 (3).
[41] *ibid*, Art. 7 (3).
[42] CETA, Art. 36 (6).
[43] Investment Treaty Working Group of the International Arbitration Committee (2016), p. 116.
[44] UN (2010), p. 17.

a disputing party from unilaterally abusing the confidentiality exception by keeping vital information away from the public eye.

In a situation where a disputing party genuinely believes that a tribunal does not sufficiently protect sensitive information, article 7 (4) of the rules allows that party to withdraw from the proceeding such document and/or information. Although article 7 (4) may undermine the balance between confidentiality and transparency, in a situation where this provision is invoked the invoking party can no longer rely on that information in the dispute.[45] The rules, therefore, build on the understanding that a disputing party may protect confidential and/or sensitive information by means of article 7(4) but, nevertheless, this action automatically takes away the possibility to use such information in the dispute.

Taking into consideration the above assesment, the chapter argues that CETA's Investment Chapter strikes the right balance between confidentiality and transparency. Despite the fact that the rules reversed the presumption for confidentiality in investment disputes over openness, provisions have been included restricting and regulating transparency in order to protect other considerations. Therefore, CETA's Investment Chapter strike a balance between the different interests at stake and successfully level the playing field between investors and host States and contribute to increasing the legitimacy of investment arbitration.[46]

In order to further level the playing field, greater transparency is expected to address the information asymmetries between disputing parties, which have been caused by closed proceedings and the lack of access to dispute-related documents. Greater transparency is also anticipated to promote more accurate and thorough decisions by arbitration as improper behavior will be discouraged. An empirical study suggests that a higher rate of publication of documents may prompt the development of systems of precedent that was suppressed by confidentiality.[47] Consequently, making other tribunals aware of other tribunals' decisions is expected to promote consistency and, ultimately, enabling both host States and foreign investors to assess their obligations, rights and legal liabilities. These expectations highlight the fact that the different elements of the Rule of Law are interdependent and, ultimately, reinforce one another.

7.2.3 Amicus Curiae *Briefs*

The extent to which third parties and non-disputing parties can effectively intervene in investment disputes under CETA was previously explored. As discussed in detail in Chap. 5, under certain conditions *amicus curiae* briefs may have a positive effect

---

[45] Augsburger (2015), p. 284.

[46] Scherer et al. (2015), p. 3. *See generally* De Chazournes and Rukia (2015).

[47] *See* Ruscall (2015), pp. 4–5.

on human rights protection in investment disputes.[48] However, the question of whether these parties have access to the arbitral proceedings is very much linked to the question of greater transparency. *Amicus curiae* briefs are not only important with respect to greater human rights protection. *Amicus curiae* briefs have been admitted, along with open hearings and access to dispute-related documents, to the effort of securing transparency in investment disputes. This section will briefly examine whether the access given to third parties and non-disputing in arbitral proceedings under CETA will enhance transparency.

Starting with, the rules state that after consultation with the disputing parties, the tribunal may allow a third person and a non-disputing party to file a written submission regarding a matter that falls within the scope of the dispute.[49] Whoever has a significant interest in a dispute can follow the arbitral proceedings and their view may be considered through *amicus curiae* brief.[50] It is also worth noting that the rules do not require the consent of the parties. According to some scholars, mechanisms of this kind constitute an effective tool to ensure public access to the proceedings and, subsequently, enhance transparency in international dispute settlement.[51] The reasoning behind such assertion stems from the fact that such mechanism allows non-disputing and third party to attend hearings and access dispute-related documents. The right to access documents improves the quality of the third-party intervention, while public participation provides credibility as it reduces the sense that proceedings are secretive.

The benefits created by *amicus curiae* briefs, nonetheless, have to be weighed against the burden or negative consequences such additional procedural requirements may have on a dispute. As article 7 stipulates, the tribunal may take appropriate measures 'to restrain or delay the publication of information where such publication would jeopardise the integrity of the arbitral process.'[52] In the same manner, Article 4 states that 'the arbitral tribunal shall ensure that any submission does not disrupt or unduly burden the arbitral proceedings, or unfairly prejudice any disputing party.'[53]

With regard to the latter, a primary concern regarding such submissions is that they could significantly add to the overall cost and/or time of conclusion of the proceedings. The concerns regarding delayed proceedings are directly related to the objective of minimising costs. In a system that is preferred over domestic proceedings, mostly because of its efficiency, any additional procedural requirements that may delay proceedings or make them more expensive should be carefully

[48] *ibid.*

[49] UNCITRAL Rules, Art. 4 (1b). In order to prevent conflicts of interest, the rules require the submitting party to disclose any connection, direct or indirect, which the third person has with any disputing party.

[50] UNCITRAL, Art. 4 (3a).

[51] Boisson de Chazournes (2004), p. 333.

[52] *ibid.* Art. 7 (7).

[53] *ibid,* Art. 4 (5).

observed. Such occasion occurred in the context of the WTO and, in particular, in *Measures Affecting Trade in Large Civil Aircraft* where the appellate body raised its concerns with respect to the time needed and the substantial workload for accommodating additional procedures.[54] The appellate body finally declared that it would not be able to circulate its report within the prescribed deadline due to the additional procedural burden.[55]

As a result of this, the tribunal should have these concerns in mind when laying out the conditions on the basis of which a third-party should submit its views. In order to mitigate this risk, a tribunal could set various limits, such as requiring succinct submissions and putting page limits.[56] Ultimately, the benefits of greater transparency should be weighted against any additional burden imposed by transparency on the arbitral proceedings.[57]

Another argument against *amicus curiae* briefs is that they risk prejudicing the arbitral proceedings since such briefs will most likely oppose an argument provided by one or both the disputing parties[58] In a similar vein, there is a fear that a home state may choose to intervene in a dispute through an *amicus* brief to support its nationals.[59] However, this argument does not justify the total rejections of *amicus* submission. It is unavoidable that such an intervention will attempt to direct a tribunal towards a particular outcome. Simply put the main objective of these submission is to inflcune the tribunal one way or another, but ultimately the impact of these submission is determined by the way the tribunal manages and interprets these submission.

The tribunal in *Pezold* case, dealing with concerns over the lack of independence of a third-party, held that despite the fact that a third-party's argument opposed the claimant's primary position in the proceedings there was no conflict of interest.[60] In other words, a situation where one of the disputing parties faces multiple opponents is not synonymous with prejudiced proceedings. Ultimately, a disputing party is free to respond to an *amicus curiae* submission.

In support of procedural fairness, the rules further state that in determining whether to allow a submission by a non-disputing party a tribunal should take into consideration 'the need to avoid submissions which would support the claim of the

---

[54] *European Communities and Certain Member States—Measures Affecting Trade in Large Civil Aircraft*, WT/DS316/40/Rev.1.

[55] *ibid.*

[56] A prominent example is the *Piero Foresti* case, where the tribunal had to balance competing interests, such as fairness and efficiency. *Piero Foresti, Laura de Carli & Others v. The Republic of South Africa,* ICSID Case No. ARB(AF)/07/01, Letter from the Secretary of the Tribunal.

[57] Art. 5 of the UNCITRAL Rules state that a tribunal shall ensure that the disputing parties are given a *reasonable* opportunity to present their observations.

[58] *See generally* Gomez (2012), pp. 551–553.

[59] Paparinskis and Howley (2015), p. 216.

[60] *Bernhard von Pezold and Others v. Republic of Zimbabwe,* ICSID Case No. ARB/10/15, Procedural Order No. 2, para. 50–53.

investor in a manner tantamount to diplomatic protection.'[61] In order to avoid 'trial by media' or any other situation that might jeopardise trust and confidence between the parties, the rules state that a tribunal may restrain or delay the publication of information where such publication would jeopardise the integrity of the arbitral process.[62] Tribunals can utilise these provisions in order to balance the transparency requirements with other considerations, such as procedural fairness.

In any case, making more information available to the public does not mean that *amicus curiae* will substantially interact in a dispute as a result of the accessible information generated. As argued by Shirlow and Caron, effective participation renders transparency meaningful with respect to *amicus curiae* briefs.[63] For example, if third parties are not able to engage with these information, in a way that will allow them to achieve their purpose, the attempt to hold the tribunals accountable through greater transparency is undermined. Regretfully, as argued in Chap. 5, these kinds of interventions are destined to have a supplementary role in investment disputes.

Despite this, the analysis undertaken in this chapter ultimately supports the notion that CETA's provisions constitute a positive development in this area as the parties have included robust and binding rules on transparency. The parties also included provisions to strike a balance between openness and confidentiality. Furthermore, the provisions governing *amicus curiae* briefs promote greater transparency as they provide to third parties the right to access dispute-related documents as well as the option to attend hearings. It is further argued that tribunals have several tools to confront the negative impact *amicus curiae* briefs may have on efficiency and procedural fairness. Setting time and content limits as well as conditioning these interventions can be used to minimize these negative side effects.

As argued in this section, the need for greater openness underscores the critical role transparency has in keeping investment tribunals under constant scrutiny. However, accessing case documents and attending hearings is one aspect of the Rule of Law. The disputing parties should also be able to afford to initiate proceedings or respond to a claim. Both the principle of transparency and access to justice are integral to the Rule of Law and necessary prerequisites to ensure that anyone who is affected by the outcome of a dispute has access to the proceedings. In

[61]UNCITRAL Rules, Art. 5 (2).

[62]*ibid*, Art. 7 (7). These circumstances include situations where publication of documents could hamper the collection or production of evidence or where such publication could lead to the intimidation of witnesses. Additionally, in *Biwater* case, the tribunal listed the following issues as failing into the scope of the integrity of the arbitral process: (1) preserve the Tribunal's mission and mandate to determine finally the issues between the parties (2) preserve the proper functioning of the dispute settlement procedure (3) preserve and promote a relationship of trust and confidence between the parties (4) ensure the orderly unfolding of the arbitration process (5) ensure a level playing field (6) minimise the scope for any external pressure on any party, witness, expert or other participant in the process (7) avoid "trial by media". *Biwater Gauff (Tanzania) Ltd. v. United Republic of Tanzania, ICSID Case No. ARB/05/22,* Procedural order No. 3, para. 135.

[63]Shirlow and Caron (2020), p. 6.

other words, the practical ability to initiate a claim or defend one renders greater transparency meaningful. Protecting the Rule of Law in investment arbitration, therefore, would not be realistic without the minimum assurances that every disputing party has the financial means to access this mechanism. This important aspect will be discussed in the next section.

7.3 Access to Justice

7.3.1 Costs and Fees

Access to justice dictates that disputing parties should have the financial resources or the ability to acquire such resources needed to bring a claim or defend one. Without such assurances, the benefits of greater transparency will not only be undermined but also the attempt to reconstruct investment arbitration in accordance with the Rule of Law will be jeopardized. Taking this Rule of Law requirement into account, a major concern that has risen during the last decade with regard to investment arbitration is the high litigation costs associated with investment disputes. The high costs of arbitral proceedings are sometimes difficult to justify for financially weak States as they pose a heavy burden. Certain investors may also struggle to meet the resources required to initiate a claim. Consequently, the high costs associated with investment disputes may put an obstacle to financially weak parties to access this mechanism.

Arbitration costs are divided into party costs (fees and expenses of counsel, experts, and witnesses) and tribunal costs (fees and expenses of arbitrators). A recent study finds that the average party costs exceed six million USD for the claimant and approximately five million USD for the respondent state, while the average tribunal costs could reach up to one million USD.[64] Attempting to reduce the length of arbitration proceedings and litigation costs of investment disputes form part of a wider attempt to address access to justice concerns. As a result of the Rule of Law concerns associated with the significant costs of investment disputes, this section examines to what extent CETA addresses excessive costs.[65]

The litigation costs are mostly related to the manner in which the arbitral proceedings are conducted and, in particular, by the length of proceedings. In other words, the longer the arbitral proceedings, the higher the costs. According to a report, the three most time-intensive stages are (1) the appointment of the tribunal (2) the disclosure, discovery or document production and (3) the issuance of the award and, in particular, the period between the final hearing and the rendering of the

[64]Hodgson and Campbell (2017).

[65]Enhancing efficiency and promoting lower costs are directly related to decisions on the costs of arbitration. However, this section is not concerned with the debate regarding the different methods a tribunal could use to allocate costs to the disputing parties (unadjusted costs order, fully or partially adjusted costs orders etc.). The focus of this section is the total amount of costs and the barriers they create in accessing justice. *See generally* Zivkovic (2018).

award.[66] In the same report, it is highlighted that the average duration of arbitrations exceeds 3 years, while the duration to issue awards after the final hearing is more or less a year.[67] It is also worth noting that the average duration of an investment dispute is comparatively higher than the duration of a dispute in the ICJ or in the WTO.[68]

Therefore, measures aiming to reduce the arbitral proceedings length and/or the litigators' workload can help to address access to justice concerns since they reduce the overall costs of a dispute. The possibility to introduce page or content limits that was discussed in the previous section could play a role in reducing costs. Along the same line, the judicial precedent that will be created, as a result of the introduction of an appellate mechanism, is expected to reduce the time it takes for the parties to prepare a case since many issues will not be unsettled.[69]

Still, the above measures are not enough to deal with high litigation costs. Taking into consideration that time is a key variable to predict costs, if not the only reliable one,[70] the promotion of dispute prevention policies,[71] the development of streamlined and simplified procedures as well as obligatory provisions for case management conferences could have been used to reduce costs.[72] Lower costs could have been realised with a fixed budget coupled with a schedule of fees and a ceiling for overall costs. As Howse rightly points out, capping costs awards for counsel fees act as a counter-incentive to law firms that might attempt to increase the length of proceedings to obtain higher chargeables.[73] Overall, the lack of timetables, time limits, clear procedures, and the absence of provisions in CETA encouraging the use of modern technology may result in unnecessary delays and costs.[74] Such measures could have also addressed the concerns that arbitrations costs are arbitrary and unpredictable.[75]

As a way to remedy high costs, Franck suggests that greater transparency and guidance with respect to costs is necessary.[76] In the absence of greater guidance and transparency the disputing parties are unable 'to appreciate the costs and benefits of their dispute resolution strategy and prevent the loss of valuable settlement

[66]Hodgson and Campbell (2017), p. 6.

[67]*ibid*, p. 12.

[68]*ibid*, pp. 14–15.

[69]United Nations Commision on International Trade Law (2018), p. 16.

[70]Franck (2019), p. 291.

[71]The EU Commision recently proposed the adoption of rules for mediation. Approval by Council, Member States and Canada is pending. *See* 'Proposal for a Council Decision as regards the adoption of rules for mediation for use by disputing parties in investment disputes (2019).

[72]*ibid*, p. 318.

[73]Howse (2017), p. 231.

[74]Scholars argue that while it is the duty of arbitrators to reduce time and costs, IIAs don't usually include any detailed rules regarding this obligation. *See generally* Mohebbi and Asgharian (2018).

[75]Franck (2019), p. 118.

[76]*ibid*, p. 303.

opportunities.'[77] Furthermore, if the members of a tribunal are aware that their decision on costs will be subject to review, this creates an incentive to be more precise and careful with such decisions.[78] Another problematic aspect of CETA with regard to high litigation costs is the absence of any provision obliging the tribunal to make public any document relating to the method used and the factors that were taken into consideration to assess costs.

Additionally, article 8 of CETA's Investment Chapter does not specify the amount to be paid to members of the tribunal, leaving this to the Joint Committee. A tribunal, therefore, will not have any guidance to decide which amount of costs is 'excessive' and which is 'necessary' as CETA provisions lack clarity on this matter. The only relevant provision on costs states that an unsuccessful party shall pay only 'reasonable costs',[79] while the Joint Committee 'shall consider supplemental rules aimed at reducing the financial burden on claimants who are natural persons or small and medium-sized enterprises. Such supplementary rules may, in particular, take into account the financial resources of such claimants and the amount of compensation sought.'[80]

That said, taking into consideration that approximately 80% of the total costs of a dispute consist of party costs (fees for counsel and legal representation, and for experts),[81] it is doubtful whether the costs of CETA's disputes will be significantly lower. Lenk argues that CETA's Investment Chapter attempts to achieve a better allocation and reduction of costs, which ultimately benefits respondent States.[82] The author makes this argument in light of the Joint's Committee capacity to cap the maximum amount for costs through supplementary rules, and because the financial resources on finding an appropriate arbitrator do not accrue in a system where arbitrators are not party-appointed.[83] However, even if one accepts that the Joint Committee will cap party costs, the drafters of CETA failed to address a key factor behind high costs, which is the length of the arbitral proceedings. Despite Lenk's argument, this chapter still maintains that CETA's provisions do not address in a satisfactory manner the high costs associated with investment disputes. In the view of the study, this is regrettable given the unique platform given to address this Rule of Law issue in investment arbitration.

[77] *ibid*, p. 304.

[78] *ibid*.

[79] CETA, Art. 8. 27 (5).

[80] *ibid*, Art. 8. 39 (6).

[81] Franck (2019), p. 5.

[82] Lenk (2019), p. 252.

[83] *ibid*, p. 253.

7.3.2 Third-Party Funding

Scenarios where disputing parties lack sufficient resources to bring a claim or defend the claim are very common in real life. The implications of such a situation are very well documented. As Nash argues, 'if neither party has adequate funding, the litigation will not happen. If only one party has adequate funding, the litigation will be a walkover and cost is a critical element in access to justice.'[84] Ensuring adequate funding for litigants is considered a way to promote access to justice.[85] With regard to investment arbitration, a usual method the disputing parties use to address this contingency is Third-Party Funding ('TPF'). TPF is a method through which another entity, natural or legal, which has no pre-existing interest in the arbitration, agrees to fund one disputing party's legal fees or other costs in return for remuneration should that party win the dispute.[86]

In addition to remuneration, a TPF provider will usually require some degree of control over the case. Therefore, a TPF arrangement is not an unconditional agreement to fund a dispute, while ongoing funding will depend on the merits of the case and upon the degree of compliance with the terms of the agreement.[87] Provisions giving to funders some degree of control are usually included in TPF agreements since if a funded party loses the arbitration, the TPF funder is usually expected to bear the expenses of the proceedings.[88] This section argues that TPF has a positive effect on international arbitration, as it may allow meritorious claims to proceed and simultaneously improve access to justice. Subsequently, this section discusses potential detrimental effects of TPF and then examines how the contracting parties have addressed these contingencies.

As already noted, TPF can provide the resources to financially weak parties to pursue arbitral proceedings that would otherwise have been impossible. In that sense, TPF is a way to provide access to justice. Nonetheless, TPF has attracted significant attention in scholarly writing since the profit potential of this method has made it a lucrative market. The business interests associated with TPF raised concerns that they might negatively affect the integrity of the arbitral proceedings.[89] It has been noted that TPF companies may direct the professional judgment of litigators of a dispute to protect their investment.[90] For example, there could be a situation where a funding arrangement was put in place as a result of the client's attorney suggestion. On that occasion, the client's attorney might find it difficult to serve his client as he best sees fit in situations where the TPF provider, from which

[84]Nash (2013), p. 98.

[85]*ibid.*

[86]*See generally* Van Boom (2011).

[87]*ibid.* p. 27.

[88]*ibid,* p. 26.

[89]There are also concerns that TPF commercialises investment arbitration and, subsequently, leads to frivolous claims. This criticism has been discussed in ch. 4 section 4 3 B (2).

[90]ICCA-Queen Mary Task Force (2018), p. 224.

the litigator rely financially, has a different opinion about the management of the case.[91]

Furthermore, a disputing party's communication with the financier—for the purpose of monitoring the investment made by the latter—may break the client-attorney privilege.[92] Critics further argue 'that TPF distorts the balance of incentives of traditional dispute settlement resolution towards speculative gain in the place of justice and the orderly settlement of disputes.'[93] This criticism, in combination with the notion that ISDS works in favor of a privileged class of investors and at the detriment of States and local populations, raise credible concerns about institutional bias.

As a result of the above concerns, CETA imposed an obligation on disputing parties to disclose if they are benefiting from third-party funding, both at the time of a claim, as well as during the duration of the dispute.[94] Additionally, the same provisions oblige the benefiting party to disclose the name and address of the funder.[95] Greater transparency with regard to TPF will assist both the tribunals and the disputing parties to assess whether there are any issues of fairness that may arise as a result of a funding facility. Disclosing the existence of a TPF facility and the identity of its provider is essential for arbitrators to make the necessary disclosures and, subsequently, assess whether there is a potential conflict of interests.

In the same manner, the IBA Guidelines state that 'when considering the relevance of facts or circumstances to determine whether a potential conflict of interest exists, or whether disclosure should be made'[96] a tribunal should take into consideration whether a disputing party sought TPF.[97] Therefore, in a situation where a conflict of interest exists the other disputing party can apply for a disqualification procedure, or even annulment of the award, even if a potential conflict of interest became known after the award was rendered. In a nutshell, the duty to disclose a TPF facility was put in place in order to avoid conflicts of interest and potential challenges of arbitral awards.

Nevertheless, the mere duty to disclose the identity of the TPF provider is not enough to enable the relevant bodies to assess whether an accusation of conflict of interest should be accepted.[98] Neither the text of CETA, nor the IBA Guidelines, proposes any specialised rules about how potential conflicts of interests between

[91]Commentators argue that TPF facilities pose risks to the integrity of the arbitral proceedings through excessive control of the dispute since 'the funded party becomes a proxy for the funder's interests'. *See* Chan (2015), p. 308.

[92]Steinitz (2011), p. 1324.

[93]Garcia (2018), p. 2912.

[94]CETA, Art. 8. 26 (1). The same obligation exists in the General Standard 7 of the IBA Guidelines.

[95]*ibid,* Art. 8. 26 (1).

[96]IBA Guidelines, General Standard 6 (1).

[97]*ibid,* Explanation to General Standard 6 (b).

[98]There are no known investment disputes where an arbitrator was disqualified or an award challenged based on conflicts of interests involving a TPF facility.

TPF providers and arbitrators should be analysed, or when a conflict of interests should lead to disqualification. Moreover, neither of these instruments oblige a party to disclose the terms of the funding arrangement, thus leaving critical aspects of the TPF agreement unknown for the purpose of assessing whether a conflict of interest exists. Despite that a disclosure order can be made by an individual tribunal,[99] it would have been preferable to include concrete provisions in the text of CETA as it falls within the discretion of tribunal to request this information.[100]

In order to address these concerns, a number of scholars argue that some of the protections and duties of the attorney-client relationship should be expanded to TPF providers.[101] Similarly, the ICCA-Queen Mary Task Force has developed a disclosure-based regime with conflict of interest rules for third party funding. The relevant rules adopted by the Task Force stipulate, among others, that a tribunal 'should assess whether any potential conflicts of interest exist between an arbitrator and a third-party funder, and assess the need to make appropriate disclosures or take other appropriate actions that may be required'.[102] In this spirit, Hong Kong enacted a code of practice that prohibits Third-Party funders 'to influence the funded party or the funded party's representative to give control or conduct of the arbitration to the third-party funder.'[103]

In addition to the conflict of interest rules, it has been suggested that if the TPF provider is considered a fiduciary of the client, the former will have to take into consideration whether non-monetary remedies better serve the interests of the client.[104] In such a situation, a TPF provider will have to take into consideration the client's interests and not only their own. Last, but not least, it has been suggested that obliging both attorneys and TPF providers to fully disclose to each other arrangements made with their clients will strengthen the integrity of the arbitral proceedings.[105] Eventually, the above will help to reduce conflict of interests between litigators and TPF providers, protect the client's ability to communicate information to both its attorneys and TPF providers, and enhance the client's control over the dispute.

To conclude, the contracting parties in CETA have missed a great opportunity to comprehensively confront the pressing challenges associated with access to justice. Further measures could have been adopted in order to reduce costs, including

[99]For examples *See Muhammet Çap & Sehil In_aat Endustri ve Ticaret Ltd. Sti. v. Turkmenistan*, ICSID Case No. ARB/12/6; *EuroGas Inc. and Belmont Resources Inc. v. Slovak Republic*, ICSID Case No. ARB/14/14.

[100]In contrast to CETA, there are treaties where the third-party funding arrangements and the funder's interests in the dispute should be disclosed. *See* IBA Arbitration SubCommittee on Investment Treaty Arbitration (2018), pp. 63–64.

[101]Steinitz (2011), p. 1328; UNCTAD (2019).

[102]Report of the ICCA-Queen Mary Task Force on Third-Party Funding in International Arbitration (2018), p. 14.

[103]Brekoulakis and Rogers (2019), p. 3.

[104]Steinitz (2011), p. 1328.

[105]*ibid.*

provisions on simplified procedures, case management conferences, and obliging tribunal to set a fixed budget and a ceiling for overall costs. With regard to TPF, it is argued that although this method may enhance access to justice for financially weak parties, it could also have some unwanted consequences, such as jeopardising the integrity of the arbitral proceedings. Moreover, conflicts of interests between a claimant's attorneys and the TPF provider may direct the professional judgment of the latter away from the strict interests of their client. Instead of regulating these issues, the parties merely included provisions on greater transparency about TPF agreements that are by no means sufficient for the purpose of protecting the integrity of the arbitral proceedings.

7.4 Conclusion

The chapter attempted to examine whether the contracting parties to CETA have achieved to provide greater transparency and remove barriers to access to justice in the context of investment arbitration. The overall argument of the chapter is that CETA provisions have the potential to ease the tension between the public law functions of investment tribunal and the lack of transparency in investment disputes. However, the same cannot be argued for access to justice since the parties have omitted to include provisions that could have reduced costs in investment disputes. Although that TPF can provide access to justice to financially weak parties, it is argued that this method is not a panacea and it may also damage the integrity of the arbitral proceedings. Although CETA's proceedings are expected to be more transparent, it is doubtful whether they will be more accessible to disputing parties. As the Rule of Law is no 'menu a la carte', the chapter argues that CETA's Investment Chapter would hardly fill the legitimacy gap. As always, halfway measures are not enough.

The analysis undertaken in this chapter is of paramount importance for study since greater transparency will support the acceptance of investment arbitration as a legitimate dispute settlement method and address the information asymmetries between disputing parties. In addition to these, greater transparency is anticipated to promote more accurate and thorough decisions by arbitration, as improper behavior will be discouraged. As noted, a higher rate of publication of documents may prompt the development of systems of precedent that was suppressed by confidentiality. Consequently, making other tribunals aware of other tribunals' decisions should be regarded as likely to promote consistency and enable both host States and foreign investors to assess their obligations, rights and legal liabilities.

It was also worth considering whether greater transparency bears any negative consequences. Given that arbitration is supposed to provide a cost-effective and fast method of resolving disputes, greater transparency may have a negative impact on the overall costs and duration of investment disputes. The negative consequences of additional procedural requirements can be mitigated by placing page and/or time limits on the *amicus curiae* brief as per the rules allow. Also, requiring several third parties to submit a single brief could ensure the effectiveness of arbitration as a dispute settlement mechanism.

Moreover, all of the documents and information that are to be made public are subject to the expectations of transparency contained in the rules. The rules seek to balance transparency requirements with other considerations. The exceptions to transparency are an innovative approach to balancing the public interest of investment disputes with the interests of the disputing parties to keep certain confidential information and trade secrets away from the public eye. Under these circumstances, the benefits of greater transparency, in combination with appropriate expectations and safeguards, outweigh its potential disadvantages. As such, the transparency requirements in CETA are in the interest of all the parties involved and indicate a process of readjustment towards a less controversial and reliable dispute settlement mechanism that functions in accordance with the fundamental principle of the Rule of Law.

However, the same cannot be argued with regard to access to justice where the parties missed an important opportunity to improve access to justice. CETA does not address lengthy proceedings, nor introduces mechanisms, such as fixed budgets and streamline procedures, that could have significantly reduced the overall costs of investment disputes. Despite that CETA includes certain provisions on costs, there is no further guidance on what 'reasonable costs' are and, most importantly, what kind of rules the Joint Committee would come up with in order to reduce the financial burden of financially weak disputing parties. In other words, the wording of CETA is too unclear to draw any concrete conclusion with regard to access to justice.

Finally, it can be expected that third-party funding will have an equalising effect between financially strong and financially weak parties as it provides the opportunity to the latter to access the arbitration mechanisms. This possibility of financing, however, remains at the discretion of the TPF provider, thus, putting limits to the expectations one could have regarding access to justice in investment arbitration. Other options, such as an Advisory Law center, similar to the WTO's version, could have been considered in order to facilitate access to justice for financially weak disputing parties. Furthermore, TPF could jeopardise the integrity of the arbitral proceedings since the control a funder could request over the dispute may result in a conflict of interest between the disputing party and its attorneys. As things currently stand, the contracting parties to CETA seem to have failed to include any concrete provisions regulating the relationship between a funder and the rest of the parties in a dispute.

References

Alexander K (2015) Article 6. Hearing. In: Scherer M et al (eds) Transparency in international investment arbitration: a guide to the UNCITRAL rules on transparency in treaty-based investor-state arbitration. Cambridge University Press, Cambridge, p 247

Asteriti A, Tams C (2010) Transparency and representation of the public interest in investment treaty arbitration. In: Schill S (ed) International investment law and comparative public law. Oxford University Press, Oxford
Augsburger T (2015) Article 7: exception to transparency. In: Scherer M et al (eds) Transparency in international investment arbitration: a guide to the UNCITRAL rules on transparency in treaty-based investor-state arbitration. Cambridge University Press, Cambridge, p 284
Bernasconi N, Johnson L (2011) Comments on draft rules on transparency in investor-state arbitration. CIEL and IISD
Bianco G (2015) Article 2. Publication of information at the commencement of arbitral proceedings. In: Scherer M et al (eds) Transparency in international investment arbitration: a guide to the UNCITRAL rules on transparency in treaty-based investor-state arbitration. Cambridge University Press, Cambridge, p 89
Boisson de Chazourne L (2004) Transparency and *Amicus Curiae* briefs'. J World Invest Trade 5 (2):333
Brabandere E (2014) Investment treaty arbitration as public international law. Cambridge University Press, Cambridge, pp 155–159
Brekoulakis S, Rogers C (2019) Third-party financing in ISDS: a framework for understanding practice and policy. Academic Forum on ISDS Concept Paper 2019/22, p 3
Calamita J (2014) Dispute settlement transparency in Europe's evolving investment treaty policy: adopting the UNCITRAL transparency rules approach. J World Invest Trade 15:645–678
Chan E (2015) Proposed guidelines for the disclosure of third-party funding arrangements in international arbitration. Am Rev Int Arbitr 26:308
De Chazournes B, Rukia B (2015) Transparency in investor-state arbitration: an incremental approach. Bahrain Chamber Disp Resol Int Arbitr Rev 2
Delaney J, Magraw D (2008) Procedural transparency. In: Muchlinski P et al (eds) The Oxford handbook of international investment law. Oxford University Press, Oxford
Feldman M (2016) International Arbitration and Transparency' (2016). SSRN Database, p 16. papers.ssrn.com/sol3/papers.cfm?abstract_id=2843140
Feliciano F as cited in Lam J and Unuvar G (2019) Transparency and participatory aspects of investor-state dispute settlement in the EU 'new wave' trade agreements. Leiden J Int Law:10
Franck S (2019) Arbitration costs: myths and realities in investment treaty arbitration. Oxford University Press, Oxford, p 291
Garcia F (2018) Third-party funding as exploitation of the investment treaty system. Boston College Law Rev 59:2912
Gomez K (2012) Rethinking the role of Amicus Curiae in international investment arbitration: how to draw the line favorably for the public interest. Fordham Int Law J 35(510):551–553
Hafner-Burton E, Victor D (2016) Secrecy in international investment arbitration: an empirical analysis. J Int Disp Settlement 7
Hodgson M, Campbell A (2017) Damages and costs in investment treaty arbitration revisited. Allen & Overy, London. www.allenovery.com/SiteCollectionDocuments/14-12 17_Damages_and_costs_in_investment_treaty_arbitration_revisited_.pdf
Howse R (2017) Designing a multilateral investment court: issues and options. Yearb Eur Law 36 (1):231
IBA Arbitration SubCommittee on Investment Treaty Arbitration (2018) Consistency, efficiency and transparency in investment treaty arbitration, pp 63–64
Investment Treaty Working Group of the International Arbitration Committee (2016) American Bar Association Section on International Law, Discussion Paper. https://shop.americanbar.org/PersonifyImages/ProductFiles/262739281/6-Proposed%20EU%20Investment%20Court.pdf
Jemielniak J, Unuvar G (2016) Participatory aspects of investor-state dispute settlement in the EU' 'New Wave' trade agreements. iCourts Working Paper Series, No. 75
Kee C (2015) Article 3. Publication of documents. In: Scherer M et al (eds) Transparency in international investment arbitration: a guide to the UNCITRAL rules on transparency in treaty-based investor-state arbitration. Cambridge University Press, Cambridge, p 92

Knahr C, Reinisch A (2007) Transparency versus confidentiality in international investment arbitration-the *Biwater Gauff* compromise. Law Pract Int Courts Tribunals 6:103
Lenk H (2019) *The EU Investment Court System: A Viable Reform Initiative?* Gothenburg University Library, Gothenburg, p 252
Maupin J (2013) Transparency in international investment law: the good, the bad, and the Murky. In: Bianchi A, Peters A (eds) Transparency in international law. Cambridge University Press, Cambridge
Mohebbi M, Asgharian M (2018) The role of arbitrators in effective time and cost reduction. Translational Disp Settlement 15:4
Mollestad C (2014) See no evil? Procedural transparency in international investment law and dispute settlement. PluriCourts Research Paper No. 14-20, p 14
Nash R (2013) Financing access to justice: innovating possibilities to promote access for all. Hague J Rule Law 5(1):98
OECD (2005) Transparency and third party participation in investor-state dispute settlement procedures. OECD Working Papers on International Investment, 2005/01
Paparinskis M, Howley J (2015) Article 5. Submission by a non-disputing party to the treaty. In: Schere M et al (eds) Transparency in international investment arbitration: a guide to the UNCITRAL rules on transparency in treaty-based investor-state arbitration. Cambridge University Press, Cambridge, p 216
Parra A (2012) The history of the ICSID. Oxford University Press, Oxford, p 104
Proposal for a Council Decision as regards the adoption of rules for mediation for use by disputing parties in investment disputes (2019) Brussels, 11.10.2019 COM
Report of the ICCA-Queen Mary Task Force on Third-Party Funding in International Arbitration (2018) p 14 www.arbitrationicca.org/media/10/40280243154551/icca_reports_4_tpf_final_for_print_5_april.pdf
Ruscall G (2015) Transparency in international arbitration: any (concrete) need to codify the standard? Groningen J Int Law 3(1):4–5
Scherer M et al (2015) Introduction. In: Scherer M et al (eds) Transparency in international investment arbitration: a guide to the UNCITRAL rules on transparency in treaty-based investor-state arbitration. Cambridge University Press, Cambridge, p 3
Shirlow E (2016) Dawn of a new era? The UNCITRAL rules and UN convention on transparency in treaty-based investor-state arbitration. ICSID Rev 31(3):626
Shirlow E, Caron D (2020) The multiple forms of transparency in international investment arbitration: their implications, and their limits. In: Thomas S, Federico O (eds) The Oxford handbook of international arbitration. Oxford University Press, Oxford, p 6
Steinitz M (2011) Whose claim is it anyway? Third party litigation funding. Minn Law Rev 95 (4):1324
Szilagyi S (2017) Transparency, investment protection and the role of the European Parliament. In: Mistelis L, Lavranos N (eds) European investment law and arbitration review. Brill Publication, Leiden
UNCTAD (2012) Transparency: UNCTAD series on issues in international investment agreements II
UNCTAD (2019) Possible reform of Investor-State Dispute Settlement (ISDS)' third-party funding - possible solution, A/CN.9/WG.III/WP.172
United Nations Commision on International Trade Law (2018) Possible reform of investor-State dispute settlement (ISDS)-cost and duration' A/CN.9/WG.III/WP.153, p 16
United Nations Commission on International Trade Law (2010) Report of working group II (Arbitration and Conciliation) on the work of its fifty-third session. A/CN.9/712, p 9
Van Boom W (2011) Third-party financing in international investment arbitration. papers.ssrn.com/sol3/papers.cfm?abstract_id=2027114
Zivkovic V (2018) The impact of cost decisions on the efficiency of arbitral proceedings. Transnational Disp Manag 15:4

Chapter 8
Conclusion

The monograph examined whether CETA constitutes a positive response to the legitimacy crisis facing investment arbitration by asking whether the reforms introduced in CETA's Investment Chapter are consistent with the Rule of Law. This endeavor ultimately paved the way for the monograph to argue that CETA's Investment Chapter is unlikely to completely overcome the legitimacy crisis facing investment arbitration. In the second chapter, it was highlighted that the reasons behind the legitimacy crisis are the lack of transparency and consistency in decision-making as well as the reluctance of arbitrators to take into consideration non-investment considerations. It was also highlighted that the high costs associated with investment disputes raise concerns over the ability of financially weak parties to access investment arbitration. The 'double-hatting' phenomenon, in combination with the party-appointed mechanisms of investment arbitration, raises further concerns about the integrity of the proceedings. The second chapter indicates that these features are rooted in history and the private law foundations of investment arbitration.

With respect to the historical origins of investment arbitration, certain events have shaped international investment law into a decentralised regime of thousands of similarly drafted IIAs that contain vaguely construed standards of treatment. It is the absence of a multilateral framework in a highly multilayered and decentralised network of IIAs that results in conceptual gaps and jurisprudential inconsistencies. This decentralization ultimately opens the system to a myriad of competing analogies. Similarly, the proliferation of investment tribunals, which frequently two or more of them have jurisdiction over the same investment dispute, slows down the process of convergence. Additionally, the vague nature of the standards of treatment led scholars to raise further concerns over inconsistency. The inconsistent awards further complicate the situation since States and affected third parties are unable to clearly identify the scope of their obligations and rights under IIAs. All the above have further led to an intrusive interference of investment tribunals over sovereign acts.

K. Dionysiou, *CETA's Investment Chapter*, European Yearbook of International Economic Law 13, https://doi.org/10.1007/978-3-030-66992-8_8

With regard to the normative foundations of investment arbitration, tribunals have demonstrated a reluctance to take into consideration human rights, which ultimately reflects the culture of commercial arbitration. Similarly, the debates about whether arbitrators should be appointed by the disputing parties are greatly influenced by the way we perceive investment arbitration. The more the private law element of investment arbitration is appreciated, the less the voices for transparent and random appointment methods in investment arbitration. Finally, the commercial law foundations of investment arbitration do not allow much room for greater openness, while concerns over accessibility and high costs are sidestepped by virtue of the commercial mindset of arbitrators and arbitral venues.

These features, however, appear to be in tension with the public element of investment disputes and the awards it delivers. Resolving whether a sovereign act has met a standard of treatment is a core element of the judicial function in public law. Quite paradoxically, in the realm of investment arbitration, the legality of sovereign acts is decided on the basis of a private law framework and in the absence of a central body that could provide consistency. In that sense, the paradox with investment arbitration is that tribunals vested with the power to review and control the exercise of public authority are largely unrestrained and inconsistent in their decision-making abilities. Compared with other dispute settlement methods, arbitration provides more flexibility and a correspondingly lower degree of predictability about the outcome of an investment dispute. Accordingly, the confidentiality of the arbitral proceedings is negatively characterised as a lack of transparency, the flexibility of the private law framework becomes arbitrariness and institutional bias, and the high costs associated with the resolution of investment arbitration raise concerns over access to justice.

Consequently, the public law function of investment tribunals, in conjunction with the criticism against investment arbitration, call for a public law framework in an effort to advance legal standards that satisfy contemporary expectations of legitimacy. With a public law framework, therefore, concerns regarding investment arbitration could be translated into meaningful public law rules and principles for debate and reform. With a closer look, one will notice that the sub-elements driving the legitimacy crisis are rooted in the fundamental principles of liberal constitutionalism: transparency; legal certainty; procedural fairness; access to justice, and human rights. These principles form part of the Rule of Law: the uniting legal principle from which the legitimacy concerns in investment arbitration stem.

On this basis, the third chapter argues that the backlash against investment arbitration reflects fundamentally a Rule of Law crisis within investment law's dispute settlement mechanism. The usefulness of this explanation lies in the fact that it provides greater clarity about the reasons behind the legitimacy crisis. In other words, such an endeavor has been of paramount importance in order to identify the deeper causes of the legitimacy crisis facing investment arbitration. This realisation, nevertheless, inherently raises further questions regarding the scope and content of the Rule of Law.

Although the concept of the Rule of Law displays much diversity in normative content, the third chapter adopts a liberal approach on its way of unfolding the Rule of Law's scope and content. The study attempted to offer a solid definition of the concept of the Rule of Law, by drawing on a variety of sources and employing the mainstream theories. Accordingly, the concept of the Rule of Law incorporates the idea that public authority should be accountable to an independent, transparent and accessible judicial body that fundamentally aims to guard human rights and provide legal certainty. It is the absence of such a mechanism that generates a legitimacy crisis in investment arbitration. In addition to constituting the principal normative and causal assumption on which existing arguments against investment arbitration are based, the third chapter argues that the Rule of Law can also infuse this system of law with legitimacy. Put simply, the clarity over the content of the Rule of Law lays the ground for the ways in which this crisis could be confronted.

Against this background, the Rule of Law could be utilized to address the legitimacy crisis facing investment arbitration. In this way, it will be possible to make arbitrators accountable and the proceedings transparent. Additionally, the possibility of third parties to participate reflects the Rule of Law notion that those who are affected should be allowed to intervene during the proceedings. Moreover, in order for arbitrators to respect the Rule of Law, they should act in an impartial and independent manner. Most importantly, for the Rule of Law to work, the parties to a dispute should be able to access investment arbitration, while human rights considerations should be taken into consideration by tribunals. Eventually, the third chapter argues that the Rule of Law may also serve as a yardstick for investment arbitration. Nonetheless, the policy implications of the arguments made in Chaps. 2 and 3 of the monograph are best understood by examining a particular case study. This is where CETA's Investment Chapter comes into play.

For this purpose, key aspects of CETA's investment chapter are examined through the Rule of Law framework. Although the monograph deemed ti neccessary to draw empirical insights, analogies, and distinctions between, other IIAs and jurisprudence in order to assess the reach and impact of CETA's Investment Chapter, this method is not adequate on its own. Evaluating CETA's Investment Chapter solely through IIAs and case-law does not allow us to focus on the 'big picture' and to analyse CETA's provisions from an external point of view.

Beginning with legal certainty, it appears that the parties to CETA have developed a consciousness about the public function of tribunals and the negative implications of the vague wording of the standards of treatment in IIAs. For this reason, the attempt made in CETA to further delineate the scope of the standard of treatment and clarify their drafting is a solid step towards greater legal certainty. Provided certain conditions are met, the joint interpretative declarations, the appellate mechanism, and the explicit reference to the Vienna Convention on the Law of Treaties can further enhance legal certainty.

With regard to amicus *curiae* briefs and human rights protection, it is argued that such interventions are meaningful to the extent that tribunals can demonstrate substantial engagement with the arguments raised by third parties. Non-disputing parties are not considered parties to the proceedings and, therefore, cannot introduce new arguments or evidence. Eventually, the limited role of these interventions prevents the full introduction of human rights law in investment disputes. As such, *amicus curiae* briefs in CETA's Investment Chapter are intended to perform a supplementary role in further integrating human rights in investment disputes.

With regard to procedural fairness, certain provisions introduced should be welcomed as a comprehensive effort to maintain an arbitrator's impartiality. Nevertheless, the method of appointment, selection, and payment of the members of the tribunal could raise criticism about a pro-state bias and, subsequently, raise concerns about a lack of institutional independence. Such features constitute an example of a wider backlash against economic globalization and signal the re-emergence of protectionism across the globe. In relation to transparency, CETA's provisions are in the interest of all the parties involved and indicate a process of readjustment towards a less controversial and much more open dispute settlement mechanism that functions in accordance with the concept of the Rule of Law.

However, the same cannot be said about access to justice where the parties have missed an important opportunity to improve access to justice. No significant effort has been made to streamline procedures or to explicitly reduce costs. Despite that TPF may provide the opportunity to financially weak parties to access this mechanism, this possibility of financing remains at the discretion of the TPF providers, thus, putting limits to the expectations one could have regarding access to justice. Furthermore, TPF could jeopardise the integrity of the arbitral proceedings since the control a funder may request over the dispute could result in a conflict of interest with the disputing party and its attorneys. It is, therefore, argued that CETA's Investment Chapter is more of a patchwork of reforms rather than a comprehensive reinvention of the substantive and procedural aspects of investment arbitration.

In addition to analysing particular aspects of CETA's Investment Chapter, the study has extracted certain general observations regarding international investment law, which are relevant for the purpose of answering the research question. In particular, it is argued that despite the ambitious attempt of the EU to reinvent the procedural and substantive provisions of IIAs, systemic reforms are necessary in order to reach closer to a situation where investment disputes are adjudicated in accordance with the Rule of Law. In other words, one should not lose sight of the fact that a single IIA is not able to completely deal with the legitimacy concerns associated with investment arbitration. In the Greek-speaking world, there is a phrase commonly used for this kind of situations: 'One swallow does not make a summer, neither does one fine day'. This phrase, which can be traced back to Aristotle, is used to highlight that a single fortunate event—or generally an effort to do something well—might not be enough to remedy a problem.

As was argued in Chap. 4, it is doubtful whether CETA's Investment Chapter will completely address the legal uncertainty associated with investment arbitration. Regardless of the fact that CETA's Investment Chapter constitutes a bold attempt in an effort to deal with the phenomenon of multiple proceedings and conflicting awards, it is unlikely that a single treaty will completely eradicate this phenomenon. The decentralised network of IIAs and arbitral venues open the system to a myriad of competing interpretations that cannot be reconciled by a single IIA i.e CETA. Concerns about legal uncertainty are therefore unlikely to completely go away. In a similar fashion, in Chap. 5, it is argued that the lack of hierarchy between different norms in international law as well as the vague formulation of several human rights norms makes their integration in investment disputes more difficult. It is therefore argued that it is highly unlikely that human rights will gain a prominent role in investment disputes.

In summary, there are several open issues regarding CETA's Investment Chapter that could raise concerns about the Rule of Law. Additionally, the observations made in Chaps. 4 and 5 highlight deeper, unsolved questions regarding international law. The lack of a hierarchy of norms and the absence of a common coordinating mechanism in international investment law set limitations from the outset to any individual attempt for the furtherance of the Rule of Law. The overall argument of the study, therefore, is that CETA's Investment Chapter does provide to a significant extent a substantial and somewhat positive response to many legitimacy concerns, yet a number of concerns associated with the concept of the Rule of Law will most likely persist. Thus, CETA's Investment Chapter is unlikely to completely overcome the legitimacy crisis facing investment arbitration. The monograph's core argument stands in sharp contrast to the contracting parties' optimistic declarations regarding CETA's ability to overcome the legitimacy crisis. The study's argument, subsequently, invites further debate about the way forward.

As a final note, therefore, it may be useful to develop some policy considerations about investment arbitration and the Rule of Law. With regard to legal certainty, the parties should consider clarifying the scope of the concept of legitimate expectations, by means of a joint interpretative declaration, in order to limit its application only in situations where a host state has given a specific promise not to alter its regulatory framework on a given area. If the contracting parties decide to proceed with a joint interpretative declaration, it is preferable to avoid giving this declaration a retroactive effect. Retroactive effective could put in jeopardy the fairness of the arbitral proceedings since it will allow a disputing party to influence the outcome of an ongoing dispute. By the same token, a retroactive declaration may also create legal uncertainty by altering the content of a provision in the middle of a dispute.

Turning to institutional independence, the parties to CETA would have been better advised to delegate the appointment of arbitrators to an independent committee. Another option is to allow greater participation during the appointment phase of other stakeholders, such as NGOs and academics. In parallel, it would have been preferable to introduce comprehensive criteria to ensure pluralist participation in the roster of arbitrators as well as a fixed salary to ensure institutional independence. As to the latter, the fixed remuneration system of arbitrators ensures only a low basic wage, while allowing additional remuneration from the disputing parties. Thus, CETA does not remove incentives to allow a high number of disputes and lengthy proceedings.

With regard to the reduction of costs, the parties to CETA should consider introducing mechanisms, such as fixed budgets and streamline procedures, to significantly reduce the overall costs of investment disputes. Further guidance should be provided by the Joint Committee on what 'reasonable costs' are in order to reduce the financial burden of financially weak disputing parties. In order to address the concerns related to TPF, some of the protections and duties of the attorney-client relationship, including a disclosure-based regime with conflict of interest rules, should be expanded to TPF providers. Furthermore, considering TPF providers as fiduciaries of the client, the former will have to take into consideration whether non-monetary remedies better serve the interests of the client.

Moreover, the observations about the systemic deficiencies of international investment law are particularly topical, given that an attempt is currently underway by both the EU and Canada regarding the establishment of a multilateral investment court. Such a court can be placed on top of international investment law in order to ensure consistency. It remains to be seen, however, how many States are willing to join this court. Depending on the number of States that are willing to join, such a multilateral court might either create more fragments in international investment law or further enhance legal certainty.

Finally, with respect to human rights protection, the parties to CETA could include specific provisions in order to clarify the normative content of human rights they are obliged to protect. Detailed provisions should also be included stipulating under what circumstances a non-disputing party may raise human rights. It is also imperative to include a method through which an appellate body could react to argumentation based on human rights law. The lack of hierarchy among different international law obligations, as well as the absence of detailed provisions stipulating what kind of human rights principles should be taken into account in investment disputes, have a negative effect on the protection of human rights. Such mechanisms are of cardinal importance as FDI projects constitute arenas of competing interests.

The policy prescriptions highlighted in the monograph are as much about correcting historical wrongs as they are about addressing the legitimacy crisis facing investment arbitration. In other words, in order to confront this legitimacy crisis, the deeper causes behind this crisis should be address rather than its symptoms. Whether the above suggestions for reform are realistic to expect—from a political point of view—is a different question that goes beyond the ambitions of the monograph.

Printed by Printforce, the Netherlands